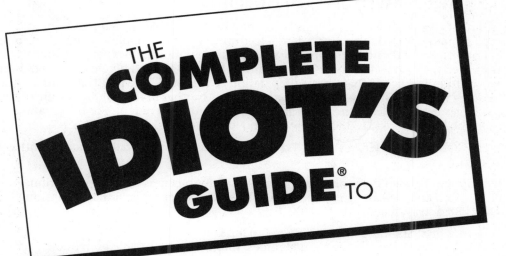

THE COMPLETE IDIOT'S GUIDE® TO

Cooking Pasta

by Natalie Danford

alpha books

A Division of Macmillan General Reference
A Simon & Schuster Macmillan Company
1633 Broadway, New York, NY 10019-6785

Copyright © 1999 by Natalie Danford

Macmillan Publishing books may be purchased for business or sales promotional use. For information please write: Special Markets Department, Macmillan Publishing USA, 1633 Broadway, New York, NY 10019.

International Standard Book Number: 0-02862330-4
Library of Congress Catalog Card Number: Information available on request

01 00 99   8 7 6 5 4 3 2 1

Interpretation of the printing code: the rightmost number of the first series of numbers is the year of the book's printing; the rightmost number of the second series of numbers is the number of the book's printing. For example, a printing code of 99-1 shows that the first printing occurred in 1999.

Printed in the United States of America

Alpha Development Team

Publisher
Kathy Nebenhaus

Editorial Director
Gary M. Krebs

Managing Editor
Bob Shuman

Marketing Brand Manager
Felice Primeau

Senior Editor
Nancy Mikhail

Editor
Jessica Faust

Development Editors
Phil Kitchel
Amy Zavatto

Assistant Editor
Maureen Horn

Production Team

Development Editor
Jim Willhite

Production Editor
Suzanne Snyder

Copy Editor
John Sleeva

Cover Designer
Mike Freeland

Photo Editor
Richard H. Fox

Illustrator
Jody P. Schaeffer

Designer
Nathan Clement

Indexer
Lisa Stumpf

Layout/Proofreading
Angela Calvert, Mary Hunt, Julie Trippetti

Contents at a Glance

Contents

Foreword

By now, I think just about everyone has ceded the supremacy of pasta as America's National Food. After all, pasta is (a) cheap; (b) easy to prepare; (c) beloved even by notoriously difficult small children; (d) can be eaten five nights a week and, with a different sauce, always deliver a new gastronomic experience; and (e) never fails to be absolutely delicious.

But all these things have long been not only known but celebrated in an obscene number of books dedicated specifically to pasta's glorification and preparation. So why are you holding in your hands yet another pasta book?

To which I answer that this is not just another book; it is *THE* book. The one that tells you, in a basic, easy-to-ingest format, what to do when you are ready to haul out those 4-quart pasta pots. Not only does it contain enough information about must-have ingredients like olive oil and grated cheese to make you sound like a verifiable expert, but its format takes you through the A to Z of pasta-making in a way that gives you enough confidence to attempt even homemade lasagne.

Sharon's approach is simple: make it accessible, make it relevant, and above all, make it fun. In fact, when I received my advance copy of this manuscript, I wound up faxing the section on fresh pasta-making to a few former students, many of whom had journied to my cooking school in Tuscany specifically to learn how to make different varieties of fresh pasta and were amazed that we still used hand-crank machines. Sharon's dictum: get your hands in there and forget about complicated gadgetry; the more you become involved with your ingredients, the more fun cooking becomes.

I recommend this book to everyone from beginners who want to learn to prepare a simple plate of pasta without having to sign up for a cooking class and end up looking like a culinary clutz; to intermediate wannabees seeking new seafood sauces or the ins and outs of cooking with Japanese noodles; to pasta connoisseurs confident of their abilities with the dried variety and ready to move on to the hallowed ground of making fresh from scratch.

To all these groups, I wish you a pleasant journey through the world of pasta and a hearty Buon Appetito!

—Anne Bianchi

Anne Bianchi is the author of numerous Italian cookbooks and the owner of the Toscana Saporita Cooking School located in Tuscany. For more information on theschool, call (212) 219-8791 school, call (212) 219-8791.

Introduction

There was a time when, to most Americans, pasta meant spaghetti and meatballs. In a short time, however, pasta has evolved from an ethnic specialty to a staple of almost every restaurant menu and dinner table in the country. Per capita consumption of pasta in the United States has risen by more than 90 percent over the last two decades. There's no mystery here (except for the mystery of what took us so long); pasta is cholesterol-free, low in fat, and quick-cooking. Best of all, it is soft, warm, and tremendously satisfying.

The year 1990 marked the first time that more pasta was consumed in the United States than in Italy; Americans now consume more than 3 billion pounds of pasta per year. The array of pasta products available has evolved tremendously, too. There is a seemingly infinite number of shapes (from tubular penne to *cuffie di papa*, or "pope's hats"), sizes, and varieties found in supermarkets and specialty stores. Not all pasta is Italian, either; more and more Americans are familiarizing themselves with toothsome Asian treats such as bean thread noodles.

The Complete Idiot's Guide to Cooking Pasta leads you through these products, as well as provides you with instructions and recipes for making your own noodles. It explains which sauces should be combined with which shapes and establishes once and for all the correct procedures for cooking dried pasta. With *The Complete Idiot's Guide to Cooking Pasta* in hand, you'll be able to whip up a dish of *Spaghetti alla Carbonara* at a moment's notice, not to mention *Cold Soba with Dipping Sauce, Orecchiette with Broccoli Rabe*, and a few specialties that are neither Italian nor Asian, such as *spaetzle*.

How to Use This Book

I'll start with the basics: some history of pasta and a few interesting stories. Then, we'll roll up our sleeves and get our pots and pans dirty, starting with the simplest pasta recipes and moving on to some more challenging ones.

Part 1: If You Knew Pasta Like I Know Pasta takes a look at what makes pasta tick, as well as some important ingredients in pasta dishes, such as Parmesan cheese.

Part 2: Saucy! flings wide the pantry doors, revealing the essential ingredients and fundamental recipes of pasta sauces.

Part 3: Pastabilities takes you past pasta with sauce to some more unusual treats: namely, soups and baked pasta.

Part 4: Rolling Your Own will teach you the age-old art of making fresh pasta. Not only will you learn to create the perfect *sfoglia*, or "sheet of dough," but you'll dabble with stuffed pastas such as tortellini as well.

Part 5: Asian Noodles moves east as we venture to China, Japan, Thailand, and other Asian countries. These are hot, quick dishes that are sure to satisfy you. It's a hungry world out there, and pasta fills a need.

Part 6: Strange Food in a Strange Land takes that idea one step further with recipes from North Africa, Germany, and even our own backyard. You'll learn to make pasta salads, couscous, spaetzle, and fidellos.

Extras

The sidebars in this book will guide you, amuse you, and keep you informed. They're separated into several different categories.

Linguine Lingo

Don't know your bucatini from your bean thread noodles? Not to worry. The Linguine Lingo sidebars will serve as your dictionary.

Pasta Practice

These hints and helpers will have you soaring through recipes without any glitches and pulling off pasta parties with aplomb.

Use Your Noodle

The Use Your Noodle sidebars feature tips for staying safe in the kitchen and keeping your wits about you in the pasta arena.

Pasta Patter

Even the Etruscans had a form of pasta! This is just one of the amazing facts you'll learn under the Pasta Patter heading.

Acknowledgments

This book is dedicated to my sisters and brothers on both sides of the Atlantic: Anna and Davide, Gabriele and Ivana, Greg and Erica, and Laura and Paul.

I'd like to thank Jennifer Griffin at Macmillan, who's as good a friend as she is an editor. Thanks are also due to Penny Kaganoff, who introduced me to Jennifer in the first place and is my guru in all things book-related.

Thanks also to the many friends who contributed ideas and support. I've learned more about Italian cooking from watching my mother-in-law, Evilia Violini, and my sister-in-law, Anna Pierleoni, than I could from any book. My friends Enrico Pontellini and Amedeo Cangiotti own a small Italian restaurant that has inspired me many times to make simple, "genuine" food. And, of course, to Paolo Pierleoni, who celebrates my successes and eats my failures without complaint.

Part 1
If You Knew Pasta Like
I Know Pasta

Pasta has made inroads all over the world, but there's no question that Italians are still the masters. Here's a close look at what makes pasta tick, some discussion on how to cook it, and an examination of dried pasta in particular.

Living in the Pasta

Pasta and noodles are an integral part of the diets of many countries. They are eaten not only in Italy, but in China, Japan, Korea, and most other Asian countries—not to mention North America. Wheat pastas exist in India and Arabia and have since the twelfth century. Germans eat egg noodles and dumplings; Greeks eat macaroni; and the couscous of North Africa is just semolina flour and water in a different shape.

Who Invented the Noodle? It's a Slippery Question

Historians have tried and always failed to determine the origins of pasta. One explanation has it that Marco Polo discovered pasta while traveling through China in the thirteenth century and brought it back to Italy. Italians scoff at this idea—how could pasta be anything other than Italian?—but offer no serious substitutes. (Recent research indicates that Marco Polo may never even have reached China but instead copied the memoirs of an earlier traveler who had.) The best explanation is probably the least romantic one: pasta and noodles (that is, foods made with some type of flour and water shaped into dough and then cooked) were most likely invented simultaneously in more than one place. This would explain the variety of noodles made in different places, as well as the fact that they existed in many different cultures before those cultures came into contact with each other.

Pasta Patter

"Italians love sun, sin, and spaghetti."

—Jennie Jerome Churchill

Pasta Patter

It's Ancient History: While the Etruscans, who lived in what is now Italy from the eighth to the first century B.C., probably ate something similar to pasta—more of a cake than a noodle—the Romans, whose era lasted from 509 B.C. until 476 A.D., apparently didn't.

Pasta Patter

That's One Explanation: An old Neapolitan legend has it that a wizard named Chico lived in Naples and stayed home all day, stirring a mysterious pot. The wizard's maid bought him no foodstuffs, but he enjoyed excellent health and appeared well fed. One day, a jealous female neighbor spied on him and saw him preparing a paste of flour and water, then rolling it quite thin and cutting it into pieces, which he cooked in a pot of boiling water. Claiming an angel had visited her in the night and given her the recipe, the neighbor presented Chico's invention to the king and immediately became rich and much admired for her creativity. Soon the entire city of Naples was enjoying this new food called *maccheroni* after the Latin *macarus,* meaning "divine food."

Macaroni Madness

There are as many explanations for the origins of the word "macaroni" as there are for the origins of pasta itself. Here are some suggested sources:

➤ A banquet was held for Emperor Frederick III (1415-1493) of Germany. Wanting to prove that he was erudite, the Emperor threw phrases from other languages into his vocabulary. When pasta was served, he described it as *makarios*, the Greek word for "happy."

➤ Initially, pasta was an expensive food because it was made by hand, so the first Italians to taste pasta commented that it was *buoni, ma caroni*, which means "good, but pricey."

➤ Mascherone is one of the characters in traditional Italian Commedia dell'arte (the name means "big mask," and this character sports one). Mascherone is a gourmand, and the word "macaroni" derives from his name.

Linguine Lingo

Macaroni (the Italian spelling is *maccheroni*, but the pronunciation is basically the same) are noodles of all types made from flour and water.

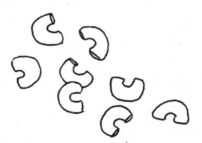

The origins of the word "macaroni" are uncertain.

Pasta Patter

Voi campari anni e annuni? Vivi vinu supra li maccaruni! Do you want to live for years and years? Drink wine and eat macaroni!

—Seventeenth-century Sicilian proverb

The term "noodles" usually refers to all kinds of long, ribbon-like pastas. The word is derived from the German *nudel,* which, in turn, probably came from the Latin *nodus,* meaning "node."

Okay, some of this is pretty far-fetched, but the history of noodles is probably less important than this: they taste pretty great, and they're always fun to eat. Noodles in all their forms—from Italian *tagliatelle* to Japanese *harusame*—provide both sustenance and comfort. Although their history may be somewhat complicated, eating them is not. They just seem to make people happy, so dig in.

The Least You Need to Know

➤ No one is sure of the origins of pasta, although many legends attempt to explain its birth.

➤ The two places most associated with pasta and noodles are Italy and Asia.

Chapter 2

The Simple Secrets of Cooking Pasta

In This Chapter

➤ What happens to pasta as it cooks?

➤ A brief description of equipment

➤ How to cook dried pasta

➤ How to cook homemade pasta

➤ How to bake pasta

Water Water Everywhere

No simple process has been exaggerated, maligned, and abused as much as that of cooking pasta. Imagine if the act of making your bed in the morning were surrounded by mystery, with all kinds of conflicting views about how it should be done. Imagine if someone told you to throw your sheets against a wall before tucking them under a mattress. Would you listen? Well, that's more or less what has happened to the cooking of pasta. Quite literally, if you can boil water, you can cook pasta. Read on to find out the right way—the easiest way, too—to do it.

Expanding Pasta's Horizons

Pasta is cooked in boiling water. It's a simple concept with complex implications: Pasta does not simply soften as it cooks, it swells and expands. Dried pasta is made from semolina flour. (You'll learn more about this special pasta flour in Chapter 3, "Your

Everyday Noodle.") The high gluten content of semolina flour strengthens pasta so that the pieces don't fragment as they grow. And pasta really grows. Dried pasta increases in volume by about fifty percent as it cooks.

As pasta swells, it also softens. Have you ever tried to eat a piece of dried pasta without cooking it? It's brittle and hard; you need to suck on it for a long time to be able to chew it. When you drop pasta into boiling water, you are softening it so that it can be chewed.

Linguine Lingo

Holy Colander, Batman!: A *colander* is a large bowl made of either metal or plastic and poked with holes. It's used for draining cooked pasta. You place the colander in the sink and pour the cooked pasta and water out of the pot. The water runs through the holes and down the drain, and the pasta is ready to go.

Use Your Noodle

Don't rest wooden spoons or other wooden utensils on the rim of a pot that is sitting on a lit burner. Most pots are made of metal, which conducts heat quickly. If left long enough on top of a hot pot, a wooden utensil can catch fire. Use a spoon rest.

Get Potted

I'm not one of those cooks who likes to have a lot of choices when it comes to equipment, or thinks that a fancy set of matching pots and pans will make my food turn out better. Most of the Italians I know have been cooking pasta in the same lightweight aluminum pot for years. I lived for a year in a studio apartment in Italy that didn't even have a kitchen. I opened a set of double doors to reveal a countertop stove with two burners, an under-the-counter refrigerator, and a sink. So when I talk about equipment, I'm talking about the most basic *batterie de cuisine* that you can imagine.

To cook pasta, you need:

> 1 large pot with a cover
>
> 1 long-handled wooden spoon
>
> 1 colander

That's it!

Assuming that you will cook a maximum of one pound of dried pasta at any given time, the pot should comfortably hold about one gallon of water (without being filled all the way to the top). When cooking pasta, always use an abundant amount of water so that the pieces of pasta can move about freely and don't stick to each other. The pot can be heavy or lightweight, it doesn't much matter. The cover for the pot need not even be the correct, tight-fitting match for that pot. It will be used to bring the water back to a boil as quickly as possible after you have added the pasta, but it will be left ajar to stop the water from boiling over.

You can use just about any type of large spoon. I prefer wooden spoons over metal because they don't heat up.

I prefer wooden spoons over hard plastic utensils because they just feel better in my hand. Although a spoon is the traditional choice, any utensil will do, as long as the handle is long enough for the end to reach the bottom of the pot without your hand hovering too close to the water and burning.

Colanders are usually made of either metal or plastic. I find metal colanders more esthetically pleasing (and I've melted more than one plastic colander by leaving it too close to the stove), but either kind will do fine. Your colander should have two handles so that you can lift it to shake the pasta gently. It should also have some type of "feet" so that it can rest upright in the sink while you pour the pasta into it. Dried pasta is strong enough to hold up to being poured out of the pot and into the colander, but if you cook homemade pasta often you may want to invest in a large slotted spoon or Chinese skimmer and use it to remove homemade pasta from the water. This more gentle method is particularly helpful when dealing with gnocchi and more delicate stuffed pasta. In most cases, however, a sturdy colander is the ticket.

Use Your Noodle

Always run a little cold water over the pieces of pasta you are going to test for doneness. Simply toss the piece or pieces into the colander and rinse briefly. Hot water can hide inside a piece of pasta and pop out to burn your lip as you bite.

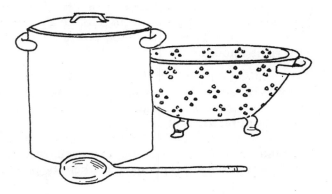

To cook pasta, you need a pot, a spoon, and a colander.

The Non-Ingredient Ingredients

It might seem strange to consider salt and water when cooking. What could be more standard, more available, than salt and water? Think again.

Rock of Ages

When it comes to Italian cooking, salt is not optional. I know many people are susceptible to hypertension and have to restrict their salt intake, but for the rest of you,

I repeat, salt is not optional. Salt is not so bad for you. Yes, excessive salt intake can do damage, but rarely does a person overindulge by salting his or her food too heavily. Excessive salt intake is almost always caused by a reliance on packaged goods such as snack foods and canned goods. So relax and pass the salt shaker.

Pasta Patter

Salt of the Earth: Sea salt, the salty deposits that remain behind when sea water dries up, has a stronger, less chemical flavor than most salt on the grocery store shelf. It is available in both rock salt and table salt forms, and is harvested in many countries, including France, Ireland, and New Zealand.

Or should I say, relax and pass the salt container? In order for salt to do its job as a flavor enhancer, you need to add it during cooking. Salt added at the end of cooking—at the table—does not blend into food as well. In Italy, few restaurants have salt and pepper shakers on the table; those seasonings are added in the kitchen during the cooking process. The best way to add salt is by hand. Pour your salt into a container and use it in pinches. You will quickly develop a feel for the right amount.

Linguine Lingo

Sale grosso ("big salt") is the rock salt used for cooking pasta. *Sale fino* is table salt.

The best salt for salting pasta water is rock salt, those big chunks of salt crystal. They melt more slowly in the water and, therefore, provide more depth of flavor. If you can't find rock salt, use kosher salt, which has larger grains than regular table salt. If throwing a handful of salt into the cooking water still scares you, keep in mind that most of the salt is poured out when the pasta goes into the colander.

Acqua: Water

Italians are nuts about water. And I don't just mean they like swimming and snorkeling. Italians choose bottled mineral water over tap water; they have well over 50 brands to choose from with varying levels of fizziness. Sometimes doctors even prescribe certain waters because of their mineral content. Italians still "take the waters" at thermal spas to cure certain ailments.

Water is important in Italian cooking, too. It is often added during cooking to keep ingredients from drying out. Water is the base for broth and other soups. And, of course, it is boiled for cooking pasta.

I'm not suggesting that you use bottled water to cook your pasta. That would be prohibitively expensive and probably ineffective. (Even in Italy, where tap water is seen with a suspicious eye, pasta is boiled in tap water.) I am suggesting, however, that you consider water quality. When filling your pot with tap water, always run cold water, which doesn't pick up traces of unwanted substances from the pipes the way hot water does. Freeing the water of impurities is another good reason to allow the pot of water to come to a free, rolling boil before tossing in the pasta. If your tap water has an unpleasant taste or smell, you may want to invest in a water filter. I use tap water for boiling pasta because so much water is required, but when it comes to soup and other dishes in which the quality of the water affects taste, I use filtered or bottled water. This seemed ridiculous to me until I tried it. The difference in taste, however, is obvious.

Use Your Noodle

Never cook pasta while barefoot. Boiling water can easily drip out of a colander or pot and burn your bare toes.

Taking the Plunge

This section discusses the specific, step-by-step instructions for cooking both short and long dried pasta and homemade pasta. The steps advise you to cook the pasta until it is just *al dente,* but what does that mean?

Al dente means different things to different people, but it generally indicates that Italian pasta should never, ever, ever be cooked until it is mushy. *Al dente* pasta is by no means still raw enough to be considered crunchy, but it is definitely firm. If pasta is going to be added to a sauce and cooked for additional time, it should be on the crunchy side of *al dente.* If it is simply going to be sauced and brought to the table, it can cook for an extra minute or so. In addition to its more savory texture, pasta that is cooked until *al dente* will also taste different from overcooked pasta. It will have an identifiable wheat flavor.

Linguine Lingo

Al dente literally means "to the tooth," indicating that the pasta should still boast some resistance so that it sticks to your teeth a little as you eat it rather than simply dissolving into mush on your tongue.

Pasta Patter

If you bite into a piece of short, tubular pasta, such as penne, when it is still *al dente*, you will see a white ring of uncooked pasta in the center. When the pasta is overcooked, it will be uniformly yellow.

Per Cucinare la Pasta Corta: Cooking Short Pasta

Here are the definitive instructions for cooking one pound of short, dried pasta:

1. Fill a large pot with one gallon of cold, clean water.
2. Bring to a boil over high heat.
3. When the water has reached a rapid boil, add one handful (a little less than $1/4$ cup) of rock salt.
4. Pour in the pasta.
5. Immediately stir the pasta thoroughly with a long-handled spoon.
6. Cover the pot to bring the water back to a rapid boil as quickly as possible, but leave the cover slightly ajar to reduce the risk of the water boiling over.
7. Continue to remove the cover and stir the pasta about every minute or so.
8. After the pasta has been cooking about five minutes, depending on the size, begin tasting a piece each time you stir.
9. After the pasta is cooked *al dente*, remove the pot from the heat and pour the water and pasta into a colander.
10. Lift the colander and shake it over the sink a few times to drain the pasta slightly.
11. Sauce the pasta and serve immediately.

Per Cucinare la Pasta Lunga: Cooking Long Pasta

A pound of long, dried pasta, such as spaghetti, is cooked in almost exactly the same way:

1. Fill a large pot with one gallon of cold, clean water.
2. Bring to a boil over high heat.
3. When the water has reached a rapid boil, add one handful of rock salt.

4. Gently place the pasta in the pot vertically and fan it out to distribute.

5. During the first minute of cooking, as the bottom ends of the pasta begin to soften, gently push the strands into the pot.

6. When all of the pasta is underwater, replace the cover to bring the water back to a rapid boil as quickly as possible, but leave the cover slightly ajar to reduce the risk of the water boiling over.

7. After 30 seconds, remove the cover and stir the pasta. You may want to use a fork to separate the strands.

8. Continue to remove the cover and stir the pasta about every minute or so.

9. After the pasta has been cooking about five minutes, depending on the size, begin breaking off pieces of a strand and tasting them each time you stir.

10. After the pasta is cooked *al dente*, remove the pot from the heat and pour the water and pasta into a colander.

11. Lift the colander and shake it over the sink a few times to drain the pasta slightly.

12. Sauce the pasta and serve immediately.

Do:

➤ Taste the pasta early and often. Many variables—temperature, water, and humidity—affect the cooking time, so consider the cooking time on a pasta package a very rough estimate.

➤ Keep the water at a rapid boil. It should slow down only when the pasta is first added.

➤ Stir often. Better to stir too much than too little and end up with clumped, sticky pasta.

➤ Always serve pasta immediately. Pasta waits for no one, so have your sauce ready to go.

Don't:

➤ Add oil to the cooking water. Oil just makes the surface of the pasta slick and unappetizing. It also makes it hard for the sauce to adhere afterward.

➤ Break spaghetti or other long pasta to fit into the pot. It will become pliable shortly after being added to the water.

➤ Rinse pasta after it is cooked. It will turn cold and flavorless.

➤ Throw pasta against the wall or attempt any other foolish exercises to check whether it is cooked. Only your mouth can tell you when it's done, so taste, taste, taste!

Per Cucinare la Pasta Fatta in Casa: Cooking Homemade Pasta

There are some minor variations for cooking fresh, homemade pastas, which are slightly softer and more delicate than dried pasta.

The most noticeable difference between the two types is cooking time. Fresh, home-made pasta is cooked in about ten seconds. That's not a typo. When just made, home-made pasta requires hardly any cooking at all. Homemade pasta that has been dried according to the instructions on page 151 will also cook quite quickly, although not quite as rapidly as when just made. That being the case, you need to keep a very careful eye on homemade pasta as it cooks. When done, homemade pasta usually floats to the top of the water and bobs there. The same rules about cooking pasta *al dente* apply to fresh pasta as well. It should have some resistance, although the texture will naturally be different than that of properly cooked dried pasta.

As previously mentioned, you may want to use a long-handled slotted spoon or Chinese skimmer to remove homemade pasta from the water to ensure that your treasures aren't damaged in the brusque movement from pot to colander.

To cook four to six eggs' worth of homemade pasta, complete the following steps:

1. Fill a large pot with one gallon of cold, clean water.
2. Bring to a boil over high heat.
3. When the water has reached a rapid boil, add one handful of rock salt.
4. Gently drop the pasta into the pot and make sure that all the pasta is covered by water.
5. Replace the cover to bring the water back to a rapid boil as quickly as possible, but leave the cover slightly ajar to reduce the risk of the water boiling over.
6. After most of the pasta has risen to the top, taste for doneness. If it is not done, continue stirring often.
7. After the pasta is cooked *al dente*, remove the pot from the heat and pour the water and pasta into a colander, or use a skimmer or slotted spoon to remove the pasta pieces (particularly when cooking gnocchi and stuffed pasta such as tortellini and ravioli).
8. Lift the colander and shake it gently over the sink a few times to drain the pasta slightly.
9. Sauce the pasta and serve immediately.

Do:

➤ Stir stuffed pasta very gently to avoid causing the filling to leak.

➤ Use a long-handled wooden fork for stirring long homemade pasta such as tagliatelle, fettuccine, and so forth.

➤ Stand by when cooking homemade pasta. It cooks almost instantly.

Don't:

➤ Overcook any pasta, including homemade. Even egg pasta, which is soft and tender to begin, should be *al dente* when properly cooked.

➤ Count on time spent in boiling water to cook the fillings for stuffed pastas. They should be thoroughly cooked before being added.

➤ Cook egg pasta in insufficient water. It will stick together in one big clump.

The Least You Need to Know

➤ Always cook pasta in plenty of water.

➤ Salt pasta cooking water (with rock salt if possible).

➤ Stir pasta occasionally while it is cooking, especially in the first few minutes.

Chapter 3

Your Everyday Noodle

In This Chapter

➤ A special flour for making dried pasta

➤ Pasta production

➤ Picking a pasta brand

➤ Dried pasta is good for you

While this book provides recipes for special occasion pasta dishes that require a certain amount of elbow grease, your everyday noodle—the pasta we all reach for again and again—is the dried pasta packed in a box or plastic bag on the grocery store shelf.

Dried pasta is an incredible invention. It is healthful: a $^1/_2$ cup serving of pasta (I know, when was the last time you ate that small a serving?) contains only about 10 calories from fat and no saturated fat. Pasta is also relatively inexpensive; even in the most expensive stores, a box of standard imported pasta rarely costs more than two dollars.

According to the government, that box should yield a meal for eight people. Even when you readjust those serving sizes to real-life appetites (a 16 oz. box feeds four in my house), pasta is still a bargain.

Pasta Patter

Pasta Is Swell/Pasta Does Swell: Dried pasta increases by 50 percent once it is cooked, so 2 cups of dried pasta will result in 3 cups of cooked pasta. Measure accordingly.

Pasta Practice

Take a Number: Italian pasta shapes not only have names, they have numbers. When buying a shape that comes in varying thickness—such as spaghetti—you can match the pasta by number to ensure that pasta from different boxes will have the same cooking time. Usually only Italian brands use the numbering system.

Linguine Lingo

Some Like It Hard: Durum wheat (its Latin name is *triticum durum*) is a spring wheat that yields a hard flour used mostly to make pasta. The word "durum" is Latin for "hard."

Pasta is inspirational, too. It is a paean to the inventiveness of human beings. When I bite into that first forkful of penne, I am often grateful that someone was creative enough to look at flour and water and come up with something that is not only satisfying, but fun to eat.

A Special Flour

Dried pasta may be our everyday noodle, but it is not made from everyday flour. Pasta is created using a special kind of flour milled from *durum wheat*. Durum wheat produces a flour that is "harder" than all-purpose white flour.

To understand what hard flour is, we need to look at the flour milling process a little more closely. In order to make flour, wheat is milled, which means the endosperm is separated from the bran and the germ, and then the endosperm is ground to a texture ranging from coarse to fine.

Durum wheat is the hardest wheat available: its endosperm has a high protein content and little starch. It also has high gluten, which means it stretches and adheres. Durum wheat is milled to make golden, gritty *semolina flour*. Although small amounts of semolina flour are used in certain breads and cakes, it is most commonly used to make dried pasta. (Conversely, the softest flours are those used for cake flour.)

If you've ever bitten into an uncooked piece of pasta, you know that dried pasta made with durum wheat is true to its name—that is, it is definitely hard. When cooked, however, the flour retains a great deal of body due to the durum wheat's high gluten content, which allows the flour to stretch while still remaining intact.

Even before pasta is cooked, that strength and endurance come in handy. The dried pasta we purchase in the grocery store is made by machine. Because durum wheat, and consequently semolina flour, is so hard, pasta dough can stand up nicely to the stretching and pulling involved.

Linguine Lingo

Semolina flour is milled from durum wheat. It has a coarser consistency than all-purpose white flour, as well as a rich yellow color. Occasionally, semolina flour is labeled simply as "pasta flour," although it is also used in certain breads and desserts, usually in combination with white flour.

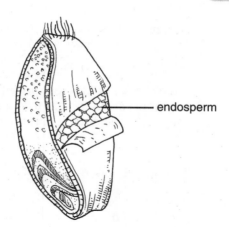

endosperm

To make wheat flour, the endosperm is separated from the rest of the grain and ground.

Pasta Production

When Italians speak of *pasta fatta in casa,* or homemade pasta, they are usually referring to egg pasta, which is covered in Part IV. The dried pasta we purchase in the grocery store is made commercially by machine, but not all machine-made pastas are alike. Italians further distinguish among dried pasta by terming certain brands *pasta artigianale,* or artisanal pasta. The difference lies in the process, the quality of semolina flour used, and the price.

Regular, industrially produced pasta is extruded through slick, Teflon-coated forms. These forms produce pasta with a perfectly smooth surface, which sounds appealing, but is actually less than desirable. Minuscule pockmarks on the surface of pasta allow sauce to cling to the pasta and coat it evenly. (More on this in Chapter 13, "You Are a

Pasta Machine.") The pasta is then dried in large rooms with hot air blowers, which speeds up the process but also results in a less supple product. Quick drying may sometimes make pasta more brittle (it is rare, for example, to come upon broken pieces of pasta at the bottom of a box of artisanal pasta, but with industrial pasta there are usually a few odds and ends lingering down there), but it is more practical, since air drying can lead to mold growth and other problems if the pasta retains moisture for too long.

Artisanal pasta also is made by machine, but the machinery is coated with brass rather than Teflon, which results in a more porous surface. If you took a piece of each type of dry pasta and examined it under a microscope, you would see that the surface of a piece of artisanal pasta is pocked with little indentations, whereas a piece of less expensive pasta is smoother. Additionally, artisanal pasta is air dried without any artificially produced hot air. The semolina flour used to make artisanal pasta is usually of a higher quality as well. The flour may be grown organically, stone-ground, or the wheat may simply be more carefully selected.

Linguine Lingo

Pasta artigianale is dried pasta made with brass-coated machinery and air dried. It is usually made of higher quality semolina flour than regular dried pasta.

Naturally, the slower drying process and the more expensive machinery add up to a higher price for artisanal pasta, but since we're still talking about a product that consists of flour and water, even artisanal pasta is not outrageously priced. I think it's worth trying the more expensive type a couple of times and deciding for yourself whether you think the difference in taste and texture is worth the difference in price.

Branded for Life

If you eat a lot of pasta, you will want to choose a favorite brand and stick with it. This is because most pasta shapes vary slightly from manufacturer to manufacturer, and you want all your *farfalle* to be the same size and shape so that they will share the same cooking time. Most industrial pasta can be stored for long periods of time. When you see your brand on sale, scoop up several boxes of the shapes you like best.

Linguine Lingo

Farfalle are butterfly-shaped pasta (sometimes called "bow ties" in the United States).

Made in the USA: Is American Pasta Really Superior?

Choosing a brand of pasta involves several different factors. The first major issue you will face is that of American-made pasta versus Italian-made pasta.

With Italians being the undisputed experts when it comes to the stuff, it stands to reason that Italian pasta will be superior to American pasta—and most gourmets would second this notion. In 1994, however, *Cook's Illustrated* magazine did a ground-breaking taste test in which a panel of tasters—including some native Italians—rated eight differ-ent brands of spaghetti. The top-ranked noodle? Ronzoni—manufactured by the Hershey Foods Company.

Author Joni Miller interviewed scientists and food manufacturers for the article and found that American durum wheat has changed over the last 20 years, and that in response to a demand from pasta manufacturers, scientists have bred wheat with higher quality gluten.

That may be so, but in my own taste test, Italian brands still come out on top. I find American pasta has a flashpoint at which it is properly cooked, and that it then moves into the overcooked stage so quickly that if I haven't happened to taste it at just the right nanosecond, all is lost. Italian pasta, on the other hand, tends to cook more gradually. I also find that it has a more pronounced "wheaty" taste.

You may want to perform your own taste test to determine which type of pasta is best for you. Naturally, imported Italian pasta is more expensive but not outrageously so.

Dried pasta brands include the following:

➤ Barilla

➤ Contadina

➤ Creamette

➤ De Cecco

➤ Delverde

➤ Mueller's

➤ Ronzoni

Use Your Noodle

Be a Careful Reader: Just because a pasta brand name ends with a vowel does not mean that it is Italian. To avoid pasta made in other coun-tries—and believe me, you want to—check packages carefully. Pasta manufacturers in Turkey, who use very low-grade semolina flour, often adopt Italian-sounding names and red, white, and green packaging to fool the consumer.

There are two brands of "industrial" Italian pasta widely available in the United States that I recommend: De Cecco and Barilla. Supermarkets often carry De Cecco pasta, which comes in a light blue box. Barilla is less well known here, but it is the best-selling pasta in Italy, which is really saying something. American brands include Ronzoni, Contadina, and Creamette.

Pasta Patter

Taking a Sun Bath: The first pasta factory in the United States was built in Brooklyn in 1848. Its owner was not Italian but French. Strands of spaghetti were spread on the roof of the factory to dry.

Artisanal Pasta

And what about those fancy artisanal pastas?

Artisanal pasta brands include the following:

➤ Latini

➤ Martelli

➤ Rustichella d'Abruzzo

➤ Viceconte

I conducted a taste test of several artisanal brands available in gourmet food stores and found that quality varied widely. My favorite of the four brands I tried was Viceconte, which had an excellent chewy texture. At close to five times the price of a box of industrial pasta, however, it was a little too rich for my blood.

The Latini brand, produced in Italy's Marche region, provided a good middle ground: it cost half as much as the Viceconte and was still toothsome and flavorful. (I also liked the text on the Latini box. Whereas most pasta boxes bear a suggested cooking time, the Latini box simply states, "Every gourmet knows how to do it!") Rustichella d'Abruzzo was also acceptable, although not quite as fresh-tasting as the Latini. I also cooked and ate a package of Martelli brand pasta, which I found quite dissatisfactory. The flour did not react like a hard flour but instead became so soft that I was amazed the noodles could hold together at all.

As the pasta market continues to grow (retail sales of pasta grew from $1.6 billion in the United States in 1991 to $2.1 billion in 1995, and are expected to reach $2.6 billion by the year 2000), new products will become available. Again, since a box of pasta doesn't cost much, it's worth your time to try new products as they become available. Only your taste buds can determine which brand of pasta is right for you.

To Your Health

Dried pasta contradicts the usual thoughts on healthy food: it tastes good and is good for you. The U.S. Department of Agriculture's food pyramid recommends that most people eat from six to eleven servings from the bread, cereal, rice, and pasta group daily. Never has being good to your body been so good to your taste buds.

A 2 oz. serving (one-eighth of a standard box or about 3/4 cup) of pasta has only 200 calories and about 1 gram of fat (that's 2 percent of your daily allowance), none of which is saturated. Pasta offers 41 grams of energy-granting carbohydrates, 2 grams of fiber, and 7 grams of protein. Furthermore, because pasta is a plant-based food, it contains no cholesterol.

Pasta Patter

Here's the Skinny: If you are concerned about calories and fat, you should opt for tomato-based sauces over cream-based sauces. See Chapter 7, "You Say Tomato," for pasta with tomato sauce.

Check out how dried pasta compares nutritionally to some other foods.

Table 3.1 Nutritional Information on Pasta and Other Foods

	Calories	Fat (grams)
$^3/_4$ cup pasta	200	1
3 oz. chicken breast	140	3
3 oz. lean beef	231	15.7
1 cup whole yogurt	139	7.4

Pasta is as versatile as you want to make it. There are recipes in this book for sauces with meat, fish, and every kind of vegetable imaginable. If you are trying to develop variety in your diet, pasta is the ticket, because it can serve as a background for so many different types of foods.

Pasta Patter

The Other Spaghetti: When people talk about spaghetti, it's not always table talk. Check out these other phrases that use the world's best-known dried pasta:

The *spaghetti league* is no pasta manufacturer's association. It's the English nickname for Italy's professional basketball league. Many American players pass a few years playing on Italian courts before moving on to the NBA.

Spaghetti squash has nothing to do with pasta, except that its edible, stringy insides resemble spaghetti. To obtain this "pasta," cut a spaghetti squash in half, steam it cut side down, and then use a fork to gently extract the yellow "spaghetti."

Spaghetti straps may sound like seatbelts made for pasta, but instead they are the thin strands of fabric that often hold up women's dresses.

Spaghetti westerns were movies set in the American West but filmed on the cheap at Cinecittà (Rome's version of Hollywood) in the 1960s and 1970s. The classic spaghetti western is Sergio Leone's 1966 film, *The Good, the Bad and the Ugly.*

What Shape Is Your Noodle?

When it comes to pasta, Italians have taken their *fantasia,* or creativity, to new heights—and lengths, and widths. Both the names and the shapes of different types of dried pasta exhibit a playful ingenuity. Many of the names are distinctly Italian as well. What other country could have invented a food called *cuffie di papa* (pope hats) or thick, chewy *strozzapreti* (priest stranglers)?

Pasta Patter

Deep Thoughts: The Philadelphia Museum of Art commemorated a 1997 exhibit of Rodin sculptures by selling pasta in the shape of the great artist's famous *The Thinker.* Art historians were outraged, but gourmands were delighted.

Despite their amazing variety, most pasta shapes fall into three general categories: small soup pasta (or *pastina*), short stubby pasta such as penne, and long string-like pasta such as spaghetti. The following table provides a sampling of the pasta shapes available. Although many have tried, no one has ever successfully categorized all the pasta shapes that exist. (The most complete lists of pasta names contain about 500 items.) With Italians still hard at work inventing new shapes, it seems a Herculean task.

Pasta Patter

Strength in Numbers: It's no coincidence that all pasta names end with either the letter "i" or the letter "e." Those letters are used to form the plural in Italian, and pasta is always discussed in the plural. When you talk about spaghetti, for example, you are talking about the many strands of spaghetti on your plate. One piece of spaghetti would be a "spaghetto," and a less-than-filling meal to boot.

Table 3.2   Dried Pasta Shapes and Names

Name	Translation	Category
Acini di pepe	Peppercorns	Soup
Anelli	Rings	Soup
Bucatini	With holes	Long
Capelli d'angelo	Angel hair	Long/soup
Cavatelli	Corkscrews	Short

continues

Table 3.2 Continued

Name	Translation	Category
Conchiglie	Snail shells	Short
Ditalini	Thimbles	Soup
Farfalle	Butterflies	Short
Fusilli	Spindles	Short
Gemelli	Twins	Short
Linguine	Little tongues	Long
Maccheroncini	Little macaroni	Short
Mostaccioli	Mustaches	Short
Orecchiette	Little ears	Short
Penne rigate	Lined quills	Short
Pipette	Little pipes	Short
Radiatori	Radiators	Short
Rigatoni	With lines	Short
Rotelle	Wheels	Short
Sedanini	Celery	Short
Spaghetti	Strings	Long
Spaghettini	Small strings	Long
Stelline	Little stars	Soup
Tortiglioni	Spirals	Short
Tubetti	Little tubes	Soup
Vermicelli	Worms	Long
Ziti	Bachelors	Short

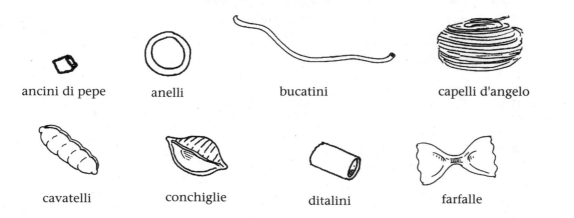

ancini di pepe   anelli   bucatini   capelli d'angelo

cavatelli   conchiglie   ditalini   farfalle

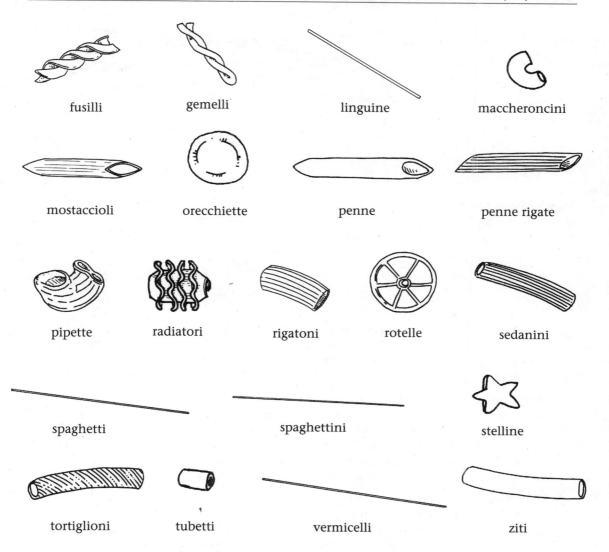

fusilli gemelli linguine maccheroncini

mostaccioli orecchiette penne penne rigate

pipette radiatori rigatoni rotelle sedanini

spaghetti spaghettini stelline

tortiglioni tubetti vermicelli ziti

Matchmaker, Matchmaker

With the embarrassment of riches available in the world of pasta, how can you be expected to marry a shape with a sauce? Once you begin to cook pasta regularly, it becomes remarkably easy.

First, with a couple of exceptions—namely meat sauces—spaghetti goes with almost anything. Both oil and tomato sauces cling nicely to strands of spaghetti (as well as to linguine and other long, string-like pastas, with the exception of angel hair, which, as noted above, are destined for the soup bowl).

Spaghetti is the most basic type of long pasta.

When you're not sure what kind of short pasta to use, reach for penne.

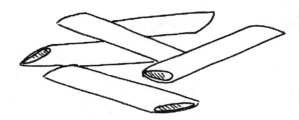

The other all-purpose pasta is penne, or for that matter any short, tubular pasta similar to penne (rigatoni, sedanini, maccheroncini, and so on). Penne also can be topped with almost anything; they are delicious under a thin blanket of meat sauce, elegant with cream, and the perfect partner for oil-based sauces.

Short, stubby types of pasta (with the exception of very small pasta for soups—for more information on these, see Chapter 10, "Pasta + Soup = Comfort[2]"), on the other hand, work best with meat sauces or other types of sauce that contain small pieces such as peas or diced carrots. This is because short, stubby pasta tends to be shaped to create a hole. Look at conchiglie (shells), for example; their small openings are perfect for harboring bits of meat or vegetable.

Then there are certain combinations of pasta and sauce that have been paired together for so long that to mix them up is almost unthinkable. Spaghetti with garlic and hot pepper (page 53) is one of these. It's not that this sauce does not taste good on other kinds of pasta (I've made it with penne in a pinch); it's just not quite the same dish.

The Least You Need to Know

➤ Dried pasta is made with special hard-wheat flour.

➤ Artisanal pasta is better tasting and more expensive than industrial pasta.

➤ Certain pasta shapes go with certain pasta sauces.

Chapter 4

The Parmesan Question: It Doesn't Make Everything Better

In This Chapter

➤ A brief history of Parmesan cheese

➤ Selecting and storing Parmesan cheese

➤ Using Parmesan cheese

➤ Other Italian cheeses

One of the "strange" American habits that puzzles Italians is our tendency to dump a cup of grated Parmesan cheese indiscriminately over any plate of pasta. To Italians, it's obvious that Parmesan cheese is a treasure to be handled delicately and used with care. Italians also believe that cheese goes well with certain foods and not with others. How, they wonder, can Americans have such ignorant palates?

Italian cheeses—including Parmesan and several other types discussed in this chapter—are an integral part of Italian cooking and, therefore, of many pasta dishes. We're all familiar with that small bowl of grated Parmesan cheese on the tables of Italian restaurants around the world. Part of the challenge inherent to using Italian cheeses is locating them; another part of the challenge lies in knowing how to use them to their best advantage.

The Birth of Parmesan

While there are numerous theories about the "discovery" of pasta, and while the discussion of which nation can claim pasta as its own rages on and arouses strong emotions, Parmesan cheese appears to have been born without much fanfare. Cheese was produced in the area around the city now known as Parma during the Roman and Etruscan periods, as recorded by Apicius, who wrote about a cheese known as *caseus parmensis,* which literally translates from the Latin as "cheese from Parma."

The inhabitants of nearby Piacenza have long tried to take credit for the creation of Parmigiano Reggiano, even though the name of their city does not appear in its title. According to them, all hard grating cheeses stem from the cheese created by monks at an abbey in that province who converted the marshlands surrounding the Pú River into pasture lands during the 1100s. Inhabitants of Parma sharply dispute this claim, and indeed, we know only that those monks made a hard cheese similar to Parmigiano Reggiano, but not that they followed the same procedures used today.

What's Up, D.O.C.?

So, no one knows exactly when the golden cheese known today as Parmigiano Reggiano was first produced. Most likely it evolved over time from various dairy ancestors. What is known is that in 1955 Parmigiano Reggiano was first established as a *d.o.c.* cheese. Certain wines and other foodstuffs in Italy carry this appellation, which stands for *denominazione di origine controllata.* Foodstuffs marked d.o.c. have been inspected by a government body charged with establishing that they respect certain rules.

Because of the "d.o.c." status of Parmigiano Reggiano, its production is regulated by the government, as well as by the *Consorzio del Formaggio Parmigiano Reggiano,* or Parmesan Cheese Consortium.

Pasta Patter

Seeing Red: Although Parmesan cheese was once made from the milk of locally indigenous cows, cows that yield a larger volume of milk are now regularly imported. Parmesan cheese made with milk from *vacche rosse,* or "red cows," a local breed, is now marked with a special symbol to indicate its higher quality.

Making the Big Cheese

Authentic Parmesan cheese can be made only in the provinces of Parma and Reggio nell'Emilia, and in accordance with the following process:

1. In the morning, fresh, unpasteurized milk is poured into large copper cauldrons with paddles and gently heated and stirred.
2. Starter—a bit of fermented milk from the day before—is added to spur fermentation.
3. When the milk has reached the proper temperature, rennet is added to cause the milk to curdle.
4. As it thickens, the mixture is agitated more rapidly and heated further.
5. The mixture is briefly heated to a high temperature to kill any bacteria and solidify the cheese.
6. This substance is wrapped in cheesecloth and left to drain briefly before it is placed in a mold.
7. The cheese is then turned out and replaced into the mold at intervals for several hours. The cheesecloth is replaced each time.
8. The cheese is placed in the final mold—which bears the words "Parmigiano Reggiano" around the sides—and left overnight to set. It is then removed from the mold and allowed to air-dry for an additional day.
9. The cheese must then sit in a brine solution for close to a month.
10. The cheese is then aged for at least one year.

During the aging process, the Parmesan Cheese Consortium sends its inspectors—a sort of cheese police squad—to inspect the large forms of cheese. Their inspection is mostly visual; they look for flaws, such as dents in the hard outer layer of the cheese, and swelling, which indicates the cheese is rotten. They also tap the cheeses with small hammers to listen for echoes; this is known as checking the "music" of the cheese.

Good cheeses are marked with the Consortium's oval-shaped seal of approval. Cheeses that don't make the grade can still be sold but are marked with a large X.

Pasta Patter

Cheese as Medicine: In earlier times, the *casaro,* or cheesemaker, was also considered a healer in Italian villages.

This description may make the process seem simpler than it is; if so, that's my simplification. The rules regarding Parmesan are myriad. There are even rules regarding the mix of feeds the cows can eat, and, until recently, only milk produced between April 1 and November 11 could be used.

Picking Parmesan

In a perfect world, all of our homes would include large cellars for storing wine, cheese, root vegetables, and all sorts of other foods that benefit from natural refrigeration.

Use Your Noodle

Don't ever buy pre-grated cheese. As the surface of cheese is exposed to air, moisture evaporates. Grated cheese, being almost all surface, has a brief period of freshness that has probably expired before it hits the store shelf. Furthermore, there's no telling what's in pre-grated cheese. Unscrupulous store owners have been known to grate in all kinds of things, including the rind.

You'd buy a wheel of Parmesan cheese and chip away at it all year long.

This isn't a perfect world, though, so we have to deal with refrigerated cheeses and unknown dates of origin. (Each wheel of Parmesan is stamped with the month and year of its creation, but you won't be able to see that when you're buying a small wedge at your local store.) When you go to the grocery store (or more likely a gourmet store) in search of Parmesan cheese, you are likely to face several triangular wedges wrapped in plastic. It's not the ideal situation, but work with what you've got.

First, *always* look for the words "Parmigiano Reggiano" stamped in dotted letters on the rind of your cheese.

Don't buy a piece of cheese that doesn't have the rind attached—a matter of freshness as well as honesty. The words Parmigiano Reggiano are repeated continuously around a wheel of true Parmesan cheese; it is impossible for them to be missing from a piece of the rind.

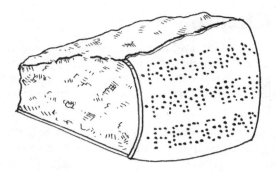

True Parmigiano Reggiano cheese always bears this distinctive mark in a continuous pattern.

Inspect the surface of a piece of Parmesan cheese carefully. It should be a golden color with small flecks of white. (Those flecks are protein deposits, which indicate slow aging.) Parmesan usually has very small holes in its surface. These are not large enough to make the surface porous-looking, but if you look very closely a few should be visible. The cheese should smell appetizing (if you can smell it through the plastic). If you can taste the cheese, it should have a slightly crumbly texture with the occasional crunchy bit, similar to a grain of sand, that dissolves in your mouth. Parmesan is by no means spicy, but it has a pleasantly salty taste. It has less of a dairy flavor than most other cheeses. Mozzarella, by way of contrast, tastes distinctly of milk.

Parmesan cheese is on the expensive side but a bargain if you use it in small amounts. The price seems justifiable when you consider that it takes about two gallons of milk to produce one pound of Parmesan cheese. Those enormous wheels, which weigh about 60 or 70 pounds, require close to 500 liters (more than 100 gallons) of milk each, which means that four cows are needed to produce the milk for one wheel of cheese in a single day. That the cheesemaking process must be executed by hand only increases the price.

Pasta Patter

All in the Family: Parmesan cheese is part of a family of cheeses known as *grana*, which are hard, yellow cheeses appropriate for grating. Aside from Parmesan, which is generally considered the most fully flavored of the grana family, the cheese known as *Grana Padano* is often available in the United States. When your Parmesan selection looks dicey, Grana Padano makes an acceptable alternative.

Making a Home for Cheese

Once you've gotten your piece of Parmesan and brought it home, unwrap it immediately. I often find that storage in plastic wrap (and I'm afraid I haven't seen wedges of Parmesan cheese stored any other way in the United States) creates a greasy film on the surface of the cheese. I pat it briefly with a clean towel, and then let it sit on its rind end for an hour or so to dry out.

Because it is an aged cheese, Parmesan stores nicely for long periods of time. If the cheese appears to be in top condition, I wrap it in aluminum foil and store it in the refrigerator for up to two weeks. If it appears dry, I wrap it in a damp cheesecloth, put a single layer of aluminum foil over the cheesecloth, and refrigerate it for about six hours (any longer and I'm afraid it will grow mold). If the cheese seems excessively wet, I still refrigerate it, but I wrap it loosely in wax paper so that some air can circulate around it. If I haven't used my hunk of Parmesan for a couple of days, I check it and moisten it or dry it using those same methods. One sign that cheese is drying out is a change in color from yellow to white. Such changes should be obvious.

Putting Parmesan to Work

Many of the recipes in this book call for grated Parmesan cheese to be either incorporated into a dish or served on the side. There are several different kinds of graters available. You can use the smallest holes on a traditional four-sided grater. You can also purchase a single, small-holed grater for use with cheese. Several companies now make a cleverly designed hand-operated grater in which you place a small piece of cheese into a drum that turns and grates the cheese.

Hand-operated cheese graters can be a boon when grating Parmesan cheese.

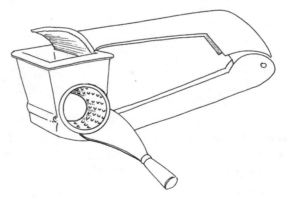

I don't recommend grating Parmesan cheese in a food processor because the pieces are never quite small enough for my taste. If you choose to go the automated route, use the steel blades rather than the perforated grating disk.

Pasta Patter

Get Fresh with Me: In the interest of utmost freshness, rather than passing a small bowl of grated Parmesan when serving pasta, place a small hunk of cheese on a plate and pass it along with a single-sided, small-holed grater. The cheese will have more flavor, and you'll have less work.

Eat It Raw

Parmesan is such an ingenious and delicious product, it would be a shame to relegate it only to pasta dishes. In Italy, it is often consumed as a table cheese. Parmesan even has its own special knife, shaped like half of a spade on a deck of playing cards. (Sometimes these knives are provided for free with a purchase of Parmesan cheese. If you can't locate such an offer, they are also available at the stores listed in Appendix B. Use the knife to break off wedges of Parmesan for eating out of hand.

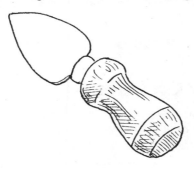

A specially shaped knife is best for breaking off pieces of Parmesan cheese.

Pasta Patter

Waste Not, Want Not: Don't throw away that Parmesan rind! When you've finished chipping off all the delicious cheese that was attached to it, scrape off the outside of the rind (the non-cheese side) and toss the rind into the soup pot. The rind adds great flavor to all kinds of Italian soups. You can even use it to make broth, although the broth will come out somewhat cloudy.

Parmesan has a place in each course of a meal. Small chunks can serve as appetizers. Italians believe that because of its great digestibility, Parmesan is one of those magical foods that opens the stomach and prepares it to welcome a meal. Accompany Parmesan with a prosecco wine (a kind of sparkling white wine), and you've got an elegant beginning. Naturally, Parmesan is served with a first course, such as a pasta or soup dish. It can also play a part in an Italian second course, such as a veal scallop. Italians serve many salads with shavings of Parmesan on top; a particularly good salad consists of raw artichoke hearts, thinly sliced raw mushrooms, and shavings of Parmesan dressed with olive oil and lemon juice. Parmesan can even be served as dessert, either as part of a cheese course or on its own. Parmesan cheese and pears are the classic fruit-and-cheese combination, but with its crinkly texture and salty taste, Parmesan contrasts nicely with almost all fruits.

Pasta Patter

Now You Can Smile When You Say Cheese: Parmesan cheese has one of the lowest cholesterol counts in the cheese family. It is also rich in protein and calcium. Because Parmesan cheese is more digestible than milk itself, Italians consider it excellent food for children and the elderly.

Altri Formaggi: **Other Cheeses**

Parmesan is, in many ways, the top Italian cheese. It accounts for about one-sixth of all cheese production in Italy, represented by 2,700,000 wheels of cheese per year, requiring 1,600 kilograms of milk. It is prized for melting evenly and for functioning equally well as a table cheese and as an ingredient. It is not, however, the only Italian cheese. Here are some other Italian cheeses you will encounter in this book and elsewhere.

Fontina is a very mild cheese from northern Italy's Valle d'Aosta region. It is similar to Swiss cheese in taste but less tangy and without the holes. Slices of fontina melt very well, making it ideal for omelets and grilled sandwiches.

Gorgonzola is an Italian blue cheese best identified by its pungent smell. You can use Gorgonzola very sparingly in salads. It is crumbly, with greenish veins running through it. Gorgonzola is usually made in the region of Lombardy (where the town of Gorgonzola is located).

Grana Padano is a hard Italian cheese similar to Parmesan cheese. It can sometimes serve as a substitute when Parmesan is not available, although I don't think Grana Padano ever has the same complexity of taste that Parmesan does. It can, however, be an acceptable substitute when high-quality Parmesan is not available. In other words,

I'd take a good piece of Grana Padano over a mediocre piece of Parmesan, but a good piece of Parmesan is still the top. Use the same criteria for judging Grana Padano as you would for judging Parmesan.

Mozzarella is probably best known outside of Italy for its use on pizza, but in Italy the best mozzarella—*mozzarella di bufala,* or buffalo's milk mozzarella—is sliced and served as a table cheese, either on its own or with sliced tomatoes. Buffalo's milk mozzarella (made from the milk of water buffalo raised in the regions of Latium and Campania) has become available in some specialty stores. Because buffalo's milk mozzarella is watery (in fact, it is packaged in water) it is not the best choice for melting. It is also quite expensive, so I feel that it should be enjoyed on its own. My first choice for use in pasta dishes is a type of Italian mozzarella known as *fior di latte,* but I almost never find that. My second choice is to buy cheese from a local producer of fresh mozzarella. If you do want to use buffalo's milk mozzarella, allow it to drain for thirty minutes or so before incorporating it. The rubbery, packaged mozzarella found in supermarkets is simply inexcusable. It has no flavor beyond saltiness, and worse, it melts into oily clumps.

Pecorino is sheep's milk cheese (*pecora* is the Italian word for sheep), and it comes in many forms. Fresh pecorino is mild and soft, almost white in color. Pecorino can be aged; it not only grows harder but develops a sharper flavor as well. Usually what we see labeled as "pecorino" is really *pecorino romano,* a very tangy grating cheese. Sometimes *pecorino romano* is recommended as a substitute for Parmesan, but I find it too sharply flavored for most dishes. Fresh pecorino, particularly from Tuscany, has recently become more widely available.

Ricotta is actually not a cheese in itself, but is made from whey, a byproduct of cheesemaking. Both cow's milk and sheep's milk ricotta are available. Italian ricotta is a real treat; in the Italian countryside it is often spread over toasted bread, topped with a sprinkling of sugar, and eaten for breakfast. Unfortunately, the ricotta available in plastic tubs in American grocery stores is far from suitable for that. Look for either imported Italian ricotta or freshly made American ricotta for the best results. If you cannot do any better than the grocery store kind, before using the ricotta, place a coffee filter in a strainer and allow some of the water to drip out before using (it should take about ten minutes).

Stracchino, which is also known as **crescenza,** is a smooth, slightly tangy Italian cheese that has a consistency somewhere between cream cheese and sour cream. Although it is most often eaten on its own or spread on bread or crackers, stracchino also can be used in baked pasta dishes. For a quick and unusual pizza: bake a crust, spread it with stracchino, and then top with chopped arugula.

Get Cooking

If you've read this far, you're ready to get into the kitchen and whip up some easy pasta dishes that allow cheese to shine as the main ingredient. When you've mastered the following recipes—a sort of "greatest hits" of pasta dishes—you're well on your way to pasta power.

Pasta al Burro e Formaggio
(Pasta with Butter and Cheese)

Butter makes a rich dish that I find quite comforting on a cold night. This is good with any kind of dried pasta, but I favor gemelli.

Serves 4

1 lb. dried pasta
6 tablespoons butter, cut into small pieces
$1/_2$ cup grated Parmesan cheese

1. Bring a large pot of water to a boil and cook the pasta according to the instructions on page 12.
2. When the pasta is done, drain it and pour it into a large serving bowl.
3. Sprinkle on the butter pieces while tossing the pasta.
4. Sprinkle on the grated Parmesan cheese.
5. Toss the pasta until it is coated evenly and all the butter has melted.

Pasta al Pomodoro e Mozzarella
(Pasta with Tomato and Mozzarella)

The mozzarella in this recipe melts deliciously when tossed with the pasta.

Serves 4

1 clove garlic, minced
2 tablespoons extra virgin olive oil
2 cups strained tomato purée
salt and freshly ground pepper to taste

1 lb. penne or other dried pasta
$1/_2$ cup diced mozzarella cheese
grated Parmesan cheese

1. Bring a large pot of water to a boil for cooking the pasta.
2. In a medium saucepan over medium heat, sauté the garlic in the olive oil until it softens, about 1 minute.
3. Stir in the tomato purée. Season to taste with salt and pepper.
4. Bring the sauce to a low simmer and cook, stirring occasionally, until thickened to the consistency of a thin sour cream.
5. Meanwhile, cook the pasta according to the instructions on page 12.
6. When the pasta is done, drain it, remove to a low, wide serving bowl, and top with the sauce. Sprinkle on the mozzarella cubes while tossing. Serve grated Parmesan on the side.

Pasta al Pomodoro e Mozzarella
(Pasta with Tomato and Mozzarella)

This is the same recipe but with ricotta in place of the mozzarella. The ricotta blends into the tomato sauce and enriches it.

Serves 4

1 clove garlic, minced	1 lb. penne or other dried pasta
2 tablespoons extra virgin olive oil	$^1/_2$ cup ricotta cheese
2 cups strained tomato purèe	grated Parmesan cheese
salt and freshly ground pepper to taste	

1. Bring a large pot of water to a boil for cooking the pasta.
2. In a medium saucepan over medium heat, sauté the garlic in the olive oil until it softens, about 1 minute.
3. Stir in the tomato purée. Season to taste with salt and pepper.
4. Bring the sauce to a low simmer and cook, stirring occasionally, until thickened to the consistency of a thin sour cream.
5. Meanwhile, cook the pasta according to the instructions on page 12.
6. When the pasta is done, drain it, remove to a low, wide serving bowl, and top with the sauce. Gradually stir in the ricotta cheese while tossing. Serve the grated Parmesan cheese on the side.

Maccheroncini ai Quattro Formaggi
(Maccheroncini with Four Cheeses)

Here is that old favorite macaroni and cheese in its original form.

Serves 4

1 tablespoon butter	$^1/_4$ cup cubed gorgonzola cheese
$^1/_2$ cup heavy cream	$^1/_4$ cup cubed mozzarella cheese
salt and freshly ground black pepper	$^1/_4$ cup grated fontina cheese
$^1/_4$ cup grated Parmesan cheese	1 lb. maccheroncini

1. Bring a large pot of water to a boil for cooking the pasta.
2. Melt the butter in a large pan over medium heat.
3. Add the heavy cream and season to taste with salt and pepper. Continue to heat the mixture until it reduces slightly, about 5 minutes.
4. Meanwhile, cook the pasta according to the instructions on page 12. When the pasta is *al dente*, drain it and transfer to the pot with the cream mixture.
5. Begin tossing the pasta over medium heat while gradually sprinkling on the cheese until all the liquid has been absorbed and the cheese is melted and evenly distributed—about 4 minutes. Transfer the pasta to a low, wide serving bowl.

The Least You Need to Know

➤ Real Parmesan cheese—called Parmigiano Reggiano in Italian—is the best cheese for grating over pasta.

➤ Always look for the Parmigiano Reggiano brand when buying Parmesan cheese.

➤ You can store a hunk of Parmesan cheese in the refrigerator for approximately two weeks.

➤ Grana Padano is the best substitute for Parmesan cheese.

Part 2
Saucy!

In Part 2, you really get up to your elbows in the kitchen with recipes. Most of these recipes call for dried pasta, although a few can also be made with fresh, homemade egg pasta. The recipes here are not just for sauces but for the entire pasta dish. Tomato sauces can be made in advance, but olive oil and cream sauces should be prepared right before serving.

A word on serving sizes: I consider a pound of dried pasta to serve four people, but if you are serving only a pasta course and nothing much else, two people could probably polish off close to a pound of pasta. If you are preparing pasta as part of a multi-course meal, one pound of pasta will suffice for six. I figure you're probably going to use these dishes as part of an American-style meal, meaning you'll serve a green salad or some other vegetable along with the pasta.

Keep in mind, too, that Italians don't serve pasta swimming in sauce. You may have grown accustomed to that arrangement over the years—many American restaurants still hold to the more sauce the better rule—but try these recipes as written (which will result in a light coating of sauce) at least once. If they're not to your liking, well, pasta recipes are never written in stone. You can easily adjust the recipes by adding more tomatoes, olive oil, or cream.

Chapter 5

You're darn Tootin'!

Olive Oil: More Than Just Popeye's Girlfriend

In This Chapter

➤ A brief history of olive oil

➤ Selecting and storing olive oil

➤ Using olive oil

➤ Olive oil and good health

Olive Oil: An Amazing Fruit Juice

Olive oil, the oil drawn from the fruit of the olive tree, is like a bed: when it's right, or comfortable, you hardly even think about it; when it's not right, your body and your palate toss and turn in discomfort.

Aside from pasta itself, no ingredient is as important to Italian cooking as a fresh, high-quality olive oil. With the exception of a few dishes, such as those classics in Chapter 4, Italians dress their pasta exclusively with olive oil. (This is a bit of a generalization: traditionally, the more dairy-rich northern half of Italy used butter on its pasta quite frequently, but in recent years, as health concerns about butter have grown, even northerners have switched to olive oil, saving butter for special occasions. Lard, too, has fallen by the wayside, also for health reasons.) When they do use butter, it serves as a condiment or adds extra flavor to a sauce cooked in olive oil. To make the classic

Ragu Bolognese (see page 154), for example, first sauté minced vegetables and meat in a combination of olive oil and butter. Olive oil always dominates, however.

Pasta Patter

Soaking It Up: Italy is second (after Spain) in worldwide production of olive oil but first in consumption. Per capita, Italians consume approximately twelve liters (more than three gallons) of olive oil each year.

It's Ancient History

Olive oil has been around a long, long time. One of the earliest references to olive oil is the Babylonian code of Hammurabi, dated 2500 B.C., which regulated the production and sale of olive oil. Phoenicians and Carthaginians sold olive oil, too. And in Greece, olive oil was believed to be a gift from the goddess Athena. The story goes like this: Athena and Poseidon found themselves in the court of Zeus and each was to make an offering to him. Poseidon pulled out his trident and created a lake of salt water to represent the ocean. Athena made the earth move and split in half, and an olive tree popped out of the crack. Needless to say, Athena won the showdown.

Although the Greeks used olive oil as a condiment, they also believed it to be effective as a medicine and a beauty enhancer. It was the Greeks who first brought olives to Italy. Greek colonists planted the trees, which flourished. By the time the '60s came around (the year 60 B.C., that is), the Etruscans boasted enormous olive groves.

Pasta Patter

Branching Out: Olive tree branches decorated the tombs of the pharaohs in ancient Egypt. They served as symbols of life and fertility. In Homer's *Ulysses*, Ulysses builds his matrimonial bed out of the trunk of an olive tree, presumably for the same reasons.

We Do as the Romans Did

During the Roman Empire, in a kind of early food stamp program, olive oil and bread were occasionally distributed to the poorest citizens for free. It was during that period that olive oil became a true business for the first time. Not only were a dozen varieties of olives already growing in what is now Italy, but the sale of olive oil was carefully regulated as well. Official *negotiatores olearii*, or oil sellers, were the only people certified to sell olive oil, and they did so at the *arca olearia*, or olive oil market.

In ancient Rome, olive oil was divided into five categories so that it could be priced more fairly. From most expensive to least, they were as follows:

1. Oil from green olives harvested by hand
2. Oil from olives harvested first stage of darkening
3. Oil from ripe olives harvested in winter
4. Oil from olives that had fallen to the ground
5. Oil from olives that had been gnawed by insects

The oil in the last two categories was most often served to slaves.

Pasta Patter

The Crown of Victory: After winning a battle, Roman emperors and generals wore crowns made of olive twigs to indicate that peace had been restored.

The Olive Doesn't Fall Far from the Tree

When it comes to picking out fruits and vegetables, selecting meat or fish, or even choosing a brand of pasta, there are few set guidelines. You have to rely mostly on your senses of taste, touch, and smell, as well as on your own common sense. You are in luck when it comes time to buy olive oil, though. Olive oil producers have created a system for labeling and categorizing their products. This system is far from foolproof, but it does help matters a great deal.

Linguine Lingo

Primary Colors: Italians often refer to olive oil as *oro verde*, or "green gold." This nickname refers to the high price of olive oil.

There are three categories of olive oil. As the following table indicates, oils are ranked by acidity and the methods used to extract the juice from the olives:

Olive Oil Categories

Type	Acidity	Extraction
Olive oil	1.5 percent	Chemical
Virgin olive oil	2 percent	Cold pressed
Extra virgin olive oil	1 percent	Cold pressed

An Oil to Avoid

At first glance, plain olive oil (sometimes labeled "pure" olive oil—although not an official category) may appear to be better than virgin olive oil, since it has an acidity of only 1.5 percent. The level of acidity in olive oil, however, has usually been reduced by means of chemical processes, which not only subtract oleic acid, but also sap the oil of its natural flavor.

Use Your Noodle

Read Carefully: Don't be taken in by labels claiming that olive oil is "light" or "pure." The only strictly regulated categories for olive oil are extra virgin, virgin, and just plain olive oil. A lighter color indicates a lesser quality oil; most "light" olive oils have been mixed with other types of oil (corn, peanut) to achieve a lighter color.

When olives are processed by industrial machinery that chugs along at increasing speed, the olives reach a high temperature and lose much of their nutritional value and flavor. Chemical processes geared to extracting every last drop from the olive are even more questionable.

In short, don't buy pure olive oil.

Dubious Virginity

Virgin olive oil has its place in the kitchen for cooking purposes—not in raw form (for dressing a salad or drizzling on soup). However, you will probably purchase only one type of olive oil, and if that is the case you should stick with extra virgin olive oil. Virgin olive oil can be used for deep frying. It is sharply acidic when raw, and has none of the fruitiness for which olive oil is prized. Although virgin olive oil can be useful, it will never be delicate.

Pasta Patter

Statistically Speaking: Today, approximately 800 million olive trees are growing around the world, 90 percent of which are somewhere along the Mediterranean basin. Thanks in large part to Italian emigrants, olive oil is now also produced in Argentina, Australia, Chile, China, Japan, Korea, New Zealand, Russia, South Africa, Ukraine, and the United States.

Go the Extra Mile

As you will have surmised by now, I advocate using extra virgin olive oil whenever possible. It tastes great. Extra virgin olive oil has a mellow flavor that goes well with almost anything. Italians agree; a few sweet cakes in Italy even have olive oil as an ingredient. Extra virgin olive oil is also the healthiest of the three types. Even within the extra virgin category, there are a few things you can look for that indicate superior quality.

Like oenophiles (that is, wine lovers), olive oil experts and others hold tastings at which they compare various extra virgin olive oils. You can do the same:

1. Decant small amounts of various extra virgin olive oils into small glasses, such as shot glasses (experts have specific containers for this, but glasses should be fine). Number the glasses as you go so that you will know which oils pleased your palate.

2. To begin, pick up a glass in one hand, cover the top with the other, and hold the glass in your hand until the oil has reached the same temperature as your hands.

3. Inspect the oil visually. Consider the color and clarity. Simply looking at an oil won't tell you much, but you should note any great imperfections like serious discoloration.

4. Smell the oil, taking in a very deep breath. The oil may smell slightly spicy but should not evidence any odor of mold or extreme bitterness.

5. To taste an oil, curl your tongue and allow a few drops to drip into the curved part towards the front. Gently suck the oil towards the back of your throat, allowing it to pass slowly over the various taste buds. Is the oil fruity? Spicy? Mellow? Also pay attention to the consistency. It shouldn't feel particularly greasy.

You Can See Clearly

There is a tendency among Americans to buy items, especially food-related items, that are light-colored or clear. When it comes to oils, however, we ought to do just the opposite. Slightly murky olive oil is difficult to find in the United States, but easy to recognize. It has a certain amount of fogginess. The difference is one of filtration. Like pasta, extra virgin olive oil can be made either industrially or by artisans. In the former case, the oil is filtered through a cellulose net, which catches any stray matter in the oil along with the olive dregs. Artisanal oils, however, have probably been strained through a cheesecloth, which catches the big chunks of matter, but not the cloudiness.

Pasta Patter

Aging Gracefully: Archeologists have discovered an olive tree in Tuscany that appears to be 3,500 years old.

Color Me Green or Mellow Yellow

A deep green olive oil is most likely younger than a gold olive oil. (Or the olives may have been harvested at a different time or be a different type.) As a rule, the greener the oil, the spicier the taste, since olive oil mellows over time. If you can get your hands on a bottle of almost emerald green *olio novello,* or "new oil," try it. None of the oils I've ever tried has smacked so distinctly of olives as *olio novello.*

This discussion of color and aging might lead you to believe that green olive oil is always better than yellow, but that is not the case. First and foremost, there is the matter of taste. Some people love the tingly taste of new, green olive oil, while others prefer the less prevalent taste of mellow, slightly aged olive oil. Those in the gourmet camp would argue that you need at least two bottles on hand at all times: a mellow oil for cooking and a spicier oil for dressing salads, cooked vegetables, and so forth. Since I am against clutter in the kitchen, and since oil does not keep forever, that seems a little silly to me. I use the greenest, most fully flavored olive oil I can find. Not only does it taste great on salads, but when heated, the flavor grows less spicy.

Under Pressure

Another factor in the creation of olive oil is the process used to extract the oil from the olives. As noted previously, extra virgin olive oil must be cold-pressed and from the first pressing of the olives. Here, too, however, there are differences from company to company.

The method for creating olive oil has not changed much over the years. An olive oil press found on the island of Santorini that dates back to the Mycenaean Age (1400–1100 B.C.), consists of a bowl-shaped stone in which workers deposited the olives, and another concave stone that was dropped on top of them. This activity created a kind of olive paste, which was then transferred to baskets that allowed the oil to leak out. The oil was then decanted.

The best olive oil is still made using old-fashioned stone presses (the price is high because the process is slow). Perhaps somewhere in the countryside of Italy there is a lonely farmer who still layers his olives between mats and extracts oil that way. Most of the olive oil sold today, however, and certainly most of the Italian olive oil that makes its way to the United States, has been pressed by machine. This is not necessarily bad news. If machines are used correctly—that is, not allowed to overheat and without the addition of hot water, which makes the process faster but also dilutes the oil—they produce excellent olive oil. If you happen to spot a bottle of oil that has been stone-pressed, however, give it a try.

Olive oil extracted with a stone press is highly valued.

What Price Virginity?

Fine olive oil is expensive. Olives are difficult to grow; a single freeze can wipe out the year's crop, and they require extensive manual labor, including pruning. While machines have been developed for extracting the oil from the olives, no machine has yet been developed that can properly coax an olive grove to produce a large number of olives. Fine olive oil is also expensive because the process for extracting extra virgin olive oil is, by definition, a slow one. In other words, you get what you pay for. Any olive oil bargain that seems too good to be true probably is.

Pasta Practice

California Dreaming: California has a climate similar to Italy. As a result, many of the same products that grow in Italy (grapes, for example) thrive in California. If you are looking to save a little money, olive oil made in California is often a good bet since it does not bear any import taxes. Use the same criteria to choose a fine olive oil from California as you would to choose one from Italy.

Use Your Noodle

Keep Spray Away: Since olive oil is very sensitive to changes in temperature, movement, and even the simple passage of time, using olive oil in a spray bottle eliminates many of its good qualities, including flavor. If you are in the habit of spraying cookie sheets and baking pans with oil to cover them lightly, try this instead: pour on a small amount of olive oil, then use a clean cotton or paper towel to simultaneously distribute the oil evenly and soak up any extra.

How to Keep a Virgin Happy

Olive oil changes over time. Its taste mellows, its color deepens, and—like all oils—it can go bad. Because of its high vitamin E content, however, olive oil can preserve itself at room temperature longer than other oils. Olive oil will keep at room temperature for about one year, although if you keep oil that long you will note some changes in the taste. If you can, buy extra virgin olive oil with a date stamped on it and then count your one-year period as beginning with that date, not with the date of purchase.

The best material for storing olive oil is certainly glass. If you buy large amounts of oil in metal canisters (it is often less expensive) immediately decant it into several glass bottles. You can also buy a small oil can and refill it from a larger bottle, but I like to store things in glass so that I can see when I am close to finishing them. Never refrigerate olive oil; it not only congeals into an unappealing cloud, it loses a great deal of flavor as well. Store your bottles in a dark, cool, dry place (a kitchen pantry is usually ideal). Light penetrates glass easily and can also affect the oil.

Pour Away!

Olive oil is so delicious it would be a shame to use it only on pasta. The recipes later in this chapter will help you make good use of a fine extra virgin olive oil. Once you've stocked up on one, you can also use it as follows:

➤ Dress a salad (along with a little vinegar)
➤ Deep fry potatoes or other foods (olive oil is stable at high temperatures)
➤ Sauté fish
➤ Drizzle on any type of soup
➤ Make *bruschetta*: toast slices of bread, rub them with garlic, salt to taste, and drizzle on olive oil
➤ Cook eggs and omelets
➤ Mix with herbs (and minced hot pepper if you like) and serve as a dip with crusty bread

➤ Make *bagna cauda*: heat the olive oil and serve with slices of raw fennel, celery, and other vegetables, then have diners dip their vegetables into the hot oil to "cook" them slightly

➤ Make your own mayonnaise

➤ Drizzle on grilled meat and fish

Some olive oil connoisseurs even drink a tablespoon or two in the morning as a kind of preventive medicine.

Say "Olive You" to Your Body

By now most people have heard the "Mediterranean diet" being vaunted as the surest way to good health and long life. While the phrase "Mediterranean diet" has been interpreted to mean many things, there is one constant in all the interpretations: the Mediterranean diet relies heavily on olive oil.

Although all oils have approximately 14 grams of fat per tablespoon, they are not all the same. Part of the magic of olive oil lies in its high percentage of monounsaturated fat (75 percent) versus its low percentage of polyunsaturated fat (9 percent). The following table compares the levels of these types of fatty acids in other cooking fats:

Fatty Acids in Various Cooking Fats

Cooking fat	Polyunsaturated fat (grams)	Monounsaturated fat (grams)	Saturated fat (grams)
Olive oil	1.5	10	2
Corn oil	8	3.5	2
Canola oil	4	8	1
Sunflower oil	9	3	2
Peanut oil	4	7	2.5

What does this mean in real-life terms, without the scientific mumbo-jumbo? It means that olive oil lowers total cholesterol. Olive oil also raises HDL cholesterol (the so-called "good" cholesterol), which serves to clean out your arteries. Olive oil, especially extra virgin olive oil, is also rich in vitamin E. (In part, it is natural vitamin E that grants olive oil such a long shelf life; vitamin E is often added to other oils as a stabilizer.) Olive oil is also highly digestible. Your body assimilates it easily.

Pasta Patter

High Marks for Olive Oil: The famous Seven Country Study of the 1950s observed the diets of inhabitants of Finland, Japan, Greece, Italy, Holland, the United States, and what was then Yugoslavia. Researchers confirmed that the so-called "Mediterranean diet," consisting of pasta, fish, fruits, and vegetables, and cooked and dressed almost exclusively with olive oil, was the most conducive to avoiding heart disease.

Get Cooking

Pasta in Bianco
(White Pasta)

When Italians are sick or exhausted, they turn to *Pasta in Bianco*, which is considered restorative.

Serves 4

1 lb. penne or other dried pasta

$1/2$ cup extra virgin olive oil

$1/2$ cup grated Parmesan cheese

1. Bring a large pot of water to a boil and cook the pasta according to the instructions on page 12.
2. When the pasta is done, drain it and pour it into a large serving bowl.
3. Drizzle on the olive oil and toss to coat thoroughly.
4. Sprinkle on the grated Parmesan cheese.
5. Toss to coat the pasta thoroughly.

Gemelli con Aglio Verde e Olio Novello
(Gemelli with Green Garlic and Young Olive Oil)

When you want to let the taste of Italy's spicy *olio novello* shine through, reach for this recipe. Green garlic is very young garlic that resembles a scallion or chive. It is available in spring when *olio novello* is also available. You can make a good facsimile of this in winter with an older olive oil and a couple cloves of garlic.

Serves 4

1 lb. gemelli or other dried pasta

1 bunch green garlic, white part minced

$^1/_2$ cup *olio novello* (extra virgin olive oil)

1. Bring a large pot of water to a boil and cook the pasta according to the instructions on page 12.
2. When the pasta is done, drain it and transfer to a large serving bowl.
3. Sprinkle on the olive oil and minced garlic.
4. Toss to coat pasta thoroughly.

Spaghetti Aglio, Olio, e Peperoncino
(Spaghetti with Garlic, Oil, and Hot Pepper)

This is *the* recipe to rely on when you've got nothing for dinner and everyone's hungry. It's also a good candidate for a *spaghettata,* a quick, late-night snack based around spaghetti. You can vary the amount of hot pepper used in this recipe. Add an entire teaspoon if you've got chile-heads coming to dinner; reduce the amount to a pinch if you're feeding the timid.

Serves 4

1 lb. spaghetti

$^1/_2$ cup extra virgin olive oil

$^1/_2$ teaspoon cracked hot red pepper

4 cloves garlic, thinly sliced

$^1/_4$ cup toasted breadcrumbs

$^1/_4$ cup chopped parsley (optional)

1. Bring a large pot of water to a boil and cook the pasta according to the instructions on page 12.
2. When the pasta is about 2 minutes from being cooked, pour about $^3/_4$ of the olive oil into a large saucepan.

continues

53

continued

3. Add the cracked hot red pepper to the pan.

4. Add the garlic slices and sauté until they just begin to turn color, and then turn off the heat. After you turn off the heat, the garlic will brown and turn crispy. If you wait until it turns brown to turn off the heat, it will burn.

5. When the pasta is done, drain it and add it to the pan. Sprinkle on the breadcrumbs while tossing the spaghetti in the oil sauce over medium heat for 2 minutes, until the strands are coated, and the garlic, hot pepper, and breadcrumbs are evenly distributed. Remove the pasta to a low, wide serving bowl and drizzle on the remaining olive oil. Top with parsley, if desired.

Spaghetti alle Erbe Aromatiche (Spaghetti with Herbs)

Italians have made simplicity into an art, and this is one of the masterpieces. *Erbe aromatiche* are Italian herbs such as oregano, basil, and parsley in their fresh (not dried) form. As the name implies, they possess a heavenly smell. Don't even consider using dried herbs in this recipe. They will impart a bitter taste.

Serves 4

1 lb. spaghetti

1 cup chopped, fresh herbs, such as parsley, oregano, basil, and rosemary

2 cloves garlic, minced

$^1/_2$ cup extra virgin olive oil

salt and freshly ground pepper to taste

$^1/_3$ cup chopped walnuts

grated Parmesan cheese

1. Bring a large pot of water to a boil and cook the pasta according to the instructions on page 12.

2. While the pasta is cooking, toss the herbs, garlic, walnuts, and about $^3/_4$ of the olive oil in a low, wide serving bowl. Season to taste with salt and pepper and set aside.

3. When the pasta is done, drain it and add it to the serving bowl. Toss the spaghetti in the oil sauce until the strands are coated and the garlic and herbs are evenly distributed.

4. Drizzle on the remaining olive oil and serve with Parmesan cheese on the side.

For a slightly more filling dish, crumble some fresh goat cheese into the herb mixture.

The Least You Need to Know

➤ Your best choice is an extra virgin olive oil.

➤ You can store olive oil at room temperature for approximately one year.

➤ Olive oil is the healthiest cooking fat; it actually lowers your cholesterol.

Chapter 6

Oil and Water: The Quickest and Easiest Italian Pasta Dishes

In This Chapter

➤ Cooking seasonally

➤ Methods for pasta with olive oil sauces

➤ Recipes for pasta with olive oil sauces

Almost every pasta dish (almost every Italian dish, for that matter) contains some olive oil. The special pasta treats in this chapter, however, feature olive oil as the starring ingredient. It is not merely used for sautéing, but serves as a sauce that coats each piece of pasta and perfumes the entire dish. Pasta with oil-based sauces are among the easiest dishes to prepare and require very little time. They can be as simple as al dente pasta tossed with herbs and an excellent, fruity olive oil. Naturally, since olive oil is the main ingredient in these sauces, using a high-quality oil is particularly key. That goes for the rest of the ingredients as well. (For more information on olive oil, please see Chapter 5, "Olive Oil: More Than Just Popeye's Girlfriend.")

Pasta Patter

Con l'olio ed il sale, si fa buono anche uno stivale. Even a boot tastes good with oil and salt. — Italian proverb

To Market, To Market

Creating pasta dishes dressed in olive oil presents a perfect opportunity for marketing the Italian way: visiting your local purveyor of vegetables, buying what looks good and what's in season, and then deciding what to do with it.

If you have a farmers' market nearby, you are in luck. Visit the stands, touch the produce (gently), and most importantly, ask a lot of questions. People who grow food almost always have hints on how to handle it.

Pasta Patter

In most places in Italy, a visit to the *fruttivendolo*, or fruit and vegetable seller, is a daily ritual.

If you need to visit a conventional grocery store, your task is harder but by no means impossible.

Use touch, smell, sight, and taste to examine the produce that's available. First, pick up the vegetables and feel their heft in your hand. Apply slight pressure to the skin. Is it too soft? Too hard? Most vegetables should yield slightly but still feel firm.

Smell your vegetables. You may get some strange looks when you try this in the supermarket, but any vegetable worth its salt (and yours) has a recognizable smell.

Examine all sides of the vegetable. Does it look fresh? Check for bruises, broken skin, and fully ripe color. (Some items, such as tomatoes, can be ripened at home.) Don't be fooled by giant-sized specimens. Although they might look impressive, they are generally less tasty than their small- and medium-sized cousins.

Pasta Patter

Many fruits and vegetables in the United States are harvested before they are ripe, and then allowed to ripen in transit.

Finally, taste a little, if possible. Now I don't expect you to bite into a tomato at your local supermarket, but you can pinch off a leaf of basil or sneak a bit of arugula. Many farmers at farmers' markets regularly offer tastes of their products. Remember, anything that doesn't taste good raw (or that simply doesn't have much taste, which is most often the case) will not improve when cooked.

Shopping seasonally and locally is the best way to ensure that you are eating the freshest foods available. Use the following list to choose foods in season (remember that seasons vary depending where in the country you live), and check the sides of cartons or ask your local supermarket manager to find out where foods are grown. Health food supermarkets often mark the name of the farm where the produce is grown.

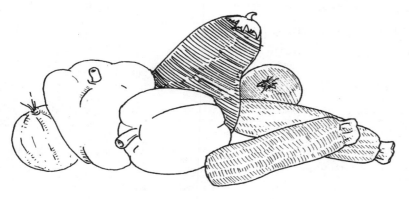

Locally grown vegetables are fresher and taste better.

Vegetables by Season

Winter

Cabbage	Potatoes	Turnips
Carrots	Sweet potatoes	Winter squash
Kale		

Spring

Artichokes	Chives	Spinach
Arugula	Green garlic	Watercress
Asparagus	Leeks	

Summer

Corn	Green beans	Radishes
Cucumbers	Peas	Tomatoes
Eggplant	Peppers	Zucchini

Autumn

Beets	Brussels sprouts	Mushrooms
Broccoli	Cauliflower	Mustard greens
Broccoli rabe	Fennel	Shell beans

When you arrive home with your bounty, spread it out on a counter or table and consider how it could best be used. Have you bought tender spring greens that need only a splash of oil to emphasize their flavor, or a bunch of kale that needs to be boiled? Generally, you can steam spring and summer produce lightly (or in some cases not at all) and toss it with oil and pasta, while fall and winter vegetables need to be cooked. Try varying your techniques and see what happens. Tomatoes, for example, are delicious raw, but can also be slow-roasted to intensify their flavor. Fennel is usually sautéed or eaten raw in salads, but it develops a whole new taste when grilled.

Don't forget the following cooking techniques:

Blanching: Food is immersed in boiling water for a few minutes, and then immersed in cold water to stop cooking.

Good candidates for blanching: artichoke hearts, peas, string beans.

Boiling: Food is cooked in boiling water for an extended period.

Good candidates for boiling: broccoli, potatoes, winter greens.

Grilling: Food is cooked close to an open flame (If you don't have a grill, you can approximate its effects with your broiler.)

Good candidates for grilling: eggplant, large mushrooms, radicchio.

Roasting: Food is cooked in the oven.

Good candidates for roasting: beets, sweet potatoes, winter squash.

Sautéing: Food is cooked on a stove with some form of fat.

Good candidates for sautéing: mushrooms, leeks, zucchini.

Serving raw: Food is left uncooked.

Good candidates for serving raw: arugula, salad greens, tomatoes.

Steaming: Food is cooked in a basket set above boiling water.

Good candidates for steaming: asparagus, carrots, spinach.

The Perfect Foil for Oil

All the olive oil sauces in this chapter can be prepared while the pasta is cooking; several of these recipes require no cooking at all beyond boiling water and cooking the pasta.

While preparing these dishes is not difficult, they are meant to be served immediately once they are ready, so set the table beforehand.

Most recipes follow the same pattern:

1. Boil water for the pasta.
2. Sauté items in some olive oil.
3. Drain the cooked pasta and add it to the pan.
4. Drizzle on additional olive oil.

Be sure the pasta is cooked until just al dente. It will cook a little more when tossed in the pan.

Linguine Lingo

In Italy, a *spaghettata* is a late-night snack consisting of simply prepared spaghetti, usually shared after a night on the town.

Pasta Patter

In Italian, tossing pasta with other ingredients in a pan is called *saltare in padella*, literally "jumping in the pan."

Don't skimp on that final drizzle of olive oil. Olive oil loses some of its flavor when heated, so that last addition of unheated oil is what you'll taste first.

So Simple, So Good

Gemelli alla Rucola e Asparagi (Gemelli with Arugula and Asparagus)

Gemelli is the Italian word for twins. This thick pasta gets its name from the two strands that twist together to form each individual piece. This dish uses the fresh flavors of early spring. Make it when the first new greens become available. If possible, buy pencil-thin wild asparagus. It has a stronger flavor and cooks more quickly than asparagus with thick stalks. If you can only find asparagus with thick stalks, cut them in half lengthwise. Arugula is tender and mild when young but spicier when more mature. Sometimes more mature arugula is steamed or sautéed briefly. In this recipe, even spicy arugula mellows when tossed with the hot pasta.

Serves 4

1 lb. gemelli

2 bunches asparagus, tough stems removed, and cut into $^1/_2$-inch pieces

$^1/_2$ cup extra virgin olive oil

1 clove garlic, minced

1 bunch arugula, cleaned and cut into ribbons

salt and freshly ground pepper to taste

grated Parmesan cheese (optional)

1. Bring a large pot of water to a boil and cook the pasta according to instructions on page 12.
2. While the pasta is cooking, in a medium pan sauté the asparagus pieces in 2 tablespoons of the oil over medium heat until tender. Use a slotted spoon to remove the cooked asparagus to a low, wide serving bowl.
3. When the pasta is done, drain and add it to the serving bowl. Add the garlic, arugula, and remaining olive oil and toss to coat the pasta and distribute the asparagus.
4. Season to taste with salt and pepper, and serve with Parmesan cheese on the side.

Linguine alle Vongole
(Linguine with Clams)

Use the smallest littleneck clams you can find for this recipe.

Serves 4

1 clove garlic, minced	$^1/_2$ cup white wine
3 tablespoons extra virgin olive oil	1 lb. linguine
24 littleneck clams, cleaned	$^1/_4$ cup chopped parsley

To clean clams, soak them in several changes of cold water until no sand appears at the bottom of the bowl. Scrub each clam briefly under cold running water.

1. Bring a large pot of water to a boil for cooking the pasta.

2. In a large pan over medium heat, sauté the garlic in 1 tablespoon of the olive oil until it softens, about 1 minute.

3. Add the clams and wine. Cover the pan and cook until all the clams have opened, about 8 minutes. Discard any unopened clams.

4. Meanwhile, cook the pasta according to the instructions on page 12. When the pasta is al dente, drain it and add it to the pan. Toss over medium heat until all the clam juices have been absorbed.

5. Drizzle on the remaining 2 tablespoons of olive oil. Sprinkle on chopped parsley.

Linguine Mare e Monti
(Linguine with Shrimp
and Mushrooms)

Mare e monti means "sea and mountains." Combining shrimp (or other shellfish) with mushrooms and tossing them over pasta is the Italian version of "surf and turf."

Serves 4

1 clove garlic, minced	salt and freshly ground pepper to taste
$^1/_4$ cup extra virgin olive oil	1 lb. linguine
1 cup sliced mushrooms	$^1/_4$ cup chopped parsley
1 lb. small shrimp, shelled and deveined	

1. Bring a large pot of water to a boil for cooking the pasta.

2. In a large pan over medium heat, sauté the garlic in 2 tablespoons of the olive oil until it softens, about 1 minute.

continues

63

continued

3. Add the mushrooms and sauté until they are soft and have given up most of their liquid.

4. Remove the mushrooms with a slotted spoon and set aside. Add the shrimp to the pan and sauté until cooked through, about 3 minutes.

5. Return the mushrooms to the pan and season the mixture to taste with salt and pepper.

6. Meanwhile, cook the pasta according to the instructions on page 12. When the pasta is al dente, drain and add it to the pan.

7. Drizzle on the remaining olive oil and toss over medium heat. Sprinkle on parsley before serving.

Spaghetti alla Carbonara
(Spaghetti with Bacon and Eggs)

This isn't exactly an oil-based sauce, but neither is it a cream or tomato sauce. The eggs cook slightly upon contact with the hot pasta. The consumption of raw eggs has occasionally caused cases of salmonella—a type of food poisoning. Use only the freshest eggs in this recipe, and follow any other necessary precautions. You can use American-style bacon in place of pancetta if you can't find pancetta, or if you simply prefer American-style bacon. Prepared that way, *spaghetti alla carbonara* makes a wonderful and unusual brunch dish.

Serves 4

1 lb. spaghetti

2 ¼-inch thick slices pancetta, diced

3 tablespoons extra virgin olive oil

3 eggs

salt and freshly ground pepper to taste

¼ cup chopped parsley (optional)

grated Parmesan cheese

1. Bring a large pot of water to a boil and cook the pasta according to the instructions on page 12.

2. Meanwhile, in a small pan, sauté the pancetta in 2 tablespoons of olive oil until just crisp, and then set aside.

3. In a small bowl, beat the eggs until the yolks and whites are thoroughly combined. Season the eggs to taste with salt and pepper.

4. When the pasta is done, drain and transfer it to a low, wide serving bowl. Add the cooked pancetta and cooking oil.

5. Pour on the egg mixture and toss it to coat the spaghetti and distribute the pancetta evenly. Drizzle on the remaining tablespoon of oil and toss again.

6. Sprinkle on the parsley, and serve grated cheese on the side.

Fusilli con Carote Piccanti
(Fusilli with Spicy Carrots)

Sweet, hot, and sour tastes meld together in this simple yet strongly flavored dish. This dish is good with almost any kind of pasta, including spaghetti and penne. *Balsamic vinegar* is made from Italian Trebbiano grapes aged through a highly specialized process. It has a distinctive, slightly sweet flavor. You can purchase balsamic vinegar in gourmet specialty stores. For an unusual switch, replace the carrots in this recipe with the diced flesh of a winter squash, such as a delicata squash.

Serves 4

1 lb. fusilli

3 cloves garlic, minced

1 small red chile pepper, minced

$1/2$ cup extra virgin olive oil

4 carrots, grated on the largest holes of a 4-sided grater

$1/4$ cup white wine

1 tablespoon balsamic vinegar

$1/4$ cup chopped parsley

1. Bring a large pot of water to a boil and cook the pasta according to the instructions on page 12.
2. Meanwhile, in a large pan over medium heat, sauté the garlic and pepper in $1/4$ cup of the olive oil just until the garlic is softened, about 1 minute.
3. Add the grated carrots and sauté until the carrots are softened, about 2 minutes. Add the wine and continue to cook, stirring frequently, until the wine has evaporated.
4. Add a ladleful of the pasta cooking water to the carrots and cook until about half of the water has evaporated.
5. When the pasta is done, drain and add it to the pan with the carrots. Tossing constantly over medium heat, drizzle on the remaining olive oil. Continue to toss over medium heat until all liquid has been absorbed.
6. Transfer the pasta to a low, wide serving bowl. Drizzle on the balsamic vinegar and toss to distribute evenly. Sprinkle the chopped parsley over the pasta.

Farfalle con Zucchine
(Farfalle with Zucchini)

Light and pretty, this is fare fit for a garden party.

Serves 4

1 lb. farfalle

1 clove garlic, crushed

³/₄ cup extra virgin olive oil

2 medium zucchini, cut into
1-inch julienne strips

salt and freshly ground pepper to taste

1 cup loosely packed basil leaves

grated Parmesan cheese

1. Bring a large pot of water to a boil and cook the pasta according to the instructions on page 12.

2. Meanwhile, in a large pan over medium heat, sauté the garlic clove in ¹/₄ cup of the oil until browned. Remove the garlic and discard.

3. Add the zucchini to the garlic-flavored oil and cook it until it just begins to brown, about 5 minutes. Remove the zucchini with a slotted spoon and set aside. Season to taste with salt and pepper.

4. When the pasta is done, drain and transfer it to a low, wide serving bowl. Add the zucchini and remaining ¹/₂ cup olive oil and toss to coat the pasta and distribute zucchini pieces evenly.

5. Tear the basil leaves onto the pasta. Serve grated cheese on the side.

Penne Primavera
(Penne with Spring Vegetables)

Celebrate spring by remaining flexible. You can use almost any green spring vegetable in this dish.

Serves 4

1 lb. garganelli or other dried pasta

2 tablespoons chopped yellow onion

¹/₂ cup extra virgin olive oil

1 cup shelled peas

1 cup chopped asparagus

4 baby artichokes, cleaned and chopped

salt and freshly ground pepper to taste

¹/₂ cup ricotta

1 cup loosely packed arugula, cut into ribbons

grated Parmesan cheese

To prepare the asparagus, grip the stalk end in one hand while holding the stalk firmly in the other. Snap off the tough end of the stalk (not the pointed tip) and discard. To clean a baby artichoke, remove all the hard outer leaves (you will feel as though you are throwing away a lot, but don't worry), then slice off the pointy top. Baby artichokes do not contain a fuzzy choke, but occasionally a downy layer does grow in their centers. Use the tip of a small paring knife to remove any hairy growth. Peel the stem and bowl-like bottom of the artichoke. Drop prepared artichokes into a bowl of cold water with a liberal dose of lemon juice to keep them from discoloring. If your ricotta contains a lot of liquid, drain it in a coffee filter set in a strainer while preparing the other ingredients.

1. Bring a large pot of water to a boil and cook the pasta according to instructions on page 12.

2. Meanwhile, in a large pan sauté the onion in $1/4$ cup of the oil until softened, about 2 minutes.

3. Add the peas and sauté until tender, adding small amounts of the pasta cooking water to the pan to keep the peas from sticking, if necessary.

4. Add the asparagus and artichokes and continue to sauté the vegetables until they are tender enough to be pierced with a fork. Again, add small amounts of the pasta cooking water to the pan if necessary. Season to taste with salt and pepper.

5. When the pasta is done, drain and transfer it to a low, wide serving bowl. Add the vegetable mixture, ricotta, arugula, and remaining $1/2$ cup olive oil, and toss to coat the pasta and distribute the vegetables evenly. Serve grated cheese on the side.

Pasta con le Sarde
(Pasta with Sardines)

This is Sicily's signature pasta dish. The version made there uses wild fennel. *Fennel* is a versatile vegetable that comes in the form of a bulb with fern-like fronds. It tastes like licorice when eaten raw; when cooked, it is much milder. *Perciatelli* are long pasta, similar to spaghetti, with a hole running down the middle. They are sometimes called *bucatini*.

Serves 4

2 tablespoons currants

1 bulb fennel with fronds (if fronds are not available, use 1 bulb fennel and 1 bunch dill)

1 lb. perciatelli or spaghetti

$1/2$ cup extra virgin olive oil

1 small yellow onion, chopped

1 lb. fresh sardines, head and tail removed, cleaned, boned, and chopped

$1/4$ teaspoon saffron threads

1 tablespoon pine nuts

1. Soak the currants in warm water, covered.

2. Meanwhile, scrub the fennel well and cut away the base and the fronds. Discard the base and any tough stalks. Soak the fronds in several changes of water to clean them. Dry the fronds, chop them roughly, and set aside.

3. Bring a large pot of water to a boil.

continues

67

continued

4. Boil the fennel bulb for 10 minutes. Remove the bulb with a slotted spoon. Leave the water in the pot, let it return to a boil, and then cook the pasta in it according to instructions on page 12.

5. While the pasta is cooking, in a large pan heat $1/4$ cup of the olive oil over very gentle heat. Sauté the onion without browning for about 5 minutes, until it is completely translucent.

6. Add the sardines and sauté for 3 additional minutes.

7. Grind the saffron threads in a mortar and pestle, then dissolve the saffron powder in 1 tablespoon lukewarm water.

8. Dice the cooked fennel and add it to the pan along with the saffron water. Stir until the fennel is evenly colored. Drain the currants and add them along with the pine nuts. The fennel should be fairly moist. If the pan seems dry, add a couple spoonfuls of the pasta cooking water.

9. When the pasta is done, drain it and add it to the pan along with the reserved fennel fronds, or dill. Toss over medium heat until all the liquid is absorbed, about 1 minute. Drizzle on the remaining olive oil and serve.

Orecchiette con le Cime di Rapa (Orecchiette with Broccoli Rabe)

This is the signature dish of Italy's Apulia region, a starkly beautiful area marked by its tall cliffs and the small, beehive-like houses known as *trulli*. Anchovies preserved in salt—available in gourmet stores—are much tastier than anchovies packed in oil. To clean salted anchovies, simply rinse off the salty coating, and then use a small paring knife to slice off the head and tail. Finally, slice the anchovy in half and remove the spine and bones. Don't worry too much about any small bones left behind; they tend to dissolve when cooked. Italians don't serve cheese on fish dishes. If you long for something to sprinkle over your orecchiette, try a spoonful of toasted breadcrumbs.

Serves 4

1 bunch broccoli rabe or other bitter greens

1 lb. dried orecchiette or fresh orecchiette for 4 people (see page 172)

$1/2$ cup extra virgin olive oil

1 clove garlic, peeled and crushed

3 anchovies, cleaned and chopped

1. Bring a large pot of water to a boil.

2. Boil the broccoli rabe until tender, about 3–5 minutes, and then remove it with a slotted spoon and run under cold water. Squeeze as much water as possible out of the broccoli rabe, chop, and set aside.

3. Leave the water in the pot and let it return to a boil. Cook the pasta according to instructions on page 12.

4. Heat $^1/_4$ cup oil in a large frying pan. Sauté the garlic clove until browned, and then discard.

5. Add the anchovies and sauté 1–2 minutes, pressing with the back of a spoon to dissolve.

6. When the pasta is cooked, drain and add it to the pan along with the remaining olive oil and the chopped broccoli rabe, and toss for about 30 seconds before serving.

Rotelle con Lenticchie e Bietole
(Rotelle with Lentils and Swiss Chard)

Rotelle are small, circular pasta that are sometimes called *wagon wheels*. Lentils work well with rotelle because they tend to get wedged in between the "spokes." Unlike other dried legumes, lentils do not need to be soaked before cooking. Simply rinse the lentils, check them for any small pebbles, and then simmer them in water (or stock if you prefer) until they are tender, about 30–45 minutes. Taste a spoonful of lentils to check for doneness. You can also use canned lentils.

Serves 4

1 bunch Swiss chard	1 cup cooked lentils
$^1/_2$ cup extra virgin olive oil	1 lb. rotelle
1 small yellow onion, chopped	salt and freshly ground pepper to taste

1. Soak the chard in several changes of cold water until clean. Tear the leaves from the ribs. Chop the ribs into $^1/_2$-inch pieces.

2. Bring a large pot of water to a boil.

3. Add the chard stalks and boil for 2 minutes, until softened but not yet tender. Add the chard leaves and boil until the leaves and stalks are tender.

4. Remove the Swiss chard with a slotted spoon and run under cold water. Squeeze as much water as possible out of the Swiss chard leaves, chop, and set aside.

5. Leave the water in the pot and let it return to a boil. Cook the pasta according to the instructions on page 12.

6. While the pasta is cooking, in a large pan heat $^1/_4$ cup olive oil. Sauté the onion until translucent, about 3 minutes.

7. Add the lentils and sauté for 3 additional minutes.

8. Add the cooked chard, separating the pieces with your hands as you do. Sauté an additional 2 minutes. Add some of the pasta cooking water if the lentils and chard seem dry.

9. When the pasta is done, drain and add it to the pan along with the remaining $^1/_4$ cup olive oil. Toss over medium heat until all liquid is absorbed, about 1 minute.

The Least You Need to Know

➤ Pasta with olive oil sauces relies on a handful of ingredients.

➤ Shopping seasonally is the best way to ensure fresh produce with peak flavor.

➤ A final drizzle of olive oil intensifies flavors.

You Say Tomato

The Golden Apple

Pomodoro, the Italian word for tomato, literally means "golden apple." (And I don't think it's an overstatement to say that tomatoes have been worth their weight in gold in Italian cuisine.) While tomatoes are indigenous to the Americas and didn't find their way to Italy until the late 1600s, they have taken on a starring role in Italian cuisine. Italians use tomatoes in many different forms; you can either purchase these tomato products or make your own.

Tomatoes are a New World food: they first grew in the Andes and were domesticated in Mexico. In fact, tomatoes were considered poisonous (as were eggplant and other vegetables in the "nightshade" family) and were much feared when first brought to Europe. They then passed into acceptance but were quite expensive and available only to the wealthy. Only after a canning method for tomatoes was perfected did they become as popular in Italy as they are today.

Pasta Patter

Something Seedy: Tomato seeds were among the many varieties of new plants that Columbus transported to Europe from the New World.

Off the Vine

Generally, tomatoes are divided as follows:

➤ Globe, or slicing, tomatoes
➤ Plum, Italian, or Roma tomatoes
➤ Cherry tomatoes

Linguine Lingo

Tomato Masquerade: Although their name means "little tomatoes," *tomatillos* are not actually tomatoes. They resemble green cherry tomatoes, but are recognized by their distinctive papery husks.

Globe, or slicing, tomatoes (which include the common beefsteak tomato), are the familiar, medium-sized tomatoes we use in salads. They are now available in many colors. Yellow globe tomatoes are slightly sweeter than the red variety. Green tomatoes are not yet ripe but are often tasty anyway.

Plum tomatoes (sometimes known as Italian or Roma tomatoes) are the smaller, elongated tomatoes often used for tomato sauce. They are not as juicy as globe tomatoes but have an intense flavor that stands up to cooking.

Cherry tomatoes (and their relatives the teardrop-shaped pear tomatoes) are smaller than ping-pong balls and sometimes come still on the vine. They are quite attractive because of their small size.

Globe, plum, and cherry tomatoes are different sizes and shapes.

Fresh tomatoes should be firm but ripe. If not yet ripe, let them sit on a windowsill for a few days. Never refrigerate fresh tomatoes; it makes the flesh fuzzy and flavorless.

Off the Shelf

The tomato season is short, so Italians have become champions of canning and conserving the golden apple so that it is available year-round. These processes do an excellent job of preserving the flavor of fresh tomatoes. They reduce the cooking times for tomato-based sauces, and since canned products can be stored for long periods of time, they make your life much easier. With a few cans of peeled tomatoes or tomato purée and a few boxes of pasta on your pantry shelves, you will never be without a filling and nutritious meal.

Peel a Meal

Many of the recipes in this book use canned, peeled tomatoes. I like that they retain some texture when cooked. Canned, peeled tomatoes are used to make somewhat chunky tomato sauces that are more rustic than their perfectly smooth cousins.

Obviously, it's hard to see inside a can, so you may want to try several brands of canned tomatoes before settling on one. I highly recommend you look for an Italian brand. Italian words on the label do not necessarily indicate the can has come from Italy; the words "imported from Italy" do. If you cannot find good Italian tomatoes, your next choice should be an organic brand from the United States. Because organic farms tend to be smaller, more care is taken with the products. The organic American tomatoes I have purchased have been noticeably more satisfactory than their non-organic counterparts.

Canned, peeled tomatoes should be a bright red and swimming in their own juices. (You will notice that recipes using canned tomatoes call for you to use some of that juice.) The tomatoes should be whole, not in pieces, and all the skin should be removed. Inferior canned tomatoes are often stringy-looking and are sometimes an underripe (pink) color rather than a deep, rich red.

Pasta Practice

Hot Tomato: The best of all canned tomatoes are San Marzano tomatoes. This name will be marked clearly on the label, along with the words "imported from Italy." San Marzano tomatoes grow in the shade of Mount Vesuvius, not far from Naples. Some have credited the volcanic mountain with providing the tomatoes with their superior flavor. San Marzano tomatoes have just the right balance of tanginess and sweetness. In Naples, they are the only tomatoes considered appropriate for pizza–making.

Use Your Noodle

Keep It Covered: Storing leftover food in open cans—even in the refrigerator—encourages the growth of mold and other organisms. After you've opened a can of peeled tomatoes—or any canned goods—pour any leftovers into a container (preferably glass—tomatoes tend to stain plastic) with a tight-fitting lid and store them in the refrigerator. They should stay good for four to five days.

Pasta Practice

Accept No Substitutes: In a pinch, you can use strained tomato purée as a substitute for tomato juice. Tomato juice is too watery to work as a substitute for tomato purée, however.

What a Strain!

When I want to make a tomato sauce with a more delicate texture, or I want to add some tomato flavor without overwhelming the other ingredients, I reach for strained tomato purée. Again, my preference is always for an Italian brand. Unscrupulous companies often water down their tomato purée or add unripe tomatoes, but taste always tells the truth. A raw tomato purée should taste of tomatoes (surprise!) and not leave a bitter aftertaste. There should be no sign of seeds or bits of skin. I use a brand that comes packaged in an aseptic box so that I can pour out the amount I need and refrigerate the rest. The only ingredients in tomato purée should be tomatoes and salt. Leave any brands with preservatives or added flavors in the supermarket.

The Plot Thickens

You would never be able to make a tasty tomato sauce using tomato paste on its own. At times, however, tomato paste adds just the right amount of tomato flavor, particularly when it comes to the *ragu* for which the region of Emilia Romagna is famous. Rather than a true tomato sauce—that is, a sauce in which an ingredient is added to a base of tomatoes— *ragu* sauce is a meat sauce flavored with tomato. Tomato paste can also be useful in soups and stews and in certain other tomato sauces that call for a concentrated flavor.

Tomato paste is most widely available in cans, but I like to buy the kind that comes in a tube, since I use it in such small amounts. The tube—like a toothpaste tube—comes with a plastic cap that can be screwed back on. If you purchase tomato paste in a can, transfer it to another container after opening.

Read the ingredients on a container of tomato paste carefully; many of these products contain unpronounceable preservatives and hefty helpings of monosodium glutamate (MSG). A high-quality tomato paste should contain only tomatoes—cooked down to a thick substance—and salt. Again, Italian products generally adhere to high standards.

Pasta Patter

Wherefore Art Thou Vegetable?: Botanically speaking, the tomato is a fruit. In 1893, however, the Supreme Court officially designated it as a vegetable since it is generally consumed as a vegetable (in salads, for example). Vegetables and fruits were taxed differently at the time.

Off Your Stove

While all of the tomato products previously discussed should be available in your grocery store, you may want to try your hand at making them yourself. Clearly, the tomato products you make will only be as good as the tomatoes with which you start. There is no making up for an unripe tomato, no matter how much you work with it. Always begin with fresh, ripe tomatoes. To do otherwise would be a waste of time.

More Than One Way to Skin a Tomato

Although you can purchase canned, peeled tomatoes (I tend to because they are inexpensive and easy to store), if you have a garden and experience a summer tomato surplus, you may want to peel your own tomatoes.

You should always start with ripe plum tomatoes. They should not be so ripe that they are mushy, however. If your tomatoes have passed peak ripeness, use them for some other purpose. Peeled tomatoes should remain whole; overripe tomatoes will disintegrate.

There are two methods for peeling tomatoes. The hot water method is slightly more complicated, but more effective. The vegetable peeler method is more time consuming but doesn't risk cooking the tomatoes.

To peel tomatoes using the hot water method, you need the following:

1 large pot

1 large bowl

1 slotted spoon

1 paring knife

1. Bring a pot of water to a boil.
2. Prepare a large bowl of ice water on the counter.

3. Cut a small X into the bottom of each tomato.

4. Pare away the stem of each tomato.

5. Drop a few tomatoes at a time into the boiling water.

6. Let the tomatoes simmer for about 10 seconds.

7. Remove the tomatoes with a slotted spoon and transfer to the bowl of ice water.

8. Remove the tomatoes from water one by one and peel. The tomato skin should lift away easily at the point where you have cut the X.

9. Allow the water to return to a boil, add ice to the bowl of ice water, and repeat the process with the remaining tomatoes.

The tomatoes should be handled in small batches, because otherwise it will take too long to remove them from the hot water and they will begin to cook.

To peel tomatoes using the vegetable peeler method, you need the following :

1 sharp vegetable peeler

1 paring knife

1. Pare away the stem of the tomato.

2. Cut a slit in the bottom of the tomato to begin.

3. Lift away the tomato skin using the vegetable peeler (as you would to peel a potato).

You can either use the peeled tomatoes immediately in a recipe or can them using a pressure canner, if you have one.

Use Your Noodle

Canning Caution: When food products are canned or preserved incorrectly, the results can be perilous to your health, even fatal. Unfortunately, detailed canning instructions are beyond the scope of this book. Healthy canning practices vary from area to area according to sea level and other factors. Before canning, be sure to contact the U.S. Department of Agriculture extension in your area to obtain the appropriate guidelines. Furthermore, never eat any canned or preserved product that looks or smells unusual, or has any signs of mold or other growth.

Don't Strain Yourself

You can also make your own tomato purée. A good tomato purée is free of seeds and skin. The best way to obtain this ideal texture is to use a food mill, which expels the skin and seeds automatically. If you don't have a food mill, you can still make a chunky-style purée. I don't recommend using a food processor or blender. The tomato pulp and liquids tend to separate, and the metal blades chop the tomatoes to a juice rather than a purée. Tomato purée made from raw tomatoes is pink in color and slightly watery. To make a more flavorful purée, you'll need to cook the tomatoes slightly.

To make a tomato purée using a food mill, you need the following:

> 1 large pot
>
> 1 hand-operated food mill
>
> 1 large bowl

1. Wash the tomatoes thoroughly.
2. Chop the tomatoes in half.
3. Place the tomatoes in the pot.
4. Place the pot on the stove over medium heat.
5. Allow the tomatoes to simmer and release their liquid. If necessary, add a small amount of water to keep the tomatoes from sticking to the pan.
6. Simmer the tomatoes until they are soft and pulpy and most of the water has evaporated, about 10 minutes.
7. Place the food mill over the bowl.
8. Process the tomatoes through the food mill. Discard the seeds and peels.

To make a tomato purée without a food mill, you need to remove the seeds and peels yourself. To do so, first peel the tomatoes using one of the two methods previously described.

To seed a tomato, you need

> 1 paring knife

1. Cut the tomato in half.
2. Holding the tomato in one hand, use the index finger of your other hand to scoop out the seeds from the indentations inside the tomato.
3. Discard the seeds.

To make the purée, prepare the tomatoes as previously directed, place them in a large bowl, and then squash them energetically with a fork until they reach the desired consistency.

One lb. of tomatoes results in about one cup of purée. Tomato purée will keep in the refrigerator for five days or so in a covered container. You can also can it.

Spaghetti al Pomodoro
(Spaghetti with Tomato Sauce)

There's a reason this is the best-known Italian dish in the world: it's delicious!

Serves 4

1 clove garlic, minced	salt and freshly ground pepper to taste
1 tablespoon minced onion	1 lb. dried spaghetti
2 tablespoons extra virgin olive oil	5 or 6 basil leaves (optional)
3 cups strained tomato purée	grated Parmesan cheese (optional)

1. Bring a large pot of water to a boil for cooking the pasta.
2. In a medium saucepan over medium heat, sauté the garlic and onion in the olive oil until softened, about 1 minute.
3. Stir in the tomato purée. Season to taste with salt and pepper.
4. Bring the sauce to a low simmer and cook, stirring occasionally, until thickened to the consistency of a thin sour cream.
5. Meanwhile, cook the pasta according to the instructions on page 12. When the pasta is done, drain and remove it to a low, wide serving bowl, and top with the sauce and basil leaves, if desired. Serve grated Parmesan on the side.

Penne al Pomodoro
(Penne with Tomato Sauce)

This chunky tomato sauce is more suited to short pasta such as penne. *Canned Goods:* One 28-oz. can of peeled tomatoes equals approximately 3 cups.

Serves 4

1 clove garlic, minced	salt and freshly ground pepper to taste
1 tablespoon minced onion	1 lb. dried penne
2 tablespoons extra virgin olive oil	5 or 6 basil leaves (optional)
3 cups peeled, chopped tomatoes, and their juice	grated Parmesan cheese (optional)

1. Bring a large pot of water to a boil for cooking the pasta.
2. In a medium saucepan over medium heat, sauté the garlic and onion in the olive oil until softened, about 1 minute.
3. Stir in the chopped tomatoes and juice. Season to taste with salt and pepper.
4. Bring the sauce to a low simmer and cook, stirring occasionally, until thickened somewhat but still moist.
5. Meanwhile, cook the pasta according to the instructions on page 12. When the pasta is done, drain and remove it to a low, wide serving bowl, and top with the sauce and basil leaves, if desired. Serve grated Parmesan on the side.

Pasta al Pomodoro Crudo
(Pasta with Fresh Tomatoes)

When tomatoes are at their ripest, they need very little embellishment. You can vary this simple recipe in any number of ways. Try adding some diced mozzarella or goat cheese, which will melt when tossed with the pasta. You can also include olives or capers to enhance the Mediterranean flavor. Juicy brandywine tomatoes are particularly good in this recipe. Be sure to mince the garlic very finely as it will not be cooked.

Serves 4

4 tomatoes

3 cloves garlic, minced

$^1/_4$ cup plus 2 tablespoons extra virgin olive oil

salt to taste

$^1/_4$ cup loosely packed basil leaves

1 lb. penne or other dried pasta

grated Parmesan cheese (optional)

1. Bring a large pot of water to a boil for cooking the pasta.
2. Dice the tomatoes and place them in a low, wide serving bowl.
3. Combine the garlic and $^1/_4$ cup oil with the tomatoes. Salt lightly, toss, and set aside. Salt helps to draw the juices out of the tomatoes, so don't skip this step.
4. Cook the pasta according to the instructions on page 12.
5. Toss the cooked pasta with the tomato mixture. Drizzle on the remaining 2 tablespoons oil. Tear the basil leaves and sprinkle them on top of the pasta. Serve with Parmesan cheese on the side.

Pasta ai Pomodorini
(Pasta with Cherry Tomatoes)

Cherry tomatoes make this dish quite visually appealing.

Serves 4

1 pt. cherry tomatoes

1 clove garlic, minced

$^1/_4$ cup plus 2 tablespoons extra virgin olive oil

1 scallion

salt to taste

1 lb. dried pasta

1. Bring a large pot of water to a boil for cooking the pasta.
2. Halve each tomato and place them in a low, wide serving bowl.
3. Combine the garlic, scallion, and $^1/_4$ cup oil with the tomatoes. Salt lightly, toss, and set aside.
4. Cook the pasta according to the instructions on page 12.
5. Toss the cooked pasta with tomato mixture, and then drizzle on the remaining 2 tablespoons of oil.

The Least You Need to Know

➤ Use plum tomatoes for making sauce.

➤ Use canned Italian tomatoes when fresh tomatoes are out of season or when you're in a hurry.

➤ Never refrigerate fresh tomatoes.

Part 3
Pastabilities

Pasta doesn't have to be served with a sauce. It can float in a soup or be baked in an oven. Soups and baked pastas are homey foods. And both can be prepared in advance and reheated just before serving, which makes them excellent choices when you're feeding a crowd.

Chapter 8

The Mother of All Pasta Sauces

In This Chapter

➤ Choosing tomato products

➤ The myth of the long-cooking tomato sauce

➤ Storing tomato sauces

➤ Tomato sauce methods

➤ Recipes for pasta dishes with tomato sauces

Most people, if taking one of those word-association psychological tests and shown the word "pasta," would come up with its frequent partner: tomato. Tomatoes and pasta are a natural match, the acidity of the former counterbalancing the blandness of the latter.

Tomatoes form a base or provide an accent for many of our classic pasta dishes—from *fettuccine alla bolognese* (wide noodles with meat sauce) to the simple *penne al pomodoro crudo* (tubular pasta tossed with fresh, diced tomatoes).

Know Your Tomatoes

The recipes in this chapter use tomatoes in the following forms:

➤ Peeled tomatoes (either canned or peeled by you)

➤ Fresh tomatoes

➤ Strained tomato purée

➤ Tomato paste

Tomato products are available in cans, cartons, and tubes.

Many of the recipes call for a combination of two or three of these products. (For more information on how to select them, how to use them, and how to prepare your own, please see Chapter 7, "You Say Tomato.")

The basic difference between a sauce made with whole tomatoes and a sauce made with tomato purée lies in texture. Whole tomatoes result in a chunkier texture that works well with rustic, heartier ingredients. Tomato purée is used for silky sauces. I often use a combination of whole tomatoes and tomato purée for a texture that falls somewhere in between. You can also purchase chopped tomatoes packaged in tomato purée. This is a good choice when a recipe calls for both tomatoes and purée.

Pasta Patter

Sun-dried tomatoes come from the southern part of Italy. They are not used in tomato sauces, however. Instead, they are conserved in olive oil (sometimes with hot pepper) and served a few at a time as an antipasto or occasionally as a sandwich ingredient.

On the Burner

Many Americans are under the impression that tomato sauces need to be cooked to death.

In Italy, however, tomato sauces—with a few exceptions such as ragu—are quick and easy to prepare. In fact, you can make most of the tomato sauces in the following recipes while your pasta is cooking.

Presumably, when Italian immigrants arrived in the United States at the turn of the century, they found tomatoes that were not of the same quality as those with which they had cooked back home. In an attempt to rectify the situation, they cooked their tomato sauces for longer periods, hoping to distill the flavor of the weaker American tomatoes.

The addition of sweeteners—most notably a pinch or two of sugar—to tomato sauces developed for the same reason.

Luckily, today we have access to high-quality Italian and American tomatoes, both canned and fresh. There's no longer any need for these little tricks. Let the flavor of your tomatoes shine through, and you won't be disappointed.

Planning Ahead

Most of the recipes in this chapter call for making a sauce while the pasta is cooking. You can, however, simply ignore the instructions for bringing the pasta water to a boil and prepare the sauce in advance.

Tomato sauce will last for about four days in the refrigerator, and three–four months in the freezer. Sauces thicken as they sit, however, so you will probably need to add a little water when you heat a made-in-advance sauce.

Use Your Noodle

Don't store tomato sauces in plastic containers. They discolor the plastic and leave behind a greasy film.

Methods for Tomato Sauces

Almost all the recipes in this chapter begin with the same step: sautéing garlic, and sometimes chopped onion, in olive oil. Garlic and onion and olive oil are as essential to Italian food as tomatoes and pasta.

After you add some form of tomato product, the next step is to reduce the tomato sauce slightly. Don't reduce the sauce to a thick paste. Once reduced, the sauce should no longer appear watery but should remain fairly moist.

Tomato sauces don't require constant supervision when cooking, but you should check in occasionally to stir the sauce and observe its progress. If your sauce does burn and stick to the bottom of the pot, don't despair. Simply spoon out the sauce that's not ruined into another pot, leaving the blackened part. Fill the pot with the burnt sauce with hot, soapy water and let it soak overnight.

Do:

➤ Use high-quality tomato products

➤ Stir the sauce occasionally while it is cooking

➤ Remember when salting a tomato sauce that the pasta is cooking in salted water

Don't:

➤ Add any ingredient to a tomato sauce that you wouldn't eat on its own

➤ Let the sauce at the bottom of the pot burn

➤ Cook the sauce to a paste

Pasta Patter

Lycopene, the substance that makes tomatoes red, is a powerful antioxidant that seems to fight cancer. Cooking tomatoes in a small amount of fat makes their lycopene even more readily available. Tomato sauce is good medicine!

You Say Tomato, I Say...Delicious

Pasta al Pomodoro e Basilico
(Pasta with Tomato and Basil Sauce)

If you are allowed to take one recipe with you to a desert island, make it this one. Not only is it uncomplicated, but it can be the source of endless variations. Almost any type of pasta is excellent with this sauce. Some classic shapes are penne and spaghetti. *Pomodoro* is the Italian word for "tomato." It literally means "golden apple."

Serves 4

1 clove garlic, minced

2 tablespoons extra virgin olive oil

2 cups strained tomato purée

salt and freshly ground pepper to taste

1 lb. dried pasta

1 cup loosely packed basil leaves

grated Parmesan cheese (optional)

1. Bring a large pot of water to a boil for cooking the pasta.
2. In a medium saucepan over medium heat, sauté the garlic in the olive oil until it softens, about 1 minute.
3. Stir in the tomato purée. Season to taste with salt and pepper.
4. Bring the sauce to a low simmer and cook, stirring occasionally, until thickened to the consistency of a thin sour cream.
5. Meanwhile, cook the pasta according to the instructions on page 12. When the pasta is done, drain and remove it to a low, wide serving bowl. Top with the sauce and basil leaves, and serve grated Parmesan on the side.

Penne al Pomodoro e Carote
(Penne With Carrot-Tomato Sauce)

Once you've got the formula down, you can embellish a basic tomato sauce any number of ways. Here's one tasty version made with ingredients you've probably got on hand.

Serves 4

1 clove garlic, minced

2 tablespoons extra virgin olive oil

2 large carrots, peeled and sliced into rounds 1/8-inch thick

2 cups strained tomato purée

salt and freshly ground pepper to taste

1 lb. dried pasta

1 cup loosely packed basil leaves

grated Parmesan cheese (optional)

1. Bring a large pot of water to a boil for cooking the pasta.
2. In a medium saucepan over medium heat, sauté the garlic in the olive oil until it softens, about 1 minute.
3. Add the carrots and sauté until they are soft enough to pierce with a fork, about 7 minutes, stirring occasionally. Do not allow the carrots to brown. If the carrots start sticking to the pan, add a small amount of water.
4. Stir in the tomato purée. Season to taste with salt and pepper.
5. Bring the sauce to a low simmer and cook, stirring occasionally, until thickened to the consistency of a thin sour cream.
6. Meanwhile, cook the pasta according to the instructions on page 12. When the pasta is done, drain and remove it to a low, wide serving bowl. Top with sauce and basil leaves, and serve grated Parmesan on the side, if desired.

Penne all'Arrabbiata
(Penne With Spicy Tomato Sauce)

This is pasta for those who like it hot. *Arrabbiata* is the Italian word for "angry." In this recipe it refers to the large quantity of hot pepper used in the sauce. Oils from hot peppers have an amazing ability to adhere to your fingers. If you have sensitive skin, wear gloves. Never touch your eyes, nostrils, or mouth after handling chile peppers. *Pancetta,* rolled and cured Italian bacon, makes a savory addition to many dishes. It is available in specialty stores. You may choose to omit it from this recipe if cooking for vegetarians, but you will sacrifice a lot of flavor. This sauce is also tasty with long pasta such as spaghetti or bucatini.

Serves 4

1 1/4-inch thick slice pancetta, diced

2 tablespoons extra virgin olive oil

1 small yellow onion, minced

1–2 small red chile peppers, minced

2 cups peeled tomatoes with their juices

salt and freshly ground pepper to taste

1 lb. penne

continues

continued

1. Bring a large pot of water to a boil for cooking the pasta.

2. In a medium saucepan over medium heat, sauté the diced pancetta in the olive oil until it begins to color, about 5 minutes.

3. Add the onion and pepper and continue cooking until the onion softens, about 2 minutes.

4. Stir in the tomatoes and their juice, breaking up the tomatoes with a wooden spoon. Season to taste with salt and pepper. If you are not a fussy cook and don't mind some cleanup afterwards, you can break up the tomatoes with your fingers as you drop them into the pan.

5. Bring the sauce to a low simmer and cook, stirring occasionally, until the juices have evaporated and the ingredients are combined.

6. Meanwhile, cook the pasta according to instructions on page 12. When the pasta is done, drain and remove it to a low, wide serving bowl, and top with the sauce.

Bucatini con le Cozze
(Bucatini with Mussels)

This pasta makes a good first course for a large meal featuring a seafood salad appetizer and a grilled tuna main course. To clean mussels, scrub each one under cold running water with a stiff brush. Remove the thick beard with a knife or by simply yanking it firmly with one hand while holding the mussel with the other.

Serves 4

1 clove garlic, minced

3 tablespoons extra virgin olive oil

2 lb. mussels, cleaned

$1/4$ cup green olives, pitted and chopped

$1/4$ cup black olives, pitted and chopped

2 cups chopped, peeled tomatoes and their juices

salt and freshly ground pepper to taste

1 lb. bucatini

$1/4$ cup chopped parsley

1. Bring a large pot of water to a boil for cooking the pasta.

2. In a large pan over medium heat, sauté the garlic in 1 tablespoon of the olive oil until it softens, about 1 minute.

3. Add the mussels and cook until they have opened, about 8 minutes. Discard any unopened mussels.

4. Remove the mussels with a slotted spoon.

5. Add the remaining 2 tablespoons of oil to the pan.

continues

continued

6. Add the olives and sauté for 2 minutes. Add the tomatoes and juices and season to taste with salt and pepper.

7. Bring the sauce to a simmer and cook, stirring occasionally, until thickened slightly.

8. Remove about half of the mussels from their shells and return them to the sauce. Add the remaining mussels with shells to the sauce as well.

9. Meanwhile, cook the pasta according to instructions on page 12. When the pasta is done, drain and remove it to a low, wide serving bowl. Top with the sauce and chopped parsley.

Spaghetti con il Tonno (Spaghetti with Tuna)

In the time it takes to make a tuna salad sandwich, you could be feasting on this satisfying pasta. *Note*: As a rule, Italians don't serve grated cheese on pasta that has fish in it.

Serves 4

1 clove garlic, minced
2 tablespoons extra virgin olive oil
2 cups strained tomato purée
salt and freshly ground pepper to taste

1 7-oz. can of tuna packed in olive oil
1 lb. spaghetti
1/4 cup chopped parsley

1. Bring a large pot of water to a boil for cooking the pasta.

2. In a medium saucepan over medium heat, sauté the garlic in the olive oil until it softens, about 1 minute.

3. Stir in the tomato purée and season to taste with salt and pepper.

4. Bring the sauce to a low simmer and cook, stirring occasionally, until thickened slightly.

5. Add the tuna to the sauce and stir to combine. Continue to simmer the sauce until thickened to the consistency of thin sour cream.

6. Meanwhile, cook the pasta according to the instructions on page 12. When the pasta is done, drain and remove it to a low, wide serving bowl. Top with the sauce and chopped parsley.

89

Spaghetti alla Puttanesca
(Spaghetti with Tomato Sauce
with Olives, Capers, and Anchovies)

Puttanesca means "of the prostitutes." Explanations for the unusual name of this pasta dish abound; the most common is that Italy's prostitutes could whip up this quick-cooking yet flavorful sauce between jobs. Anchovies preserved in salt—available in gourmet stores—are much tastier than the kind packed in oil. To clean salted anchovies, simply rinse off the salty coating, and then use a small paring knife to slice off the head and tail. Slice the anchovy in half and remove the spine and bones. Don't worry too much about any small bones left behind; they tend to dissolve when cooked. Use the big, juicy capers of the Italian island of Pantelleria if you can find them. If the sauce dries out too much, ladle some cooking water from the pasta pot into the pan.

Serves 4

2 cloves garlic, thinly sliced	1 teaspoon capers, rinsed
2 tablespoons extra virgin olive oil	$1/3$ cup black olives, pitted
4 anchovies, cleaned and minced	salt and freshly ground pepper to taste
2 cups peeled tomatoes with their juices	1 lb. spaghetti

1. Bring a large pot of water to a boil for cooking the pasta.
2. In a medium pan over medium heat, sauté the garlic in the olive oil until it just begins to color, about 2 minutes.
3. Add the anchovies to the pan and continue cooking, stirring often, until anchovies have melted, about 3 minutes.
4. Stir in the tomatoes and their juice, breaking up the tomatoes with a wooden spoon.
5. Bring the sauce to a low simmer and cook, stirring occasionally, until thickened slightly.
6. Stir in the capers and olives. Season to taste with salt and pepper, keeping in mind that the anchovies, capers, and olives are all salty ingredients. Cook until the ingredients are combined but not all the liquid has evaporated.
7. Meanwhile, cook the pasta until just al dente according to the instructions on page 12. When the pasta is done, drain and add it to the pan with the sauce. Turn the heat to medium-high and cook, stirring constantly, until all the liquid has been absorbed, about 2 minutes.

Spaghetti Bandiera
(Spaghetti with Tomato Sauce
with Eggplant and Zucchini)

This sauce is so full of brightly colored vegetables that it resembles a flag, or *bandiera*. To drain an eggplant of its bitter juices, place the eggplant pieces in a colander or strainer, sprinkle with salt, and let sit for 20 minutes or so. When the eggplant no longer drips, rinse the pieces and pat them dry.

Serves 4

2 cloves garlic, minced

1 small carrot, peeled and finely grated

1 rib celery, minced

3 tablespoons extra virgin olive oil

1 zucchini, diced

1 eggplant, diced, drained, rinsed, and patted dry

2 cups strained tomato purée

salt and freshly ground pepper to taste

1 lb. spaghetti

1. Bring a large pot of water to a boil for cooking the pasta.

2. In a medium pan over medium heat, sauté garlic in the olive oil until it just begins to color, about 2 minutes.

3. Add the carrot and celery and sauté an additional 2 minutes.

4. Add the zucchini and eggplant and sauté until soft, about 5 minutes.

5. Stir in the tomato purée and season to taste with salt and pepper. Bring the sauce to a simmer.

6. Meanwhile, cook the pasta just until al dente according to the instructions on page 12. When the pasta is done, drain and add it to the pan with the sauce. Turn the heat to medium-high and cook, stirring constantly, until all the liquid has been absorbed, about 2 minutes.

Pasta con le Lenticchie
(Pasta with Lentils)

Serve this robust peasant dish with crusty bread and a salad of grated carrots tossed with lemon juice and olive oil. In Italy, as in many other countries, superstition says that if you eat lentils on New Year's Day, you'll be rich by the end of the year. Look for Le Puy or Castelluccio lentils, which have a more delicate flavor than the regular brown variety.

Serves 4

2 tablespoons extra virgin olive oil

1 small yellow onion, minced

1 carrot, peeled and chopped

1 cup lentils, rinsed

1½ cups chopped peeled tomatoes with their juices

½ cup tomato purée

salt and freshly ground pepper to taste

1 lb. rotelle or other dried pasta

1. In a heavy pot over medium heat, sauté the onion in the olive oil until softened, about 2 minutes.

2. Add the carrot and celery and cook until softened, about 3 minutes.

3. Add the lentils and sauté for 2 minutes.

4. Add enough cold water to cover the lentils by about 1 inch. Bring the pot to a boil, and then turn down to a simmer.

5. Simmer the lentils gently over low heat until soft, 30–45 minutes. If necessary, add 1–2 tablespoons of water at a time to keep the lentils from drying out.

6. When the lentils are cooked, add the tomatoes and purée, and season to taste with salt and pepper. Simmer until the liquid has evaporated, about 20 minutes.

7. When the sauce is ready, cook the pasta according to the instructions on page 12. When the pasta is done, drain and transfer it to a low, wide bowl, and then top with the sauce.

The Least You Need to Know

➤ Pasta and tomatoes are a natural match.

➤ With a few exceptions, tomato sauces need not be cooked for a long time.

➤ Tomato sauces can be made in advance and reheated.

Chapter 9

Cream Sauces: The Most Luxurious of Italian Dishes

In This Chapter

➤ Types of cream

➤ Nutritional information about cream

➤ Cream sauce methods

➤ Cream sauce recipes

There's something special about cream. It's rich, silky texture elevates even a simple plate of pasta to a special occasion.

He Ain't Heavy

It must be admitted right off the bat: cream has fat. In fact, fat is cream's most distinguishing characteristic, since cream is defined as milk with a higher concentration of fat, created when the fat rises to the top.

Cream is categorized by fat content. There are generally three types of cream available today:

1. Light cream (18–30 percent butterfat)
2. Light whipping cream (30–36 percent butterfat)
3. Heavy whipping cream (36–40 percent butterfat)

I've used heavy whipping cream in all the recipes in this chapter. It responds more reliably to heat. (Again, that's the fat at work.) If you choose to experiment with light cream or light whipping cream, you may end up with a curdled sauce or skin forming on top of the sauce.

Seek out high-quality cream to use in cream sauces.

If you have access to high-quality cream that has not been homogenized or stabilized in any way, by all means use it. These "gourmet" creams are likely to be locally produced and are sometimes found at farmers' markets or in health food stores. They are well worth the extra expense.

Cream's No Crime

So cream has a high percentage of fat, and about 50 calories per tablespoon. It's not diet food, but neither is it an everyday food. In Italy, pastas with cream sauces are a special treat, not something to be enjoyed every day, or even every week.

That said, there is also something truly luxurious about cream. Maybe it's just because we know that it's not an everyday food, but serve anyone a cream sauce and watch them coo. If tomato sauces are daily fare, and olive oil sauces are the fastest and easiest to prepare, surely cream sauces for pasta are the "fanciest." Make these dishes when you're having important company (or company you want to make feel important). Fresh pasta with cream sauce is particularly decadent.

Linguine Lingo

The word "cream" derives from the Greek word *chriein*, meaning "to anoint."

Cream Dreams

Cream sauces are "of the moment." Never try to prepare a cream sauce in advance; it will separate and will never taste right. Sometimes, however, you can sauté other ingredients in advance, then add the cream and reduce it just before serving.

All the following recipes call for reducing cream sauces slightly before tossing them with the pasta. To reduce a cream sauce, bring it to a gentle simmer so that a few bubbles break to the surface at one time. Stir the cream occasionally while it is reducing, and keep an eye on it to be sure it is not bubbling too rapidly.

In most of these recipes, you will first sauté an ingredient, then add cream and reduce the sauce. Generally, you can follow these steps while the pasta is cooking. With all these sauces, leave the pasta slightly al dente, as it will be tossed in the pan with the cream sauce for a few minutes as a final step, which will cook it a little further.

Linguine Lingo

Panna is the Italian word for cream. Don't be confused by the word *crema,* which refers to the pastry cream used in desserts such as zabaglione.

Penne Pasticciate
(Penne with Tomato-Cream Sauce)

These penne sport a pretty pink coating. In Italian, something *pasticciato* is something that has been made a mess of. This dish earns that title because it has a little of everything that might be thrown over pasta: olive oil, tomato, garlic, and cream. You can make a heartier version of this recipe by removing and discarding the casing from one small, high-quality sausage, and then sautéing the sausage along with the garlic.

Serves 4

1 clove garlic, minced	salt to taste
2 tablespoons extra virgin olive oil	1 lb. penne
$^1/_3$ cup strained tomato purée	grated Parmesan cheese (optional)
$^2/_3$ cup heavy cream	

1. Bring a large pot of water to a boil for cooking the pasta.
2. In a large pan over medium heat, sauté the garlic in the olive oil until it softens, about 1 minute.
3. Stir in the tomato purée and cream. Season to taste with salt.
4. Bring the sauce to a low simmer and cook, stirring occasionally, until thickened slightly.
5. Meanwhile, cook the pasta according to the instructions on page 12. When the pasta is al dente, drain and transfer it to the pan. Toss over medium heat until all the liquid has been absorbed, about 2 minutes. Serve grated Parmesan on the side, if desired.

Maccheroncini e Radicchio
(Maccheroncini with Radicchio)

Radicchio is one of those vegetables that tastes completely different in its raw and cooked forms. If you've eaten radicchio only as a bitter salad component, you're in for a treat when you taste the sweet, cooked version. Any of the shorter pastas will work with this recipe.

Serves 4

1 clove garlic, minced
2 tablespoons extra virgin olive oil
1 head radicchio, chopped into 1-inch pieces
$^1/_3$ cup strained tomato purée

$^2/_3$ cup heavy cream
salt to taste
1 lb. maccheroncini or other dried pasta
grated Parmesan cheese (optional)

1. Bring a large pot of water to a boil for cooking the pasta.
2. In a large pan over medium heat, sauté the garlic in the olive oil until it softens, about 1 minute.
3. Add the chopped radicchio and sauté until wilted, about 3 minutes.
4. Stir in the tomato purée and cream. Season to taste with salt.
5. Bring the sauce to a low simmer and cook, stirring occasionally, until thickened slightly.
6. Meanwhile, cook the pasta according to the instructions on page 12. When the pasta is al dente, drain and transfer it to the pan. Toss over medium heat until all the liquid has been absorbed, about 2 minutes. Serve grated Parmesan on the side, if desired.

Maccheroncini alla Boscaiola
(Maccheroncini with Mushrooms)

When you see the word *boscaiola* on an Italian menu, it's no guarantee of a specific recipe. All *boscaiola* sauces contain mushrooms; the other ingredients are more flexible.

Serves 4

1 clove garlic, minced
2 tablespoons extra virgin olive oil
4 oz. ground lamb
1 cup shelled peas
8 oz. mushrooms, cleaned, trimmed, and thinly sliced
$^1/_2$ cup white wine

1 cup heavy cream
salt and freshly ground black pepper to taste
1 lb. maccheroncini or ziti
$^1/_4$ cup chopped parsley
grated Parmesan cheese (optional)

1. Bring a large pot of water to a boil for cooking the pasta.
2. In a large pan over medium heat, sauté the garlic in the olive oil until it softens, about 1 minute.

3. Add the ground lamb and cook, stirring constantly, until it loses its rawness, about 4 minutes.
4. Add the peas and mushrooms and sauté an additional 2 minutes.
5. Pour in the wine. Bring to a boil, reduce to a simmer, and cook until the wine has evaporated. The peas and mushrooms should be tender.
6. Add the cream. Turn down the sauce to a low simmer and cook, stirring occasionally, until thickened slightly. Season to taste with salt and pepper.
7. Meanwhile, cook the pasta according to the instructions on page 12. When the pasta is al dente, drain and transfer it to the pan. Toss over medium heat until all the liquid has been absorbed, about 2 minutes. Remove to a low, wide serving bowl. Sprinkle with chopped parsley. Serve grated Parmesan on the side, if desired.

Penne con i Funghi
(Penne with Mushrooms)

This is one of the most basic cream sauces for pasta. Pair it with a rustic salad of roasted beets and fennel. You can use cultivated white mushrooms or a mix of more exotic types such as crimini and portobello. Fresh porcini mushrooms represent the zenith of the mushroom world. Some mushrooms are toxic. Never gather wild mushrooms without the assistance of a practiced mycologist (mushroom expert).

Serves 4

2 cloves garlic, chopped

2 tablespoons extra virgin olive oil

8 oz. mushrooms, cleaned, trimmed, and sliced

1 cup heavy cream

salt and freshly ground black pepper

1 lb. penne or other short pasta

1/4 cup chopped parsley

grated Parmesan cheese

1. Bring a large pot of water to a boil for cooking the pasta.
2. In a large pan over medium heat, sauté the garlic in the olive oil until it softens, about 1 minute.
3. Add the mushrooms and sauté until they are soft and have given up their liquid. If the mushrooms stick to the pan initially, add a little of the pasta cooking water to the pan.
4. Add the cream. Bring the sauce to a low simmer and cook, stirring occasionally, until thickened slightly. Season to taste with salt and pepper.
5. Meanwhile, cook the pasta according to the instructions on page 12. When the pasta is al dente, drain and transfer it to the pan. Toss over medium heat until all the liquid has been absorbed, about 2 minutes. Transfer the pasta to a low, wide serving bowl and sprinkle on the parsley. Serve grated Parmesan on the side.

Penne alla Vodka
(Penne in Vodka Sauce)

This is another classic pasta preparation found on the menu of almost every *trattoria* in the north of Italy. One of my favorite casual restaurants in Italy serves this dish with thin strips of Speck (a smoked meat from Germany) in place of the shrimp, resulting in a smoky dish.

Serves 4

1 clove garlic, minced	$^1/_3$ cup strained tomato purée
2 tablespoons extra virgin olive oil	1 cup heavy cream
6 oz. rock shrimp	salt to taste
$^1/_3$ cup vodka	1 lb. penne

1. Bring a large pot of water to a boil for cooking the pasta.
2. In a large pan over medium heat, sauté the garlic in the olive oil until it softens, about 1 minute.
3. Add the shrimp and sauté until cooked through, about 1 minute.
4. Add the vodka to the pan, bring to a boil, and allow it to evaporate.
5. Add the tomato purée and cream. Bring to a low simmer and cook, stirring occasionally, until thickened slightly. Season to taste with salt.
6. Meanwhile, cook the pasta according to the instructions on page 12. When the pasta is al dente, drain and transfer it to the pan. Toss over medium heat until all the liquid has been absorbed, about 2 minutes.

Conchiglie ai Piselli e
Prosciutto Cotto
(Conchiglie with Peas and Ham)

Shell-shaped pieces of pasta give peas the perfect hiding place. *Prosciutto cotto* is ham that has been baked rather than salted and air-cured like *prosciutto crudo*.

Serves 4

1 tablespoon butter	1 cup heavy cream
1 tablespoon extra virgin olive oil	salt and freshly ground black pepper
1 clove garlic, minced	1 lb. conchiglie or other shell-shaped pasta
1 cup shelled peas	grated Parmesan cheese
1 $^1/_4$-inch thick slice prosciutto cotto, diced	

1. In a large pan over medium heat, melt the butter and olive oil.
2. Sauté the garlic until softened, about 1 minute.

continued

3. Add the peas and sauté until tender, about 5 minutes for frozen peas, 10 minutes for fresh peas. If the peas appear to be getting dry, add a small amount of pasta cooking water to the pan.

4. When the peas are tender, add the prosciutto cotto and cream to the pan. Bring the cream to a low simmer and allow to thicken slightly. Season to taste with salt and pepper.

5. Meanwhile, bring a large pot of water to a boil and cook the pasta according to the instructions on page 12. When the pasta is al dente, drain and transfer it to the pan.

6. Toss the pasta over medium heat until all the liquid has been absorbed and the peas are evenly distributed, about 2 minutes. Serve grated cheese on the side.

The Least You Need to Know

➤ Heavy cream is the most stable kind of cream.

➤ Cream should be an occasional indulgence in a balanced diet.

➤ Cooked pasta is added to the pan in which a cream sauce has been slightly reduced, and then tossed until all the liquid has been absorbed.

Chapter 10

Pasta + Soup = Comfort^2

Surely one of the reasons we love pasta so is that it provides comfort. Time and time again, that first bite of soft noodles erases all cares. Soup, too, is a restorative meal. When the two are combined, nothing could be more soothing, more satisfying, more comforting. If you want to forget a bad day, stop a cold in its tracks, or just feel pampered, any of the recipes in this chapter will do the trick.

In This Chapter

➤ Appropriate pasta for soup

➤ Types of Italian soup

➤ Soup techniques

➤ Soup recipes

Pasta Goes for a Swim

Pasta for soup should be small enough that one or more pieces of the pasta can fit on a soup spoon at one time. The Italian word for the small dried pastas that are cooked directly in soup is *pastina*. (The *-ina* suffix makes Italian words diminutive, so it literally means "small pasta.") The following table illustrates some of the many varieties of pastina available.

Can You Name That Floater?

Pastina	Translation
Acini di pepe	Peppercorns
Anellini	Little rings
Ditalini	Little thimbles
Farfalline	Little butterflies
Lumachine	Little snails
Nastrini	Ribbons

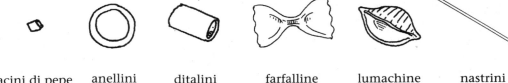

acini di pepe   anellini   ditalini   farfalline   lumachine   nastrini

Sometimes pastina is simply a smaller version of a larger type of pasta. For example, farfalline are miniatures of farfalle.

Beyond dried pastina, Italians often cut a sheet of egg pasta into small pieces and add it to soup. These shapes are usually very informal. The larger pieces are called *stracci* or *maltagliati*.

There is a third type of pasta that is served in soup: stuffed pastas such as tortellini and cappelletti (see page 168) are often floated in broth for a simple, yet delicious, first course. Sometimes eating these carefully made pastas in broth is the best way to appreciate their complex flavors. Larger stuffed pasta such as ravioli would be inappropriate to serve in soup.

Linguine Lingo

Stracci and *maltagliati* are irregular pieces of pasta that are usually cooked in soup. The former Italian word means "rags," the latter "poorly cut."

Savory Italian Soups

There are basically two types of Italian soups: broth soups and bean soups. Broth soups are clear; bean soups are more filling and usually contain several types of vegetables.

Brilliant Broth

Italian cuisine is tremendously thrifty. It makes use of all kinds of scraps, and almost magically makes something special out of a few humble ingredients. How else do you explain the creation of pasta with only eggs and flour? That same thrifty spirit has inspired Italians to become expert broth makers.

Pasta Patter

Gallina vecchia fa buon brodo. An old hen makes good broth.— Italian proverb

Italians have the distinct advantage of excellent, old-fashioned butchers who will save scraps and bones for their loyal customers. If you can locate an old-style butcher shop, ask to purchase soup bones. They will be inexpensive, possibly free.

You can also save various bones and scraps in a large container in your freezer. Depending how much meat you consume, it will take a few months to save a good amount. Supplement your collection of bones and scraps with a few pieces of meat.

The key to a good broth is balance. For a mellow yet rich flavor, keep in mind the following guidelines:

Use liberally in broth:

➤ Beef shank
➤ Beef knuckles
➤ Beef leg bones
➤ Beef neck
➤ Beef ribs
➤ Capon
➤ Steak bones
➤ Turkey wings

Use sparingly in broth:

➤ Chicken bones
➤ Chicken giblets
➤ Oxtail
➤ Veal bones

Don't use in broth:

➤ Lamb
➤ Pork

Full of Beans

Beans play a special role in Italian soups. They add heft, since beans are very filling, but they also add creaminess. In keeping with the emphasis on rustic foods in Italy, cream soups are not as common as simple broths or chunky bean soups. When the latter are puréed, the smooth consistency of beans gives them a creamy feel.

Because of this special aspect to bean soups, all the recipes in this chapter use dried beans, which need to be soaked the night before to rehydrate before cooking.

In a pinch, you can substitute rinsed, canned beans for beans that have been soaked overnight. When using canned beans, don't add them until about 10 minutes before the end of the cooking time. And remember that dried beans thicken soup as they cook; soups made with canned beans will be slightly thinner.

To soak dried beans:

1. Look through the beans and eliminate any small pebbles.
2. Rinse the beans once or twice to remove dust.
3. Place the beans in a large bowl and add a large amount of cold water. The beans should be well covered. If you live in a warm climate or will be soaking the beans for more than eight hours, refrigerate them to avoid the growth of bacteria. If bacteria do grow in your bean bowl, the water will smell sour.
4. Before using the beans, drain the soaking water and rinse the beans one more time.

Soaking dried beans overnight eliminates some of the complex sugars that may cause digestive problems. Although all dried beans may seem the same, they do age. Therefore, soaking and cooking times for beans are hard to pinpoint. Relatively fresh dried beans may need to soak for only three or four hours, whereas harder, older beans can require eight hours or more. If you're not sure of the age of your beans or whether they are sufficiently rehydrated, cut one in half and inspect the cut side. If it is a uniform color, the beans are probably ready; if there is still a white circle at the center of the beans, they need a little more soaking time.

Some people also cook beans using the "quick soak" method, but I'm not one of them. I find it too much trouble and would rather use canned beans when I haven't put beans to soak the night before. Here's how it works, though:

1. Place the beans in a pot and cover with water.
2. Bring the pot to a boil for a few minutes.
3. Remove the pot from the heat and let the beans soak in the hot water for at least one hour.
4. Drain and rinse the beans, and then use them as you would a fully soaked bean.

Pasta Practice

Don't Slow It Down: Salt and acidic items like tomatoes can slow down the cooking time for beans; add them only when the beans are already tender.

Never reuse bean soaking water, whether you've soaked them overnight or used the quick soak method. All those indigestible sugars you're trying to get rid of will go right into your system.

You can also use a pressure cooker to speed up the cooking time for beans, but you'll need to use less liquid. I still prefer soup cooked on a standard stovetop to that prepared in a pressure cooker; the flavors seem to meld better with longer cooking. The pressure cooker is a tremendous time-saver, however.

> **Use Your Noodle**
>
> Always consult your owner's manual when adapting recipes to the pressure cooker. The owner's manual should give a recommended maximum (as in, don't fill the pressure cooker more than three-quarters full) that will guide you in adjusting the amount of liquid to be used.

Soup Secrets

The key to great soup is, in most cases, long, slow cooking. Fortunately, most soups also freeze nicely, so you can make them in advance. Never cook pasta in a soup until you are ready to serve it, however.

> **Pasta Patter**
>
> *La minestra è la biada dell'uomo.* Soup is man's fodder. —Italian proverb

Soups are also an extremely forgiving type of food. Do you have a different type of bean on hand? Two extra carrots but not enough potatoes? A little less broth than is required? Don't worry about it. As long as the proportions are more or less the way they appear in these recipes, and as long as the ingredients in the soup remain covered with liquid, you're safe. And if you enjoy experimenting, soups are a good place to start. No soup need ever taste the same way twice.

When pasta is to be served in soup, it should be cooked in the soup as well. It makes no sense to boil pasta in water and then add it to the soup later. When pasta cooks in soup it absorbs the soup's flavors.

Generally, broth soups are heated to a simmer and then the pasta is added. With bean soups, the ingredients are sautéed in oil, and then liquid (either broth or water) is added and brought to a simmer. Once everything is in the pot, your work is basically done. When the vegetables and beans are thoroughly cooked, you'll add the pasta. Just keep an eye on everything and stir the soup occasionally to keep solid pieces from sticking to the bottom.

Recipes

Basic Broth

This basic broth serves as an ingredient in several of the recipes in this chapter. Italians serve the boiled meat from the broth as a second course after soup. You can reserve the leftover meat and even the cooked vegetables, and do the same. Always leave a very small amount of fat in the broth. When the broth is reheated, this fat forms small circles on the surface known as the *occhi*, or eyes, of the soup.

Makes about 3 quarts

7 lbs. soup bones and meat

1 small yellow onion, peeled and roughly chopped

3 large carrots, peeled and roughly chopped

3 ribs celery, roughly chopped

1 bay leaf

1 bunch parsley

1. Place all the ingredients in a stock pot with about 4 quarts of cold water. (The water should cover the ingredients by an inch or two.)
2. Place the cover slightly ajar, bring to a boil, and then turn down to a gentle simmer. Simmer until the meat has given up all its flavor, at least 4 hours. Add small amounts of boiling water, if necessary, to keep the bones covered. Every 20 minutes or so, use a skimmer to remove any foam from the surface.
3. Pour the broth through a sieve into a bowl and refrigerate for at least 2 hours, preferably overnight. Remove the solidified fat from the surface and discard. This broth will keep for a few days in the refrigerator, or it can be frozen for as long as a few months.

Pastina in Brodo (Broth with Pastina)

There is no easier first course than this.

Serves 6

3 quarts basic broth (see above)

salt and freshly ground pepper to taste

1 cup pastina

grated Parmesan cheese

1. Bring the broth to a boil in a large pot. Season to taste with salt and pepper.
2. Add the pastina to the broth and boil gently until the pasta is cooked, about 5 minutes. Serve with grated Parmesan cheese.

Passatelli in Brodo
(Broth with Passatelli)

This soup makes an unusual first course for a winter supper.

Serves 6

3 quarts basic broth (see page 106)

salt and freshly ground pepper to taste

$^2/_3$ cup grated Parmesan cheese, plus additional grated Parmesan cheese to serve on the side

1 $^1/_2$ cups untoasted breadcrumbs

$^1/_2$ teaspoon freshly grated nutmeg

1 teaspoon grated lemon zest

2 eggs

1. Bring the broth to a boil in a large pot. Season to taste with salt and pepper.

2. Combine $^2/_3$ cup cheese, breadcrumbs, nutmeg, and zest in a small bowl.

3. Add the eggs and knead until thoroughly combined. The dough should be damp but firm, the same consistency as regular pasta dough. You may need to incorporate additional breadcrumbs or a few drops of water to achieve the right consistency.

4. Pinch off a piece of the dough and roll it between your palms. (If it is too wet or too dry it will fall apart or crumble.) As you roll it into a cylinder about $^1/_4$-inch thick, the dough will break into pieces about $^1/_2$-inch long. Each of these small logs is called a *passatello*. In the Romagna half of the Emilia-Romagna region, you can purchase a type of food mill designed specifically for making passatelli. Assuming you can't get your hands on that tool, I think they hold together best when made by hand. You can also place a ball of dough in a potato ricer fitted with the disk with the largest holes and push it through so that the passatelli fall directly into the boiling broth.

5. Add the passatelli and boil gently for 5 minutes, occasionally stirring carefully. Serve with additional grated Parmesan cheese on the side.

Minestrone
(Vegetable Soup)

This is another dish that you will find prepared in almost every home in Italy (and in a slightly different way in each one). This soup's diverse ingredients have enough flavor that it will work with plain water. Broth makes it richer and more satisfying, however. Pastina is the generic term for small types of pasta made for soup. There are endless varieties, with most of their names ending -*ini* or -*ine* (the Italian diminutive). Some of the more common types are acini di pepe, anellini, ditalini, stelline, farfalline, and quadratini.

Serves 6

1 cup dried borlotti beans
1 small yellow onion, chopped
2 tablespoons extra virgin olive oil
1 clove garlic, minced
2 large carrots, peeled and diced
1 rib celery, diced
2 potatoes, peeled and diced
1 bay leaf

1/2 cup chopped parsley
3 quarts basic broth (see page 106) or water
1 cup peeled tomatoes and juices
salt and freshly ground black pepper to taste
4 cups loosely packed Swiss chard
1 cup pastina
grated Parmesan cheese

1. Rinse the beans in abundant water and soak them overnight.
2. In a large, heavy soup pot, sauté the onion in olive oil until translucent, about 2 minutes. Add the garlic and sauté until softened, an additional 2 minutes.
3. Drain and rinse the soaked beans, add to the soup pot, and sauté 2 minutes.
4. Add the carrots, celery, and potatoes. Sauté 2 minutes.
5. Add the bay leaf and parsley. Pour in the broth or water. (If the vegetables are not covered, add cold water to cover.)
6. Bring the soup to a boil, and then turn down to a simmer. Cover the pot and simmer until the beans are very soft, about 90 minutes.
7. Remove the bay leaf. Roughly chop the tomatoes and stir in along with the tomato juices. Season to taste with salt and pepper. Simmer until the tomatoes have broken down, about 20 minutes.
8. Strip the chard leaves from their ribs. Chop the leaves roughly and add to the soup. Before adding the pasta, you have a decision to make. You can either purée the soup (an immersion blender is handy for this) or leave the diced vegetables and beans whole.
9. Stir in the pastina. Simmer until the pastina is cooked and the greens are tender, about 5 minutes. Serve with grated cheese on the side.

Zuppa di Cannellini
(Cannellini Bean Soup)

Bean soup is, by definition, a humble food, but this one is pretty with its white and green color scheme. *Cannellini beans* are about ¹/₂-inch long and white. They are creamy and nutty when cooked. Dried cannellini beans are available yearlong and may be sold fresh in their pods in the spring in some areas.

Serves 6–8

1 ¹/₂ cups dried cannellini beans	2 cloves garlic, peeled and crushed
1 small yellow onion, peeled	4 tablespoons extra virgin olive oil
2 bay leaves	salt and freshly ground black pepper to taste
3 sprigs parsley	4 oz. spaghetti
3 sprigs thyme	grated Parmesan cheese

1. Rinse the beans and soak them overnight in abundant water.
2. Enclose the onion, bay leaves, parsley, and thyme in a small piece of cheesecloth and tie with a piece of kitchen twine. Set aside.
3. In a large, heavy soup pot, sauté the garlic in 2 tablespoons of the olive oil until it just begins to turn color, about 4 minutes.
4. Drain and rinse the soaked beans, add them to the soup pot, and sauté 2 minutes.
5. Add enough water to cover the beans by 2 inches. Place the cheesecloth packet in the pot.
6. Bring the soup to a boil, and then turn down to a simmer. Cover the pot and simmer until the beans are very soft, about 90 minutes.
7. Remove the cheesecloth packet. Season to taste with salt and pepper. Break the spaghetti into pieces about 1 inch long and drop them directly into the pot. Simmer until the pasta is cooked, about 5 minutes. Drizzle on the remaining 2 tablespoons of olive oil. Serve with grated Parmesan cheese on the side.

The Least You Need to Know

➤ Only small pastas are appropriate for most soups.

➤ Pasta should be cooked directly in the broth or soup just before serving.

➤ Dried beans need to be soaked overnight before cooking.

Chapter 11

Something in the Oven: Baked Pasta

In This Chapter

➤ Types of baked pasta dishes

➤ How to make baked pasta dishes

Italian baked pastas are grouped in the category *pasta al forno,* which literally means "pasta from the oven." That is about all these various dishes have in common. Some use fresh, homemade noodles; some use dried macaroni. For most of these recipes it's up to you which kind of pasta to use.

There's something highly comforting about baked pastas. They usually have at least one kind of cheese that melts in the oven. They are also convenient to make ahead. You can refrigerate a casserole of assembled, unbaked pasta for a day or two, or even freeze it, carefully wrapped in aluminum foil. Just thaw to room temperature before baking. You can also freeze individual servings of pasta in aluminum foil after baking. Baked pastas make particularly impressive party dishes. When you carry a steaming casserole to the table, you are sure to elicit some oohs and aahs.

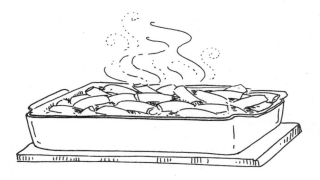

Baked pasta dishes can go right from the oven to the table.

Baking Without Shaking

Baked pastas don't take much more work than pastas prepared on the stovetop, but they do take a little more time. In most cases, the pasta is cooked, tossed or otherwise arranged with the other ingredients, and then baked. Usually some kind of cheese topping or filling melts in the oven. There are a few different kinds of baked pastas, as follows:

➤ Layered baked pastas

➤ Stuffed baked pastas

➤ Tossed baked pastas

Layered baked pastas include *lasagne* and *millefoglie*. Layers of pasta alternate with layers of sauce and other ingredients. These are particularly impressive when sliced, since you get a side view of all the layers.

Stuffed baked pastas include dishes such as *cannelloni*. You can either purchase these large pieces of pasta or make them yourself. They are boiled, filled, and then baked until crusty and hot.

Tossed baked pastas are the easiest of the baked dishes to prepare. These are similar to layered pastas but less carefully arranged. They still look nice when brought to the table, though, and still sport the most coveted part of any baked pasta: that crusty, browned layer that forms on top and around the sides of the casserole.

Pasta Practice

Making It Pretty: It's worth the trouble to invest in a few pretty ceramic and glass dishes that can go directly from the oven to the table.

Pasta Practice

Timing and Temperature: If you don't already have them, invest in a good timer and oven thermometer before you begin working on baked pastas. They are inexpensive and can make a big difference. Your oven's temperature can fluctuate as much as 100 degrees from what it says on the dial, and it's too easy to lose track of time not to have a timer with a nice loud beep to alert you.

Layered baked pastas such as lasagne form pretty layers.

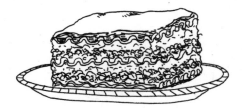

Baked Pasta Equipment

Because the pasta for baked pasta dishes is usually cooked in boiling water before being baked, you need the usual equipment for cooking pasta (a large pot, a skimmer for removing large pieces from the boiling water), as well as at least one good, heavy baking dish. Although you can certainly bake pasta in a dish with rounded sides—and such dishes are often more attractive—you should really bake dishes such as lasagne that have angular corners in a dish that matches that shape.

The sides of your pasta baking dish should be fairly high so that in the heat of the moment no sauce or cheese bubbles up and spills onto the oven floor. You can be pretty flexible about the size and shape of your baking dishes, but don't fill a dish all the way to the top, and remember that if you use a dish larger than the one indicated in the recipe, the pasta will probably need to bake for a shorter period of time.

Many baked pasta dishes call for heating through first with the dish covered by aluminum foil, and then removing the foil and cooking another 10 minutes or so to brown the top. Keep a close watch on your dish during these last few minutes as it can burn easily.

Pasta Practice

Beauty Counts: It's a good idea to keep a large spatula on hand for serving baked pastas such as lasagne. Although the first piece is usually a little messy, succeeding pieces should remain intact.

Lovin' the Oven

Lasagne

Although the American version of this dish is usually loaded with cheese, the original Italian version is as much about pasta as it is about dairy. Don't be tempted to double the cheese. In Emilia-Romagna, the birthplace of lasagne, it's rare to see this dish with any cheese other than Parmesan cheese. In Naples, however, mozzarella cheese is sometimes incorporated. For a delicious and easy variation, make this lasagne with spinach noodles rather than plain egg noodles. The red, white, and green match the colors of the Italian flag.

Serves 6

1 yellow onion, chopped

1 tablespoon extra virgin olive oil, plus oil for pan

1 carrot, peeled and minced

1 stalk celery, minced

$\frac{1}{2}$ lb. ground veal

1 tablespoon fresh thyme or 1 teaspoon dried thyme

1 cup white wine

2 cups peeled tomatoes, chopped, with juice

salt and freshly ground pepper to taste

1 recipe pasta dough (pages 142-143), rolled out and cut into noodles about 4×8 inches wide, or 1 lb. dried lasagne noodles

$\frac{1}{2}$ cup grated Parmesan cheese

$\frac{1}{2}$ cup diced mozzarella cheese

1. In a large skillet, sauté the onion in olive oil until soft, about 2 minutes.

2. Add the carrot and celery and sauté until soft, about 2 minutes.

3. Add the ground veal and thyme to the pan and sauté until the meat loses its rawness, about 7 minutes.

continues

continued

4. Pour in the white wine and cook until the wine has evaporated and the meat is cooked through, about 5 minutes.

5. Add the tomatoes and cook until the tomato juice has evaporated, about 10 minutes. Season to taste with salt and pepper and set aside to cool.

6. Lightly oil a 13×9-inch baking dish and set aside. Preheat the oven to 350 degrees.

7. Cook the lasagne noodles in abundant boiling water as instructed on page 12. Drain and set aside.

8. Spread about 1 tablespoon of the tomato sauce on the bottom of the pan.

9. Cover the tomato sauce with 1 layer of the noodles, overlapping them slightly.

10. Top the noodles with about $1/3$ of the tomato sauce, spreading it evenly with the back of a spoon.

11. Top the sauce with $1/3$ of the mozzarella and $1/3$ of the Parmesan cheese.

12. Top with another layer of noodles, then sauce, and then cheese.

13. Form another layer of noodles, then sauce, and then cheese. The lasagne may be three or four layers thick as long as you end with sauce and then cheese on top.

14. Cover the baking dish with foil and bake for 45 minutes.

15. After 45 minutes, remove the foil and bake for an additional 10 minutes or until browned on top.

16. Allow the lasagne to settle for 10–15 minutes before cutting. You can use just about any meat sauce in this lasagne. Try the *ragu* on page 154 or any leftover tomato sauce you have on hand. If you want your lasagne to be even heartier, try layering in some thinly cut vegetables as well.

Lasagne Bianche (White Lasagne)

This elegant lasagne contains no tomatoes and no meat. Serve it as an appetizing first course in a vegetarian meal.

Serves 6

1 clove garlic, chopped

1 tablespoon extra virgin olive oil, plus oil for pan

1 lb. mushrooms, cleaned and sliced

1 cup peas, fresh or frozen

1 cup white wine

salt and freshly ground white pepper to taste

2 tablespoons butter

3 tablespoons flour

2 cups milk

1 recipe pasta dough (pages 142–143), rolled out and cut into noodles about 4×8 inches wide, or 1 lb. dried lasagne noodles

$1/2$ cup grated fontina cheese

$1/2$ cup grated Parmesan cheese

1. In a large pan, sauté the garlic in olive oil until soft, about 2 minutes.
2. Add the mushrooms and sauté until they begin to give up their liquid, about 7 minutes.
3. Add the peas and sauté until softened, about 4 minutes.
4. Add the wine and cook until it has evaporated and the vegetables are cooked. Season to taste with salt and pepper. Remove from the heat and set aside.
5. To prepare the béchamel sauce, melt the butter in a small, heavy-bottomed pan.
6. Add the flour a very little bit at a time, stirring over low heat until incorporated. The mixture should thicken but not brown.
7. Add the milk very slowly, whisking constantly. Bring the sauce to a simmer and continue to cook, stirring constantly, until it reaches the consistency of sour cream. This should take about 5 minutes. You can prepare the béchamel sauce in advance, but it will thicken as it stands. Before arranging the lasagne, heat the béchamel sauce in a double boiler until thin again, adding a small amount of milk to thin it if necessary.
8. Lightly oil a 13×9-inch baking dish and set aside. Preheat the oven to 350 degrees.
9. Cook the lasagne noodles in abundant boiling water as instructed on page 12. Drain and set aside.
10. Spread about 1 tablespoon of the béchamel sauce on the bottom of the pan.
11. Cover the béchamel sauce with 1 layer of the noodles, overlapping them slightly.
12. Top the noodles with about $^1/_3$ of the béchamel sauce, spreading it evenly with the back of a spoon.
13. Top the sauce with $^1/_3$ of the vegetables, $^1/_3$ of the fontina, and $^1/_3$ of the Parmesan cheese.
14. Top the mixture with another layer of noodles, then sauce, then vegetables, and then cheese.
15. Form another layer of noodles, then sauce, then vegetables, and then cheese. The lasagne may be three or four layers thick, as long as you end with sauce and then cheese on top.
16. Cover the baking dish with foil and bake 45 minutes.
17. After 45 minutes, remove the foil and bake an additional 10 minutes or until browned on top.
18. Allow the lasagne to settle for 10–15 minutes before cutting. Although béchamel sauce is universally known by its French name, it was actually an Italian invention. The original name was *balsamella*.

Millefoglie

Millefoglie are one of my favorite foods of all time. They are, I think, even better than lasagne because they are crispier and somewhat lighter. Although you can make decent lasagne with store-bought noodles, I highly recommend making your own noodles when you try your hand at millefoglie. You can use 1 lb. of ground lean beef or a combination of beef and veal in this recipe. You can prepare the meat sauce in advance and either refrigerate it for a couple of days or freeze it for longer. Bring to room temperature before using.

Serves 6

1 clove garlic, minced
2 tablespoons extra virgin olive oil
1 small yellow onion, minced
2 carrots, peeled and finely grated
1 stalk celery, minced
1 lb. ground meat
$^3/_4$ cup white wine
1 tablespoon tomato paste, dissolved in 2 tablespoons water

$^3/_4$ cup milk
1 pinch nutmeg
2 cups chopped peeled tomatoes with their juices
salt and freshly ground pepper to taste
1 recipe pasta dough (pages 142–143) rolled out and cut into noodles about 4×8 inches wide, or 1 lb. dried lasagne noodles
$^3/_4$ cup grated Parmesan cheese

1. To make the meat sauce, in a heavy pot over medium heat, sauté the garlic in the olive oil until it softens, about 1 minute.
2. Add the onion and sauté until it softens, about 2 minutes.
3. Add the carrot and celery and cook until softened, about 3 minutes.
4. Add the meat to the pot and cook just until it is no longer red.
5. Stir in the wine and the dissolved tomato paste. Turn the heat down to low and cook, stirring occasionally, until the liquid has evaporated.
6. Add the milk and the nutmeg and allow the milk to evaporate slowly.
7. When the milk has evaporated, add the tomatoes and their juices. Season to taste with salt and pepper. Cook at a low simmer until the sauce has thickened considerably, about $1^1/_2$ hours.
8. Lightly oil a 13×9-inch baking dish and set aside. Preheat the oven to 350 degrees.
9. Cook the lasagne noodles in abundant boiling water as instructed on page 12. Drain and set aside.
10. Spread about 1 tablespoon of the tomato sauce on the bottom of the pan.
11. Cover the tomato sauce with 1 layer of the noodles, overlapping them slightly.
12. Top the noodles with about $^1/_3$ of the tomato sauce, spreading it evenly with the back of a spoon.
13. Top the sauce with $^1/_3$ of the Parmesan cheese.
14. Top with another layer of noodles, then sauce, and then cheese.
15. Form another layer of noodles, then sauce, and then cheese. You can have three or four layers, as long as you end with sauce and then cheese on top.
16. Cover the baking dish with foil and bake for 30 minutes.
17. After 30 minutes, remove the foil and bake an additional 10 minutes or until browned on top.
18. Allow the millefoglie to settle for 10–15 minutes before cutting.

Cannelloni
(Cannelloni)

Cannelloni are cylinders of pasta that are cooked, filled with some kind of stuffing, and then baked. *Cannelloni* means "tubes" or "pipes," which perfectly describes the shape of these pieces of Italian pasta.

Serves 6

1 cup ricotta cheese

$^1/_2$ cup diced mozzarella cheese

$^1/_4$ lb. prosciutto, trimmed and minced

2 eggs

salt and freshly ground pepper to taste

1 tablespoon extra virgin olive oil

2 cups peeled tomatoes, chopped

1 tablespoon fresh basil, minced

1 recipe pasta dough (pages 142–143) rolled out and cut into 5×5-inch noodles, or 1 lb. dried cannelloni

1 tablespoon butter

$^1/_4$ cup grated Parmesan cheese

1. Combine the ricotta, mozzarella, prosciutto, and eggs. Season to taste with salt and pepper. Set aside.

2. Heat the olive oil in a medium pan and cook the tomatoes over medium heat until reduced to the consistency of a sauce, about 8 minutes. Add the basil and season to taste with salt and pepper.

3. Lightly oil a 13×9-inch baking dish and set aside. Preheat the oven to 350 degrees.

4. Cook the fresh or dried cannelloni as instructed on page 14, and then drain and dry them thoroughly with a clean towel.

5. If you are using fresh pasta, place one piece on a clean work surface and place a heaping tablespoon of the cheese mixture in a line about 1 inch from the edge of the square. Roll the square around the mixture and place in the dish with the fold facing down. If you are using dried cannelloni, stuff them using a small spoon and pushing with your fingers so that the filling reaches the middle. Place them in the baking dish so that the sides of the tubes touch but are not pushing on each other.

6. When all the cannelloni have been filled, spread the reserved tomato sauce evenly over the surface.

7. Dot the surface of the sauce with butter.

8. Sprinkle Parmesan cheese evenly over the surface.

9. Bake the cannelloni until browned, about 30 minutes.

Fusilli alla Ciociara
(Fusilli Ciociaria Style)

This casserole of cooked pasta couldn't be simpler; the final trip through the oven makes it special. *Ciociaria* (pronounced *cho-cha-ree'-a*) is a part of the region of Latium that falls to the south of Rome. Even if you haven't heard of the place, you surely know its most famous native: Sophia Loren.

Serves 4

4 tablespoons extra virgin olive oil

1 lb. dried fusilli or other short dried pasta

6 plum tomatoes, peeled, seeded, and diced

2 cups diced mozzarella cheese

3 tablespoons grated pecorino romano cheese

1 tablespoon fresh oregano or 1 teaspoon dried oregano

salt and freshly ground black pepper to taste

1. Oil a 2¹/₂-quart ceramic baking dish with 1 tablespoon of oil and set aside. Preheat the oven to 350 degrees.

2. Cook the pasta in abundant boiling water until just al dente, following the instructions on page 12.

3. Meanwhile, prepare the sauce. Sauté the tomatoes in the olive oil until softened, about 5 minutes.

4. Add the mozzarella cheese and cook, stirring constantly, until it melts.

5. Add the pecorino romano cheese and oregano and season to taste with salt and pepper. Cook an additional 5 minutes, until the ingredients are well combined.

6. When the pasta is just al dente, drain and toss it with the sauce.

7. Transfer the pasta to the prepared baking dish and bake until lightly browned, about 15 minutes. Since the pasta and sauce will be hot when you put them in the oven, it shouldn't take long for the top to brown. If you are preparing the casserole in advance and then cooking it, bake for about 30 minutes covered with aluminum foil to heat the whole thing through, and then remove the foil and bake an additional 15 minutes to brown.

Maccheroni Gratinati
(Maccheroni au Gratin)

This hearty casserole makes a nice, casual winter supper. I like to use spicy salami in this dish; the flavor cuts through the richness of the béchamel and cheese.

Serves 6

3 tablespoons butter

1 lb. dried maccheroni or other short dried pasta

3 tablespoons flour

2 cups milk

$^1/_4$ cup grated Parmesan cheese

salt and freshly ground white pepper to taste

$^1/_4$ teaspoon grated nutmeg

$^1/_4$ lb. salami, diced

1. Grease a 2 $^1/_2$-quart ceramic baking dish with 1 tablespoon of butter and set aside. Preheat the oven to 350 degrees.

2. Cook the pasta in abundant boiling water until al dente, following the instructions on page 12.

3. Meanwhile, to prepare the béchamel sauce, melt the remaining 2 tablespoons of butter in a small, heavy-bottomed pan.

4. Add the flour a very little bit at a time, stirring over low heat until incorporated. The mixture should thicken but not brown.

5. Add milk very slowly, whisking constantly. Bring the sauce to a simmer and continue to cook, stirring constantly, until it reaches the consistency of sour cream. This should take about 5 minutes.

6. Stir the nutmeg into the sauce, season to taste with salt and pepper, and set aside.

7. When the pasta is cooked al dente, drain and toss it with the béchamel, half of the Parmesan cheese, and the salami.

8. Pour the pasta into the prepared baking dish, top with the remaining Parmesan cheese, and bake, uncovered, about 25 minutes or until browned on top.

Pizzoccheri alla Valtellina
(Pizzoccheri Valtellina Style)

Pizzoccheri are an unusual pasta made with buckwheat flour. You can make your own by following the recipe on page 174 or buy dried *pizzoccheri* in a specialty store. If you need to substitute dried pasta, look for a whole wheat variety. Valtellina is an area of Italy near the Italian-Swiss border with a tradition of rich, warming foods. *Savoy cabbage,* also known as *curly cabbage,* is a ruffled, green cabbage. It remains bright green when cooked and has a less funky smell than other cabbages.

Serves 6

3 tablespoons butter

2 potatoes, peeled and cut into $1/2$-inch slices

1 small head Savoy cabbage, thinly sliced

1 recipe Pizzoccheri (see page 174) or 1 lb. dried pizzoccheri

1 cup grated fontina or Swiss cheese

2 cloves garlic, minced

4 fresh sage leaves, minced, or $1/2$ tsp. dried sage

salt and freshly ground black pepper

1. Grease a $2^1/2$-quart ceramic baking dish with 1 tablespoon of butter and set aside. Preheat the oven to 350 degrees.
2. Prepare a large pot of water for the cooking pasta, following the instructions on page 12.
3. When the water is boiling, boil the potato slices and cabbage. When the potatoes are almost cooked through, add the pizzoccheri. (Fresh pizzoccheri cooks in about 5 minutes; dried pizzoccheri takes about 10 minutes.)
4. Meanwhile, in a small pan, melt the remaining butter and add the garlic and sage. Cook over low heat for 2 minutes.
5. When the pasta and vegetables are cooked, drain and toss with the fontina and melted butter. Season to taste with salt and pepper.
6. Pour the pasta mixture into the prepared dish and bake, uncovered, about 15 minutes or until browned on top.

The Least You Need to Know

➤ Most types of baked pasta can be assembled in advance.

➤ Pasta is usually boiled before being added to a baked pasta dish.

➤ The size and shape of your baking dish may affect the cooking times.

Part 4
Rolling Your Own

This is the big stuff, homemade pasta. The recipes in Part 4 are, by far, the most challenging in this book; they're the most rewarding, as well.

Keep in mind that you can prepare many of the recipes here with dried pasta if you are in a hurry. You can also purchase fresh pasta in gourmet stores, although I promise that the pasta you make at home will taste far superior.

It's pretty ironic that homemade pasta has become seen as a great feat of gourmet cooking, since one source of its appeal is its rough unevenness. You are about to enter the homemade pasta zone, but don't be nervous. Roll up your sleeves, get out your flour, and enjoy the work and the rewards.

Chapter 12

Fresh Pasta: Why Go to All This Trouble?

In This Chapter

➤ A brief history of fresh pasta

➤ Traditional pastas: where do they belong?

➤ Different types of fresh pasta

Now that I've gone on and on about the virtues of dried pasta—not the least of which is that it is inexpensive and widely available—you may wonder why you should go to the trouble of making your own pasta. Why buy the eggs when you can get the chicken for free, or something like that? The answer is that even Italians don't eat homemade pasta every day. No special occasion passes in most parts of central and northern Italy without pasta being made in the home, to be shared by the whole family. Dried pasta has its virtues, but fresh pasta has its special points, too. It tastes fresher, not to mention richer. Plus, homemade pasta is *de rigueur* with certain sauces. Finally, the fact that it is different from dried pasta and requires a little more effort makes it a special occasion any time you take the time to make your own pasta.

A Place Pasta Calls Home

Whereas fresh egg pasta is made in several of the central and northern regions of Italy, the Emilia-Romagna region can really boast of being the "home" of fresh egg pasta. The wheat of the Emilia-Romagna region has long been recognized for its softness, which suits it particularly for fresh pasta. (As we have already seen, hard wheat, such as durum wheat, is particularly suited to making dried pasta.)

Pasta Patter

Assembly Line Pasta: In 1587, a man named Giovanni dall'Aglio opened the first pasta factory in Bologna, Emilia-Romagna's largest city.

Although pasta is often thought of as peasant food, the fresh egg pasta of Emilia-Romagna was eaten by the rich originally, since wheat and eggs were expensive commodities. Today even the inhabitants of Emilia-Romagna fall back on packaged dried pasta, but fresh egg pasta is featured in restaurants and hits the table like clockwork every Sunday, as well as on holidays.

Pasta Patter

It's a Compliment, Sort Of: The city of Bologna, located in Emilia-Romagna, is known as *la grassa*, or "the fat one," because of its reputation for gastronomy and particularly for its excellent handmade pastas.

No one can pinpoint a date for the creation of egg pasta, but menus and records of court banquets during the Italian Renaissance indicate that people ate something akin to homemade pasta, usually with some kind of sweet sauce, and often as a side dish (a big "no-no" in Italy today). When you roll out a sheet of egg pasta, you are not just making food; you are making history as well.

Are You My Pasta?

Although nominally Italy is a single country, Italians still have a vision of their homeland that is much more akin to the many city-states that existed on the same land during the Renaissance. That is, someone from the city of Parma is much more likely to identify himself as a *parmigiano* (inhabitant of Parma) than as an Italian. This is partly the result of a culture in which people tend to stay put, and partly a result of those many years before the end of the nineteenth century when all the cities and regions combined into one country (with the exceptions of San Marino and the Vatican City, which remain their own separate city-states).

All this is a long prelude to the idea that Italians never eat "Italian food." What they eat is the food of their regions and cities and even neighborhoods. You are no more likely to find a plate of Sicily's famous *bucatini alle sarde* (bucatini with sardines) on the table of someone from Milan than you are to be served some endangered species at a Greenpeace fundraiser. When Italians venture out of their home territory, they are exposed to a cuisine completely different from that to which they are accustomed. Things are confused further by the fact that the same pasta may exist in two different regions under two different names, and that the same name in a different city does not necessarily indicate the same dish. The *cappelletti* of the town of Rimini, for example, differ from those of Ravenna, although these two towns are only about 30 miles from each other.

The different regions of Italy have different types of pasta.

Almost every city has its signature *primo*, or first course: usually pasta but sometimes rice or soup. These classic dishes are served again and again on holidays, particularly Christmas and Easter. In the Emilia-Romagna region, all special-occasion pastas are made with fresh egg dough.

Traditional Pastas of Some Italian Regions

Region	*Pasta*
Abruzzi	Maccheroni alla chitarra
Emilia-Romagna	Cappellacci, cappelletti, tortellini, tagliatelle, lasagne
Latium	Fettuccine
Liguria	Trenette
Lombardy	Pizzoccheri
Molize	Cavatelli
Piedmont	Agnolotti
Apulia	Orecchiette
Tuscany	Pappardelle

There's Nothing Like Homemade

Generally, the Italian pasta you can make at home is divided into the following categories having to do with shape and finishing.

➤ Egg noodles

➤ Soup pastas

➤ Stuffed pastas

➤ Baked pastas

➤ Miscellaneous pastas

Noodling Around

The simplest Italian pastas to make are noodles. If you have never made your own pasta, I highly recommend starting with these, since after you have kneaded the dough the only other step is cutting it. Noodles can be made with egg dough or spinach dough, but egg dough is the most common. The "standard" egg noodles are *tagliatelle*.

Egg Noodles

➤ Fettuccine

➤ Pappardelle

➤ Tagliatelle

➤ Tagliolini

Pasta Overboard!

Soup pastas are also very simple to make, mostly because their shape is not so important. If you feel unsure about your cutting abilities, start with these. Don't, however, try to dress soup pastas with sauce. They just don't stand up to it.

Soup Pastas

➤ Quadretti

➤ Stracci

Stuff It

Stuffed pastas are more tricky and involve a lot of detail work. They are often floated in broth (in which case you need fewer of them). They are a challenge for even the most confident cook.

Pasta Patter

All Hands On Deck: In the regions where stuffed pastas such as *cappelletti* and *tortellini* are eaten on holidays, the day before Christmas sees a virtual assembly line of women and children—whose small hands are particularly adept at shaping these minuscule forms—working to make enough pasta to feed a family.

Stuffed Pastas

➤ Agnolotti

➤ Capellacci

➤ Capelletti

➤ Ravioli

➤ Tortellini

➤ Tortelloni

Baked and Bountiful

As a rule, the pieces of pasta for baked dishes such as lasagne are large and easy to cut. The assembly of the entire dish, however, can take a fair amount of time. Luckily, you can prepare most of the ingredients in advance, and assemble all the dishes prior to baking. Baked pastas are easier to cut and serve if they "set" for 20 minutes or so after coming out of the oven, so working ahead is no problem.

Baked Pastas

➤ Cannelloni

➤ Crespelle

➤ Lasagne

➤ Millefoglie

The Outsiders

Some homemade pastas are not made with traditional egg pasta or spinach pasta dough. These are generally less well known outside of Italy, but they are often easier to make.

Other Homemade Pastas

➤ Gnocchi

➤ Orecchiette

➤ Passatelli

➤ Pizzoccheri

Linguine Lingo

Get It Right: The word "lasagne" is persistently misspelled in North America. The singular "lasagna" indicates only one noodle, whereas the famous dish that consists of layers of noodles and tomato sauce and some form of dairy—either béchamel sauce or cheese—is properly known as "lasagne" because it contains more than one noodle.

The Least You Need to Know

➤ Fresh pasta entails some extra work, but it's worth it.

➤ Noodles and soup pastas are the easiest kinds of fresh pasta to make.

You Are a Pasta Machine

When it comes to most culinary activities, an expert is marked by his or her large array of equipment. When it comes to pasta, however, an expert is marked by his or her lack of equipment. In other words, the most authentic way to make pasta is with the least amount of equipment possible. For generations upon generations, people have rolled out pasta dough with wooden rolling pins and cut it using sharp knives, and that's it. We modern pasta-makers have a wider choice when it comes to machinery, but being more equipped can sometimes stop you from developing pasta-making skills. On the other hand, having that equipment around may mean that you make pasta more often. The choice, in the end, is up to you.

Arming Yourself for the Pasta Battle

We live in a modern world where produce is available out of season and there's no longer any real need to bake our own bread or make our own pasta. Fine artisanal loaves are available even in grocery stores, and imported pasta packs the shelves. I've always found, though, that making very basic foodstuffs myself is relaxing, even fulfilling. Sure, I'm impressed by a professional pastry chef who can whip up a fancy cake, but someone who bakes his or her own bread—even occasionally—really bowls me over.

Maybe that's why when I'm making pasta, I prefer to do it all by hand. It's a tradeoff, to be sure. If I'd become accustomed to machine-made pasta at some point (and yes, you can taste the difference), I might make pasta more often, because the machine-made kind doesn't require quite as much labor. On the other hand, when I pull out my wooden board and begin cracking eggs, I know I'm repeating a process that has been performed for hundreds of years. I know, too, that I'm going to spend some time without answering the phone or thinking about anything much except a big hunk of dough. That is often its own kind of satisfaction.

You do need some equipment to make pasta by hand, though. Here are the basics:

➤ A wooden cutting board

➤ A wooden rolling pin

➤ A knife

Let's take each of those one at a time.

The *wooden cutting board* should be smooth and large, preferably 2×2 feet square. The best kind of cutting board for making pasta has a "lip" about 1 1/2 half inches long on one end that hangs over the side of the table. This lip locks the board in place so that when you're kneading the pasta dough the board doesn't slide all over the table. If you can't get a board with a lip on it (and you don't want to nail a piece of wood onto your wooden cutting board to make one), you'll need to place the board against at least one wall, preferably two, when kneading to hold it in place. In a pinch, you can knead your pasta dough on a marble cutting board. The stone surface is really too cold, however. You need the warmth of wood to do the job right. You may also want to purchase a dough scraper or other small, sharp blade to help you lift the pasta dough off the board. If you have the right ratio of flour to egg, this shouldn't be necessary. If your pasta dough is even slightly sticky, however, it can adhere to the board and tear as you lift it up. The dough scraper is also good for cleaning the board thoroughly once you've finished.

Pasta Practice

Grease Monkey: A brand new rolling pin needs to be oiled before it will work correctly. To do so, rub some olive oil on the rolling pin, sprinkle it with some flour, and then let it rest for a day or two. Repeat this process a few more times until the surface of the rolling pin feels smooth to the touch. You may have to oil it again every few years.

Like the cutting board, the *rolling pin* that you use to flatten the pasta dough into a sheet should be made of wood and quite smooth. A well-worn rolling pin grows smoother over time, but you can oil a new pin to speed up the process. The best kind of rolling pin for making pasta is a cylinder made of a single piece of wood. It should have a diameter of about 1 inch and should be about 20 inches long. You can use the traditional rolling pin with handles (the kind that women always seem to threaten their husbands with in old cartoons), but make sure the diameter of the central cylinder is not too large.

The *knife* you use for cutting pasta should be (unsurprisingly) sharp. A small- or medium-sized paring knife is the best choice. A table knife won't make a clean cut through the dough. If you want to make pasta with fluted edges (such as *pappardelle*), you need a fluted pastry wheel. If you like your ravioli and other pasta to have fancy triangular-cut sides, you need a smaller pastry wheel with a serrated edge.

Getting Cranky

Sometimes we all need a little help. If you want to make pasta the old-fashioned way but don't want to go to the trouble of rolling it out and cutting it, a hand-cranked pasta machine is for you. Using a hand-cranked pasta machine ensures more consistent results than rolling pasta by hand and cutting it with a knife. All of your *tagliatelle* will be exactly the same thickness and width.

A hand-cranked pasta machine produces a somewhat more slippery pasta to which sauces, particularly tomato sauces, don't adhere quite as well as they do to handmade pasta. The reason for this is elementary: Although you probably can't see them, your rolling pin and cutting board have thousands of tiny irregularities in the wood; items made by hand and rolled out on a wooden cutting board with a wooden rolling pin develop pockmarks in the surface. When you use a hand-cranked pasta machine, the pasta is squeezed between metal rollers. The metal surface isn't porous, so neither is the surface of the pasta. Once the pasta is cooked, there's nowhere for the sauce to gain a foothold.

Pasta Practice

Erase the Grease: A pasta machine may come covered in a film of oil applied in the factory to protect it. To clean the machine, make a very stiff dough of flour and water and pass it through all of the slots, making sure to run it through the corners of each slot as well. When you're done, the chunk of dough should be black with grease, and the machine should be clean. You need to perform this routine the first time you use the machine only.

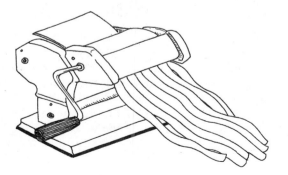

A hand-cranked pasta machine is a labor-saving device.

Pasta Practice

Cleaning House: To clean a hand-cranked pasta machine after using it, place the crank into the indentation matching the slot or slots you have used and crank backwards rather than forwards. Small pieces of dough should fall out of the slots. Use a clean brush such as a pastry brush to clean the rollers as you do this. Next, hold the machine upside down and shake it gently to remove any other pieces that are trapped inside. Again, use a brush to clean the machine more thoroughly. Always perform this ritual immediately after you have finished using the machine; if you let it sit for an hour or so before you clean it, the dough will dry into small bits and clog the machine.

Use Your Noodle

Keep It Dry: Never use water to clean a hand-cranked pasta machine. It will result in a rusty, unusable machine. Store your pasta machine in a dry spot for the same reason.

To make pasta using a hand-cranked machine, you need the following:

➤ A wooden cutting board

➤ A knife

➤ A hand-cranked pasta machine

See the preceding section for information on wooden cutting boards. The knife you use here is not so crucial; you use it only to separate chunks of dough, which are then fed through the machine. Therefore, the knife need merely be sharp.

A hand-cranked pasta machine is an ingenious little tool. It has two purposes really: it both flattens out pasta dough to the appropriate thickness and cuts the dough into noodles. Your machine should be sturdy, yet the crank should turn smoothly and easily in both directions. The slot for flattening out pasta dough is opened and closed in increments using a notched wheel, and I find it helpful for those notches to be numbered. After you've identified the best thickness for a certain type of pasta, you can record it and use it again. Unfortunately, the numbers on different brands of pasta machines do not match each other. The machine should be outfitted with various size cutters; you choose the size by setting the crank in the correct indentation.

Your pasta machine should also have some kind of system on its base (usually a clamp but sometimes a set of screws or suction cups) to attach it to a surface. Make sure that it will hold steady. If the pasta machine uses a clamp to hold itself in place, make sure the clamp fits on the edge of your counter or table.

Man and Machine

I'm a huge fan of the food processor. When it comes to kneading bread dough, whipping up a quick pizza crust, or chopping vegetables, I reach for my own food processor again and again. I don't, however, use the food processor for kneading pasta dough, although I do provide instructions for that here. The food processor has one big defect: heat. If you've ever kneaded bread dough in the food processor, you've probably noticed (and maybe even followed) the instructions in a recipe to allow the dough to sit between spurts of kneading. This is because dough can be ruined by overheating just as easily as it can be ruined by too cold of a temperature. (That's why you're instructed to let the dough rise in a warm, draft-free environment.) During a long, slow kneading by hand, pasta dough heats up slowly as it absorbs the warmth of human hands. In the food processor, the dough heats up quickly. And the metal or plastic blades are a far cry from the porousness of human hands; as with a hand-cranked pasta machine, dough kneaded in the food processor is slick and slippery, and does not "grasp" its sauce very firmly.

On the other hand, not everyone enjoys kneading for 15–20 minutes at a time. I'd encourage you to try kneading by hand a few times (it may take a few tries to get it right) before you give up and turn to the food processor. I'd especially caution against kneading dough in a food processor and then cranking it through a pasta machine. At some point, your hands need to get involved.

To make pasta using a food processor, you need the following:

➤ A food processor

➤ A metal blade for the food processor

➤ A plastic blade for the food processor

➤ A wooden cutting board

➤ A wooden rolling pin

➤ A knife

A standard food processor has a base that rests on a counter (or, in the case of mine, travels merrily across the counter as it works) and a plastic work bowl that rests on top. The most common size found in home kitchens has a bowl that holds 14 cups. You don't accommodate more food in the bowl by changing to a larger bowl but by changing blades. The metal blade is used to mix the ingredients in pasta dough; the plastic blade is used for kneading. Check your food processor's instructions

Use Your Noodle

The Electric Slide: Never turn on your food processor and then leave the room. Not only is it impractical since the processor does its work in mere seconds, but it can be dangerous. When handling large loads, a food processor can move across a counter and fall on the floor. Food processors also overheat easily, although modern models are equipped to turn themselves off when this happens.

Pasta Practice

The Processor Process: A food processor outfitted with a metal blade can also be useful for chopping ingredients for pasta sauces. It is great for cutting up cured meats such as prosciutto and pancetta; I also use it to grind my own meat for ragu. A food processor grates three or four carrots in mere seconds, and it purées soups as well. (Don't pour liquid into the food processor, though. Remove any solids with a slotted spoon, purée them, and then return them to the pot.) Do not, however, use the food processor to chop onions. Its high speed mushes the onions rather than chopping them, and they turn into a soggy mess.

Use Your Noodle

Look Sharp!: The metal blade used by a food processor is extremely sharp. Always use great care when handling it. This includes storing it in a spot where you cannot touch it by mistake and keeping it far out of reach of children. It is best to wash the metal blade in a dishwasher; you can accidentally slice yourself when washing it by hand.

Pasta Practice

Making a Clean Sweep: Always disassemble your machine as soon as you are done using it. Otherwise, the dough will dry up and clog the machine. Every part of the machine except for the part housing the motor and the extruding dies should be soaked in warm, soapy water. The manufacturer usually suggests wiping down the outside of the machine with a damp cloth (check your manual). If you are having trouble cleaning the die, let it sit until the dough dries (about two hours), or freeze it for about 15 minutes, and then tap it on a hard surface until the dried pieces of pasta fall off.

to learn the maximum amount of flour your bowl can hold. If you're making huge amounts of pasta dough, you'll have to knead it in batches regardless of whether you're using your hands or a machine.

Pasta Robots

It had to happen. With our mania for all things electric, Americans have discovered the electric pasta machine. The electric pasta machine mixes dough in a container and then forces it through a die to shape it. Electric pasta machines don't require any effort on your part; a motor turns all the parts. Your only responsibilities are choosing and inserting the die, and catching the pasta as it comes out. I don't use an electric pasta machine, and I don't particularly recommend them. If your choice is between never making pasta at all or making it with this gadget, however, it's worth a try. Maybe tasting fresh pasta will inspire you to have a go at making it by hand.

What's Out There?

You can find electric pasta machines in kitchen equipment stores. There are basically three companies that make electric pasta machines:

➤ Cuisinart

➤ Vitantonio

➤ Simac

How Does It Work?

The requirements for making pasta dough in a machine may be slightly different from those for making pasta dough by hand; be sure to read the instructions that come with your machine. Dry ingredients such as flour and spices are added to the mixing container first. Some machines require a wetter dough, so water and oil are added with the eggs. Most machines come with a measuring cup for the liquid ingredients. Liquid ingredients are added to the container slowly with the machine running.

You should ensure the dough is consistent and smooth before beginning the extruding process. The dough should hold together when you pinch off a piece between your fingers.

The Least You Need to Know

➤ Pasta made by hand has superior taste and texture to that made by machine.

➤ A hand-cranked pasta machine can be used for rolling and cutting dough.

➤ An electric pasta machine mixes the dough and extrudes it.

I think I can, I think I can...

Chapter 14

Egging Ourselves On

In This Chapter

➤ Step-by-step instructions for making fresh egg pasta

Perhaps no other image has defined Italian cooking quite so indelibly as that of the hefty Italian *mamma* rolling out a big sheet of pasta dough and cutting it into clever shapes to feed her family. There is some truth to this image: In all the years I've lived in and visited Italy, I have never witnessed a man making pasta in his own house. It's not that Italian men don't cook; they do. Many are the principal chefs in their own homes. But pasta, it seems, is women's work. And it's the work of older women, too. The new generation raising children in Italy today considers itself too busy, too mobile, and just plain too modern to worry about acquiring the old skill of making egg pasta. That's a terrible shame. Pasta-making is a valuable skill, and it's not a difficult one. Your first few batches of pasta may be less then optimum, but after a couple of tries you are sure to learn the rhythm. Once you have caught on and begun creating the softest, freshest, most inviting pasta you've ever tasted, you'll be hooked, because nothing, not even fresh pasta in the finest four-star restaurants, compares to pasta made fresh in your own home and cooked soon afterward.

Le Uova: Eggs

At this point, it really goes without saying that the eggs you use to make pasta should be the freshest, healthiest eggs you can find. It is worth it to seek out organic eggs at a health food store or, better yet, fresh eggs from a farm. Like dried pasta, fresh egg pasta has very few ingredients (eggs and flour), so you want those ingredients to be their best.

Size Does Matter!

Eggs are ranked by two different standards in the United States: size and thickness. Eggs are sized as follows:

Size	Weight per Egg (ounces)
Jumbo	30
Extra Large	27
Large	24

I usually use large eggs (the smallest size) because that's what I can buy from a farmer at a nearby farmers' market, but you should purchase whatever size is freshest. You will use slightly more or less flour to make the pasta depending on the size of the eggs. Some eggs are simply more absorbent than others and will require more flour anyway, even though they are small.

Making the Grade

Egg grades are different from size and are meant to reflect quality (not freshness). Eggs are graded as follows:

Grade	Quality
AA	Thick white and strong yolk membrane
A	Medium white and medium yolk membrane
B	Thin white and weak yolk membrane

You are unlikely to find B-grade eggs in your grocery store. Although grade-AA eggs are superior to grade-A eggs, freshness is still more important than grade. If you like to eat fried eggs with the yolk intact, these grades are something to keep in mind.

Incredible and Edible, Too

Eggs are often given a bad rap for being high in cholesterol, but they are also nutritional powerhouses. A large egg contains 6.5 grams of protein and is rich in iron, phosphorus, thiamin, and vitamins A, D, E, and K. Also consider that when you eat fresh pasta you are consuming a maximum of one egg per person.

When purchasing eggs, follow the usual precautions, including checking that none of the shells are cracked or broken.

La Farina: Flour

Although they share the same name, in some ways dried pasta and fresh egg pasta are opposites. Dried pasta is made with hard flour so that it will remain *al dente* even when cooked. It is meant to provide a plain taste and chewy texture that serve as a backdrop for numerous sauces. Fresh egg pasta, on the other hand, is rich and soft. It cooks in mere seconds and almost melts in your mouth.

Because you are seeking softness when making fresh egg pasta, you will use a softer flour, not the hard semolina flour used to make dried pasta (with the exception of the orecchiette on page 172). Italians find a range of different flours in their grocery stores that are marked "for pasta,""for pastry," and so forth, but our standard unbleached white flour is quite similar to their pasta flour.

Unbleached, all-purpose flour should be available in every supermarket. Bleached flour just won't cut the mustard. The bleaching process is an unnecessary step taken to "whiten" wheat flour, which is naturally yellowish in color. At the same time, the chemical processing used to bleach flour reduces its wheaty flavor. Bleaching also removes some of the vitamin E from wheat.

Store unbleached white flour in an airtight container. Whole grain flours need to be stored in the refrigerator, but white flour should be fine on the kitchen counter almost indefinitely, as long as it is not exposed to extreme temperatures, extreme humidity, or lots of direct sunlight. I like to store my flour in a glass container with a wide mouth. That way, I can see when I'm running low and I can comfortably fit both my hand and a one-cup measuring cup into the jar.

Measure for Measure

Most professional cooks will tell you that they prefer weighing over measuring; it is much more accurate. When you are baking something delicate like a cake or even a loaf of bread, you are probably

Pasta Practice

Storing Eggs: Always store eggs in their cardboard carton in the refrigerator, not in those little built-in egg cups in the door. They will stay fresh longer. Egg shells are very porous, which means that they absorb odors rapidly. (To make truffle-flavored scrambled eggs, chefs often leave fresh eggs in a basket together with a truffle, and soon the eggs have absorbed the truffle's flavor through their shells.) Keep eggs away from strong-smelling foods and, most importantly, use them quickly.

Pasta Practice

Hearts and Flours: It may surprise you to learn that flour, which seems like such a basic element in food, can be judged comparatively. Your pasta will come out fine if you use unbleached white flour, but try making pasta with organic, stone-ground flour and you *will* notice a difference. The less a food is processed, the more flavor it retains.

better off using a small kitchen scale. Pasta is not such an exact science, however. I think measuring with a dry measuring cup is fine in this case, since you will need to gauge the exact amount of flour to be used anyway. The measuring cup can certainly provide a rough estimate.

Use a dry measuring cup to measure flour.

Use Your Noodle

The Dry Look: Be sure that you are using a dry measuring cup to measure flour, and not a liquid one. "Dry" does not mean that the measuring cup need not have droplets of water on it. It should be a scoop made of metal or plastic with "1 cup" marked on it some-where. A "liquid" measuring cup is made of glass or plastic and has a spout and various measurements marked on its side.

To measure flour using a measuring cup:

1. Either sweep the measuring cup into a container of flour and bring it up full, or gently spoon the flour into the measuring cup until it is full. The flour should rest in a mound that is higher than the top of the measuring cup.

2. Hold the measuring cup over the flour container (or over a sheet of wax paper).

3. Grasp a knife in your other hand and hold the blade vertically with the blunt side against the edge of the measuring cup closest to you.

4. Briskly sweep the knife across the top of the measuring cup so that the excess flour spills either back into the flour container or onto the wax paper.

5. If using the wax paper method, pinch one side of the piece of paper to create a "spout" and pour the flour back into your flour container.

If you prefer using a scale rather than a measuring cup, one cup is equal to four or five ounces of flour. As you will see in the following recipe, I recommend beginning with the smaller amount of flour and incorporating more if necessary.

Pasta Patter

La farina del diavolo va tutta in crusca. "The devil's flour is all bran." – Italian proverb

L'Impasto: **The Dough**

The standard measurements for making homemade pasta are as follows:

➤ 1 egg per person

➤ 1 cup of flour per egg

I do things a little differently, however. I encourage you to begin with less flour, especially if you don't have a lot of kneading experience, since less flour will make a softer dough that's easier to work with. It is much easier to add flour to a wet dough than it is to moisten a dry dough. I also think that the measurement of one egg per person makes a lot of pasta. If you are making pasta as part of a multi-course meal, the following recipes will serve six people. If you are making pasta only, you may want to stick to the one egg per person rule.

After reading so much about the making of fresh egg pasta, you must be ready by now for some action. The first step in making fresh egg pasta is creating the dough, which is made of eggs and flour. You can do this either by hand (preferred), using a food processor, or using an electric pasta machine.

Pasta Practice

Watching the Clock: Making fresh egg pasta is not terribly time consuming, but if you want to schedule it, allow yourself about 30 minutes to make simple egg pasta, such as tagliatelle, by hand. Using one of the various pasta machines can cut 10–20 minutes off of that time frame. Luckily, fresh egg pasta need not be made the very second before it is going to be cooked; most types of fresh egg pasta benefit from sitting for an hour or longer before cooking.

In the Palm of Your Hand: Mixing and Kneading Pasta Dough

Pasta Dough (by Hand)

4 cups unbleached flour

4 eggs

1. Mound about 3 ¹/₂ cups of the flour on a large wooden cutting board.
2. Shape the flour into a well with a deep indentation in the center.
3. Crack the eggs into the well.
4. Use a fork or your fingers to break up the yolks and mix the eggs. *Avoiding a Leak:* The trickiest part about making pasta dough by hand is not letting the eggs seep out through the walls of the flour "well" while you're mixing them in. To prevent this, keep one hand cupped around the side of the flour while you work with the other. If you are really having trouble with this step, you can beat the eggs in a small bowl in advance, and then pour them into the well.
5. Draw in a little bit of the flour and mix it with the eggs.
6. Continue drawing in a little bit of flour at a time and mixing it in until a paste has formed in the center of the well.
7. When the paste has formed, move all the remaining flour on top of the dough.
8. Squeeze the dough between your fingers to incorporate the remaining flour.
9. At this point, you need to evaluate your dough. It should be dry enough that it doesn't stick to the board as you knead. If it still feels somewhat gummy, incorporate more flour, but only about 1 tablespoon at a time. Remember that it's much easier to add flour to an overly wet dough than it is to moisten a dry dough.
10. When the dough has reached the right consistency and forms a ball, clean off your work surface (a dough scraper works best) and wash and dry your hands.
11. Return the ball of dough to your clean work surface and begin kneading. To knead pasta dough, press into the ball of dough with the heel of your hand and push away from yourself. Next, fold the far end of the dough back over the top of the dough and turn it a quarter turn. Repeat this action of pushing into the dough, folding it, and turning it. This will go fastest if you use one hand to press and the other to fold. The dough may feel resistant at first, but it will grow more tender as you work it. Kneading takes a fair amount of strength; don't worry about being too rough with the dough.
12. Knead until the dough is soft and firm. It should be a bright, consistent yellow color with no lumps of flour. The surface of the dough should be soft and smooth. Vigorous kneading by hand will take about 8 minutes.

Working the Blades: Mixing and Kneading Pasta Dough

Pasta Dough
(by Food Processor)

4 cups unbleached flour

4 eggs

1. Place 3 ¹/₂ cups of the flour in a food processor equipped with the metal blade.
2. Crack the eggs on top of the flour.
3. Run the processor on "pulse" a few times to break up the eggs.
4. Turn on the processor and watch carefully. In about 30 seconds the dough should form a ball on top of the blades and clean the sides of the bowl. If the dough remains too crumbly, add a teaspoon of water at a time through the feed tube until a ball forms. If the dough remains too wet, add a teaspoon of flour at a time through the feed tube until a ball forms.
5. When the dough forms a ball on top of the blades and cleans the sides of the bowl, remove the dough and set aside.
6. Replace the metal blade with the plastic dough blade.
7. Return the ball of dough to the processor and process for 2 minutes to knead. Be sure to check the capacity of your food processor. You may need to make the dough in two batches.

Get Your Motor Running: Mixing and Kneading Pasta Dough

Pasta Dough
(by Pasta Machine)

Man versus Machine: Naturally, you should read the manufacturer's instructions that came with your particular machine and follow them to the letter. These are just basic guidelines for using a pasta machine. Most pasta machines call for a more liquid dough than other pasta-making methods. Read your machine's instruction booklet and add water to create the amount of liquid you need.

3 cups unbleached flour

4 eggs

1. Measure the flour into the mixing container.
2. Crack the eggs into a measuring cup with a spout and beat them.
3. Slowly pour the eggs into the mixing container.
4. Mix the dough as instructed in the manual.
5. Turn off the machine and check the consistency of the dough. If it is too wet, add a teaspoon of flour at a time. If it is too dry, add a teaspoon of water at a time. Mix the dough between additions, checking the consistency before continuing.

How Green Was My Pasta

Adding cooked, chopped spinach to your pasta dough makes it a pretty, green color. You can actually taste the spinach in fresh spinach pasta (as opposed to the spinach in the dried green pasta you can buy, which adds color but little flavor). Adding spinach also makes your pasta softer and more malleable.

Using Your Green Thumbs

Spinach Pasta Dough (by Hand)

Cooking Spinach: If you are using frozen spinach, be sure to thaw it first. If you are using fresh spinach, clean it by soaking it in several changes of water. Cook the spinach over medium heat with a small amount of water until very soft, about 5 minutes, and then set aside to cool. When the spinach is cool, squeeze out as much water as possible with your hands.

$3/4$ cup cooked spinach, drained

3 cups unbleached flour

4 eggs

1. Chop spinach as finely as possible. Puréeing spinach in the food processor or blender makes it too watery. This is better done by hand.
2. Mound the flour on a large wooden cutting board.
3. Shape the flour into a well with a deep indentation in the center.
4. Crack the eggs into the well.
5. Use a fork or your fingers to break up the yolks and mix the eggs.
6. Add the spinach to the well and mix with the eggs.
7. Draw in a little bit of the flour and mix it with the eggs and spinach.
8. Continue drawing in a little bit of flour at a time, mixing it in until a paste has formed in the center of the well.
9. When the paste has formed, move all the remaining flour on top of the dough.
10. Squeeze the dough between your fingers to incorporate the remaining flour.
11. At this point you need to evaluate your dough. It should be dry enough that it doesn't stick to the board as you knead. If it still feels somewhat gummy, incorporate more flour, but only about 1 tablespoon at a time. Remember that it's much easier to add flour to an overly wet dough than it is to moisten a dry dough.
12. When the dough has reached the right consistency and forms a ball, clean off your work surface (a dough scraper works best) and wash and dry your hands.
13. Return the ball of dough to your work surface and begin kneading.
14. Knead until the dough is soft and firm. It should be a bright, consistent green color with no lumps of flour or large chunks of spinach. The surface of the dough should be soft and smooth. Vigorous kneading by hand will take about 8 minutes.

Give Spinach a Whirl

Spinach Pasta Dough
(by Food Processor)

³/₄ cup cooked spinach, drained

3 cups unbleached flour

4 eggs

1. Chop the spinach as finely as possible.
2. Place 1 ¹/₂ cups of the flour in a food processor equipped with the metal blade.
3. Crack 2 of the eggs on top of the flour. Add about ¹/₂ of the spinach.
4. Run the processor on "pulse" a few times to break up eggs.
5. Turn on the processor and watch carefully. In about 30 seconds the dough should form a ball on top of the blades and clean the sides of the bowl. If the dough remains too crumbly, add a teaspoon of water at a time through the feed tube until a ball forms. If the dough remains too wet, add a teaspoon of flour at a time through the feed tube until a ball forms.
6. When the dough forms a ball on top of the blades and cleans the sides of the bowl, remove the dough and set aside.
7. Replace the metal blade with the plastic dough blade.
8. Return the ball of dough to the processor and process for 2 minutes to knead.
9. Remove the first batch of dough and repeat with the remaining flour, eggs, and spinach.

Spinach Flies into the Mix

Spinach Pasta Dough
(by Pasta Machine)

Damp Dough: Most pasta machines call for a more liquid dough than other pasta-making methods. Read your machine's instruction booklet and add water to create the amount of liquid you need.

³/₄ cup cooked spinach, drained

3 cups unbleached flour

4 eggs

1. Chop the spinach as finely as possible.
2. Measure the flour into the mixing container.
3. Crack the eggs into a measuring cup with a spout and beat them. Stir in the spinach.
4. Slowly pour the spinach-egg mixture into the mixing container.
5. Mix the dough as instructed in the manual.
6. Turn off the machine and check the consistency of the dough. If it is too wet, add a teaspoon of flour at a time. If it is too dry, add a teaspoon of water at a time. Mix the dough between additions, checking the consistency before continuing.

145

Extras! Extras!

Although spinach is by far the most common addition to egg pasta dough, you also can use other foodstuffs to vary the color and flavor of your pasta. Try some of the following:

➤ Saffron for brighter yellow pasta

➤ Beet juice for pink pasta

➤ Tomato paste for orange pasta

➤ Chopped fresh herbs for speckled pasta

➤ Squid ink for black pasta

La Sfoglia: The Sheet

Once you've made your pasta dough, you need to roll it out into a thin sheet known as *la sfoglia*, or "the sheet." You can do this with a rolling pin or with a hand-cranked pasta machine. Pasta that is made in an electric pasta machine is not rolled out but extruded through a die shaped like the pasta you wish to create; if you are using an electric pasta machine, you can skip this section.

Pinning It Down

To roll pasta dough into a sheet by hand, you need a wooden cutting board and rolling pin (see page 130).

Pasta Practice

Half and Half: When making pasta for the first time, you may find it easier to work with only half of the dough at a time. Cut the ball of dough in half with a sharp knife or cleaver. Set one half aside and either cover it with a bowl or wrap it in a clean, damp, cotton cloth. It will still be moist when you're done with the first half.

1. Dust your work surface (wooden cutting board) very lightly with flour.

2. Place the ball of dough on the center of the work surface.

3. Use your hands to flatten the ball of dough slightly.

4. Place the rolling pin on the center of the dough and roll it away from you.

5. Turn the dough a quarter turn and repeat.

6. Continue rolling the dough away from you, turning a quarter turn each time, until you have a large circle about $1/8$ inch thick. It is important that you retain the dough's circular shape.

7. Picture the circle of dough as a clock. Roll the 12 side of the clock towards you, wrapping about $1/3$ of the circle around the rolling pin, and then rapidly unroll the sheet, smoothing the pasta with your hands as you go.

8. Repeat this action about 10 times, rolling up more and more of the circle as you do, until the last time you roll up the entire circle.

9. Turn the sheet slightly and repeat.

10. You should repeat this final thinning action about 10 times around the entire circle of dough. If the dough sticks to the rolling pin or to itself, sprinkle it very lightly with flour.

11. The sheet should be so thin that it is almost transparent. Keep in mind that egg pasta expands when cooked, so pasta that seems the right thickness in its raw state needs to be thinned further.

12. Allow the sheet of pasta to dry slightly before cutting. Spread a clean towel on your work surface and lay the pasta on top of it. When the surface of the pasta dough begins to look dry and has slightly visible lines running through it, it is ready to cut.

Flat as a Board

A hand-cranked pasta machine certainly makes rolling out the dough a lot easier, but it also results in a certain loss of texture on the surface of your pasta, making it more difficult for the sauce to adhere to the pasta. To roll out dough using a hand-cranked pasta machine, you need only the machine itself, plus a little extra flour.

1. Set the rollers on your hand-cranked pasta machine to the widest setting.

2. Take a golf-ball sized piece of pasta dough and store the remaining dough under an inverted bowl or wrapped in a clean, damp, cotton cloth.

3. Lightly flour the piece of dough.

4. Put the piece of dough through the rollers and turn the crank evenly. A flattened piece of dough will emerge from the other side.

5. Remove the flattened piece of dough, fold it in half, lightly flour it again, and feed it through the rollers again, leaving them on the same setting.

6. Repeat the preceding step 5–6 times until the pasta dough is perfectly smooth and does not shred or show "fringe" on its sides.

7. Turn the dial on the pasta machine to the next thinnest setting (say from 8 to 7), lightly flour the piece of dough, and pass it through the rollers.

8. Continue to move the rollers closer and closer together. Do not fold the piece of dough, but do flour it each time you pass it through the rollers.

Pasta Practice

Speed It Up: Although you do not have to work lightning fast when dealing with pasta dough, you shouldn't dawdle or interrupt your work for a phone call, either. You want the pasta dough to remain moist and pliable, so work at a quick and steady rate.

9. Continue until you have passed the pasta through the thinnest or second-thinnest level (depending on the machine and how thin you want your pasta).

10. Set each piece aside on a clean towel as you finish.

11. Repeat until all the pasta dough has been thinned.

Tagliare: Cutting

The final step in preparing pasta is cutting it. This is fairly simple to do by hand, but using a hand-cranked machine results in more consistently sized pieces. When using an electric pasta machine, you don't roll out the dough at all, but press it through an extruder, which shapes it.

The Kindest Cut

To cut pasta by hand, you need a sharp knife or, if you want curly edges on wide pasta such as pappardelle, a fluted pastry cutter.

Pasta Patter

Pretty, But Not So Tasty: Bologna is the birthplace of *tagliatelle*. It is also the place where you will find the "official" measure for these noodles. A case in Bologna's city hall houses a single golden noodle created by the local culinary academy that is $5/16$ of an inch wide and $1/32$ of an inch thick.

To cut tagliatelle, fettuccine, and tagliolini by hand:

1. Spread the sheet of dough on a clean work surface.

2. Roll the dough up into a flat cylinder about 3 inches wide.

3. Use your left hand (assuming you are right-handed) to hold the roll of dough steady while you cut it into strips with your right hand. Use the following measurements:

Noodle	Width
Tagliatelle	$1/4$ inch
Fettuccine	$1/8$ inch
Tagliolini	$1/16$ inch

Don't worry about measuring your pasta with a ruler. These are simply guidelines.

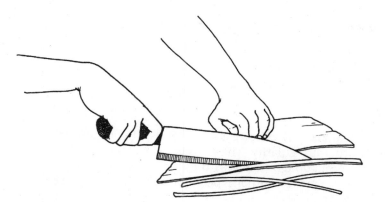

Always tuck in your fingers when cutting noodles.

4. Fluff the noodles by hand to separate them.
5. Transfer the noodles to a clean, dry towel until you are ready to cook them.

Pappardelle are wide noodles with fluted edges. To cut them, lay the sheet of dough flat and cut it into strips about $1/2$ inch wide using a fluted pastry wheel. Cut the noodles in half so that they won't be unwieldy.

Quadretti are little squares of fresh pasta that you can toss in soup. To cut quadretti, lay the sheet of dough flat and cut into squares about $1/4$ inch $\times$ $1/4$ inch. Alternately, you can cut the pasta into tagliatelle and then slice them off at $1/4$-inch intervals. Use only about half of the pasta dough to make quadretti for 6 people. You can use the rest to make another type of pasta, or you can make quadretti and store them in the refrigerator or freezer to toss into soups at the last minute.

Use Your Noodle

Blade Etiquette: Always curl the fingertips of the hand you are holding the pasta with underneath your fingers to avoid the risk of cutting yourself. The side of the knife blade should rest against the lower joints of your fingers as you cut.

Pasta Patter

Cruel Inspiration: Bologna's *tagliatelle* are said to have been inspired by the blond hair of Lucretia Borgia, a noblewoman and murderer.

Quadretti are small squares.

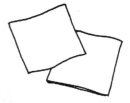

Stracci, or *maltagliati,* are haphazardly cut pieces of pasta, usually vaguely triangular in shape; their beauty lies in their irregularity. They should be $1/4$ inch to $1/2$ inch wide. Use only about half of the pasta dough (made with four eggs) to make stracci for 6 people. You can use the rest to make another type of pasta, or you can make stracci and store them in the refrigerator or freezer to toss into soups at the last minute.

Smooth as...Pasta?

After you have pressed your pasta dough into sheets using the machine, you can cut it easily. Most pasta machines come with three or four sizes, corresponding (from smallest to largest) to *tagliolini, fettuccine,* and *tagliatelle.*

Pasta Patter

Dry Up!: Make sure your sheets of pasta are fairly dry before passing them through the machine. Flour them lightly before beginning.

To cut pasta using a hand-cranked machine:

1. Switch the crank to the hole corresponding to the size pasta you want to make.
2. Feed one sheet of the pasta through the cutters while you use the other hand to crank at a steady pace.
3. As the pasta begins to emerge from the other end, switch your feeding hand to the front to catch and spread out the noodles as they fall.
4. Fluff the noodles by hand to separate them.
5. Transfer the pasta to a clean, dry towel until you are ready to cook it.

Extrude, Dude

When the dough you made in your electric pasta machine has been kneaded enough, set the machine to begin forcing the dough through the die to create the pasta. Before you begin making the dough, select and install the die you want for the noodles you are making. Then just sit back and watch the machine force out your pasta.

At first, the machine will eject little bits of pasta (you can return these to the dough container), but soon the shape will become recognizable. Pasta from an electric pasta machine comes out in one long piece. Either hold a knife over and parallel to the die and cut the pieces as they come out or spread them on the counter as they emerge and cut them there. Transfer the pasta to a clean cotton towel. That's all there is to it.

Saving Pasta for a Rainy Day

If you plan to cook and eat your pasta within the same day, you can leave it resting on its clean towel. In fact, I think pasta tends to improve a little if left to dry for a couple of hours after it is made; I often make pasta in the morning that I will use for lunch, or early in the afternoon if I want it for dinner.

If you want to store noodles, such as tagliatelle, for longer than that, allow them to dry thoroughly (in humid places this can take up to 2 days) on a pasta drying rack or a clean towel, and then store them in a tin or plastic bag. If kept in a cool, dry environment, noodles will keep for a couple of weeks or even an entire month.

Quadretti and stracci can also be dried and stored this way, or they can be refrigerated in a plastic bag. Be sure that the pieces are fairly dry before tossing them together, however, or they will stick together.

A Few Recipes for Fresh Pasta

The following are some ways to use your new-found fresh pasta skills. You can also use fresh pasta to prepare some of the dishes in Part 2, "Saucy."

Quadretti in Brodo
(Broth with Quadretti)

After a hard day, nothing soothes more than a steaming bowl of broth with simple pasta squares.

Serves 6

3 qt. Basic Broth (page 106)   fresh quadretti for 6 people (page 149)
salt and freshly ground pepper to taste   grated Parmesan cheese

1. Bring the broth to a boil in a large pot. Season to taste with salt and pepper.
2. Add the quadretti to the broth and boil gently until the pasta is cooked, about 4 minutes. Serve with grated Parmesan cheese.

Pasta e Fagioli
(Pasta and Bean Soup)

This thick purée with its unevenly cut pieces of pasta is the essence of home-cooked food.

Serves 6

1 1/2 cups dried borlotti beans

1 small yellow onion, chopped

2 cloves garlic, peeled and crushed

2 tablespoons extra virgin olive oil

1 carrot, peeled and roughly chopped

1 rib celery, roughly chopped

1 bay leaf

2 sprigs fresh sage

3 quarts Basic Broth (page 106)

2/3 cup peeled tomatoes and juices

salt and freshly ground black pepper

fresh maltagliati for 6 people (page 150)

grated Parmesan cheese

1. Rinse the beans and soak them overnight in abundant water.

2. In a large, heavy soup pot, sauté the onion and garlic in olive oil until translucent, about 2 minutes.

3. Drain and rinse the soaked beans and add them to the soup pot. Sauté for 2 minutes.

4. Add the carrot and celery. Sauté for 2 minutes.

5. Add the bay leaf and only the leaves from the sage. Pour in the broth. (If necessary, add cold water to cover the vegetables by about 2 inches.) Bring the soup to a boil, and then turn down to a simmer. Cover the pot and simmer until the beans are very soft, about 90 minutes.

6. Remove the bay leaf. Add the tomatoes and tomato juices. Season to taste with salt and pepper. Simmer until the tomatoes have broken down, about 20 minutes.

7. Purée the soup. There are two ways to purée soup. You can use an immersion blender and purée it right in the pot (with the stove turned off). Alternately, you can use a slotted spoon to move the solid pieces to a blender or food processor, process them, and then stir the purée back into the pot.

8. Stir in the pasta and simmer until it is cooked, about 5 minutes. Serve with grated cheese on the side.

Zuppa di Ceci
(Chick Pea Soup)

Here is another classic bean soup with homemade pasta. This one is made with sweet, nutty chick peas.

Serves 6

1 ½ cups dried chick peas
1 small yellow onion, chopped
2 cloves garlic, peeled and crushed
leaves of 1 sprig rosemary, minced
4 tablespoons extra virgin olive oil

3 qt. Basic Broth (page 106)
²/₃ cup peeled tomatoes and their juices
salt and freshly ground black pepper to taste
fresh stracci for 6 people (page 150)
grated Parmesan cheese

1. Rinse the chick peas and soak them overnight in abundant water. Chick peas need extra-long soaking and cooking time. You may want to start soaking them a full 24 hours before you want to make this soup.

2. In a large, heavy soup pot, sauté the onion, garlic, and minced rosemary leaves in 2 tablespoons of olive oil until the onion is translucent, about 2 minutes.

3. Drain and rinse the soaked beans and add them to the soup pot. Sauté for 2 minutes.

4. Pour in the broth. (If necessary, add cold water to cover the beans by about 2 inches.) Bring the soup to a boil, and then turn down to a simmer. Cover the pot and simmer until the beans are very soft, about 2 hours.

5. Add the tomatoes and tomato juices. Season to taste with salt and pepper. Simmer until the tomatoes have broken down, about 20 minutes.

6. Purée the soup. There are two ways to purée soup. You can use an immersion blender and purée it right in the pot (with the stove turned off). Alternately, you can use a slotted spoon to move the solid pieces to a blender or food processor, process them, and then stir the purée back into the pot.

7. Stir in the pasta and simmer until it is cooked, about 5 minutes. Drizzle on the remaining 2 tablespoons of olive oil. Serve with grated cheese on the side.

Fettuccine alla Bolognese
(Fettuccine with Tomato-Flavored Meat Sauce)

Any pasta with the word "Bolognese" in the title is topped with ragu, the meat sauce that reigns supreme in the Emilia-Romagna region where the city of Bologna is located. *Ragu* (tomato-flavored meat sauce) is an ancient food with recipes dating all the way back to the sixteenth century. Early versions were usually sweet. In this recipe, you can use either 1 lb. of ground lean beef or a combination of beef and veal. Some ragu also use chicken meat and chicken livers. Ragu is excellent served over tubular pasta such as rigatoni. It also marries well with tortellini (page 168) and fresh spinach pasta (page 144).

Serves 4

1 clove garlic, minced

2 tablespoons extra virgin olive oil

1 small yellow onion, minced

2 carrots, peeled and finely grated

1 stalk celery, minced

1 lb. ground meat

$3/4$ cup white wine

1 tablespoon tomato paste, dissolved in 2 tablespoons water

$3/4$ cup milk

1 pinch nutmeg

2 cups chopped peeled tomatoes with their juices

salt and freshly ground pepper to taste

fresh fettuccine for 4 people (page 148) or 1 lb. dried pasta

grated Parmesan cheese (optional)

1. In a heavy pot over medium heat, sauté the garlic in the olive oil until softened, about 1 minute.

2. Add the onion and sauté until softened, about 2 minutes.

3. Add the carrot and celery and cook until softened, about 3 minutes.

4. Add the meat and cook just until it is no longer red. Do not brown the meat at this point. It will become tough.

5. Stir in the wine and the dissolved tomato paste. Turn the heat down to low and cook, stirring occasionally, until the liquid has evaporated.

6. Add the milk and nutmeg and allow the milk to evaporate slowly.

7. When the milk has evaporated, add the tomatoes and their juices. Season to taste with salt and pepper. Cook at a low simmer until the sauce has thickened considerably, about $1^1/2$ hours. Ragu is an exception to tomato sauce rules because of its long cooking time.

8. When the ragu is ready, cook the pasta according to the instructions on page 12. When the pasta is done, drain and transfer it to a low, wide bowl. Serve grated Parmesan on the side.

Tagliatelle con i Fagioli
(Tagliatelle with Beans)

Sauces like this one that use beans or other legumes in place of meat are often described as *magro*, or "lean," in Italy. *Borlotti beans* are brown beans with red markings related to kidney beans. They are sometimes labeled as "cranberry" or romano beans. Borlotti beans are available dried year-round and may be purchased fresh in their pods in some areas in the spring. This sauce is also excellent over short, dried pasta such as penne and rigatoni. Conchiglie are another good choice.

Serves 4

1 cup dried borlotti beans	1 $1/2$ cups chopped peeled tomatoes with their juices
1 small yellow onion, minced	$1/2$ cup tomato purée
2 tablespoons extra virgin olive oil	salt and freshly ground pepper to taste
2 carrots, peeled and finely grated	fresh tagliatelle for 4 people (page 148)
1 stalk celery, minced	grated Parmesan cheese (optional)
$1/2$ cup white wine	

1. Soak the beans overnight in abundant water. If you can find fresh borlotti beans still encased in their bright pink pods, by all means use them. Simply skip the overnight soaking, shell the beans, and begin this recipe with step 3.
2. The next morning, drain and rinse the beans, and then set aside.
3. In a heavy pot over medium heat, sauté the onion in the olive oil until softened, about 2 minutes.
4. Add the carrot and celery and cook until softened, about 3 minutes.
5. Add the beans and sauté for 1 minute.
6. Add the wine and allow to evaporate.
7. Add enough cold water to cover the beans by about 1 inch, bring to a boil, and then turn down the heat to a simmer.
8. Simmer the beans gently over low heat until very soft, 1–1$1/2$ hours. You should be able to crush a bean between your tongue and your palate with very little effort. If the beans appear to be drying up, add additional water in small amounts. The beans should remain covered.
9. Add the tomatoes and purée. Season to taste with salt and pepper. Simmer until the liquid has evaporated, about 20 minutes. Because the tomatoes and salt will retard the cooking, don't add them until the beans are thoroughly tender and creamy.
10. When the sauce is ready, cook the pasta according to instructions on page 12. When the pasta is done, drain and transfer it to a low, wide bowl, and then top with the sauce. Serve grated Parmesan on the side, if desired.

Tagliatelle al Caviale
(Tagliatelle with Caviar)

This rich dish fits perfectly at an elegant supper. It can easily be halved to serve only two people. Dark sevruga caviar is lovely against pale tagliatelle. If you are feeling flush, you can buy the expensive beluga caviar. With this recipe, it is better to economize by buying a smaller amount of pricier caviar than by buying more of a cheaper grade of caviar. Inexpensive caviar will clump together.

Serves 4

fresh tagliatelle for 4 people (page 148)

1/3 cup extra virgin olive oil

1 small red onion, chopped

1 oz. caviar

1 bunch chives, minced (optional)

1. Bring a large pot of water to a boil and cook the pasta according to the instructions on page 12.
2. When the pasta is done, drain and transfer it to a low, wide serving bowl.
3. Drizzle the oil over the pasta and toss to coat. Sprinkle on the chopped onion and toss again.
4. Sprinkle the caviar over the pasta, separating the grains as much as possible. Top the pasta with the chives, if desired. Toss the pasta at the table before serving.

Trenette al Pesto
(Trenette with Pesto)

Pesto originates in Italy's Liguria region where the city of Genoa is located. This area boasts a particularly fragrant type of basil that does not grow anywhere else in the world. You may also use grated pecorino cheese or a combination of Parmesan and pecorino. Because bunches of basil can vary in size, you may need more or less olive oil than this. Your final product should be creamy but not too liquid. *Trenette* are slightly narrower than tagliatelle. If you want to use dried pasta in this recipe, you can substitute 1 lb. of linguine.

Serves 6

1 large bunch basil

salt and freshly ground pepper to taste

3 cloves garlic, lightly crushed

1 tablespoon pine nuts

3/4 cup grated Parmesan cheese

3/4 cup extra virgin olive oil

2 boiling potatoes

8 oz. green beans, trimmed

fresh trenette for 6 people (page 259)

1. To make the pesto, place the basil leaves in a mortar. A mortar and pestle—basically a fancy bowl and a stubby stick—are ancient tools used to pound and rub ingredients into a paste. (You can also make pesto in a food processor or blender. Follow the next six steps, adding the oil through the feed tube with the machine running. Metal blades have a tendency to overheat the basil, however, so the best results still come from using a mortar and pestle.)

2. Add a pinch of salt, the garlic, and the pine nuts.

3. Work the combination with the pestle until the basil leaves are in fine pieces and the garlic and pine nuts are crushed.

4. Add 3 tablespoons of the oil, drizzling it in very slowly while continuing to work the mixture with the pestle.

5. Stir in the grated cheese.

6. Slowly incorporate the remaining oil until the mixture is creamy.

7. Season the mixture to taste with additional salt and pepper.

8. Meanwhile, boil the potatoes until soft. As soon as the potatoes are cool enough to handle, peel and dice them, and set aside.

9. Blanch the green beans. After shocking them with cold water, cut the beans into 1 inch pieces and set aside.

10. Bring a large pot of water to a boil and cook the pasta according to the instructions on page 12.

11. When the pasta is done, drain and transfer it to a low, wide serving bowl. Immediately mix in the pesto and toss to coat. Add the green beans and potatoes and toss again.

Pappardelle con Finocchio e Vitello (Pappardelle with Veal and Fennel)

Wide noodles and small pieces of veal combine to create an elegant dish. Serve this with a dry white wine and follow it with poached pears. If you want to avoid unsightly black flecks on your pasta, use white pepper rather than black pepper.

Serves 4

4 oz. veal scaloppini, pounded
1 clove garlic, minced
2 tablespoons extra virgin olive oil
2 bulbs fennel, trimmed and chopped
1 cup heavy cream

salt and freshly ground pepper to taste
fresh pappardelle for 4 people
1 tablespoon minced fresh sage
grated Parmesan cheese (optional)

continues

continued

1. Bring a large pot of water to a boil for cooking the pasta.
2. Cut the veal scaloppini into $1/2$ inch squares and set aside.
3. In a large pan over medium heat, sauté the garlic in the olive oil until softened, about 1 minute.
4. Add the fennel and sauté until tender but not quite cooked through.
5. Push the fennel pieces over to one side of the pan, add the veal, and sauté until cooked through, about 2 minutes.
6. Add the cream. Bring to a low simmer and cook, stirring occasionally, until thickened slightly. Season to taste with salt and pepper.
7. Meanwhile, cook the pasta according to the instructions on page 12. When the pasta is al dente, drain and transfer it to the pan. Sprinkle on the sage and toss over medium heat until all the liquid has been absorbed, about 2 minutes. Serve grated Parmesan on the side, if desired.

Fettuccine Alfredo
(Fettuccine in Cream Sauce)

Fettuccine Alfredo came under fire a few years ago for being a high-fat dish. The Surgeon General will never recommend a sauce made with butter and cream, but keep in mind that this is special-occasion fare in Italy, not an everyday meal. An actual person named Alfredo, a Roman restaurateur, invented this dish. Legend has it that he used a gold fork and spoon to toss the pasta. *Fettuccine* are medium-width egg noodles. Their name in Italian literally means "little ribbons."

Serves 4

1 tablespoon butter

1 tablespoon extra virgin olive oil

1 cup heavy cream

salt and freshly ground black pepper to taste

fresh fettuccine for 4 people

$1/2$ cup grated Parmesan cheese, plus additional grated Parmesan to serve on the side

$1/4$ cup chopped parsley

1. Bring a large pot of water to a boil for cooking the pasta.
2. In a large, heavy pot over medium heat, melt the butter and olive oil.
3. Add the cream and salt to taste. Bring to a low simmer and cook, stirring occasionally, until thickened slightly. Season to taste with salt and pepper.
4. Meanwhile, cook the pasta according to the instructions on page 12. When the pasta is al dente, drain and transfer it to the pot. Sprinkle on the Parmesan cheese. Toss over medium heat until all the liquid has been absorbed and the cheese is evenly distributed, about 2 minutes. Transfer the pasta to a low, wide serving bowl and sprinkle on the chopped parsley. Serve additional grated cheese on the side.

The Least You Need to Know

➤ Pasta measurements are very variable: be flexible.

➤ Pasta dough can be kneaded, rolled out, and cut in various ways.

➤ Egg pasta can be colored and flavored with edible ingredients.

Chapter 15

Filling Out: Stuffed Italian Pastas

In This Chapter

➤ How to make stuffed Italian pasta

➤ Recipes for stuffed pasta

Italians make all kinds of stuffed pastas in all sorts of shapes. Fillings are made from vegetables, cooked meat, cheese, and herbs, or some combination of those. Many of these types of pasta are labors of love. They are in no way difficult, but they do take some time because individual pieces must be fashioned one by one.

Tricks of the Trade

The following are a few things to keep in mind as you make stuffed pasta:

➤ Be sure all the pieces are carefully sealed, or the stuffing will leak out while the pasta is being boiled. If you have trouble sealing the pasta dough when making stuffed pastas, try adding a teaspoon or so of milk to the dough when you are making it. This makes the dough somewhat softer and more pliable.

➤ All stuffings that include meat should be cooked in advance.

➤ Stuffings should be prepared and set aside to cool, if necessary, before you begin making the pasta dough.

➤ Pieces from the same batch will vary slightly in appearance but should be approximately the same size so that they require the same amount of cooking.

➤ Stuffed pastas are already flavored, so they don't require complicated sauces.

➤ Stuffed pasta is great for using up leftover vegetables.

➤ If you want to make your own stuffed pasta but don't feel like making the dough, you can sometimes purchase sheets of pasta dough in specialty stores.

This recipe calls for a pastry crimper.

Ravioli agli Spinaci
(Ravioli with Spinach)

Ravioli are square pillows of pasta usually filled with some type of greens. The name derives from the Genoese dialect word *rabiole*, meaning "rubbish." Presumably, these tasty squares were a handy way for using up leftovers. This is a great stuffed pasta to start with. The filling is simple to prepare, and ravioli are not fussy. To highlight the fresh taste of the filling, top these with butter and a few fresh sage leaves. You can vary the following recipe by using different greens. A combination of mild greens, such as spinach, and bitter greens, such as broccoli rabe, is especially good. To steam spinach, first clean the leaves by soaking them in abundant water in a large bowl or clean sink. Lift the leaves gently out of the water, fill the bowl or sink with clean water, and return the leaves to the clean water until no more sand rests at the bottom of the bowl when you remove the spinach. (Even if you are using pre-cleaned spinach, rinse it once to refresh it.) Shake any excess water off the leaves, and then place the damp leaves in a pot and cook over medium-low heat, covered, until they have wilted.

Serves 4

6 cups loosely packed spinach	salt and freshly ground pepper to taste
$1/4$ teaspoon nutmeg	1 recipe Pasta Dough (pages 142–143)
$1/4$ cup grated Parmesan cheese	

1. Soak the spinach in several changes of water. When the water runs clear, remove the spinach leaves but don't dry them.
2. Steam the spinach until wilted, about 5 minutes.
3. When the greens have cooled, squeeze out as much water as possible and chop them finely.
4. In a small bowl, combine the cooked greens, nutmeg, and cheese and season to taste with salt and pepper.
5. Lightly flour your work surface.
6. If you are using a hand-cranked machine, roll out a piece of pasta dough into a strip about 2 inches wide. If you are rolling the dough by hand, roll it out into a sheet and cut the sheet into 2-inch strips.
7. Place about 1 teaspoon of the stuffing 1 inch from the top of the strip, and then place additional teaspoon of the stuffing along the strip, all about 1 inch apart.

8. Place a second strip of pasta on top of the first strip.

9. Press the two layers of dough together between the portions of filling. Trim the sides of the strips to make them straight.

10. Cut the ravioli into squares using a knife or pastry crimper to cut between the places where stuffing is.

11. Gently press the edges together a second time with your fingertips to be sure they stick, and then remove the ravioli to a floured plate. Repeat with the remaining dough and stuffing. When pressing the edges of ravioli together, wet your fingertips to be sure they really stick.

12. For cooking ideas, see pages 14 and 117.

Ravioli agli Spinaci e Ricotta
(Ravioli with Spinach and Ricotta)

The addition of ricotta cheese makes these ravioli a little lighter than those in the preceding recipe. Try these with a simple tomato sauce like the one on page 78.

Serves 4

5 cups loosely packed spinach

$1/4$ teaspoon nutmeg

$1/4$ cup grated Parmesan cheese

$1/2$ cup ricotta cheese, drained if necessary

salt and freshly ground pepper to taste

1 recipe Pasta Dough (pages 142–143)

1. Soak the spinach in several changes of water. When the water runs clear, remove the spinach leaves but don't dry them.

2. Following the directions on page 162, steam the spinach until wilted, about 5 minutes.

3. When the greens have cooled, squeeze out as much water as possible and chop them finely.

4. In a small bowl, combine the cooked greens, nutmeg, and cheeses and season to taste with salt and pepper.

5. Lightly flour your work surface.

6. If you are using a hand-cranked machine, roll out a piece of pasta dough into a strip about 2 inches wide. If you are rolling the dough by hand, roll it out into a sheet and cut the sheet into 2-inch strips.

7. Place about 1 teaspoon of the stuffing 1 inch from the top of the strip, then place additional teaspoon of the stuffing along the strip, all about 1 inch apart.

8. Place a second strip of pasta on top of the first strip.

continues

continued

9. Press the two layers of dough together between the portions of filling. Trim the sides of the strips to make them straight.

10. Cut the ravioli into squares using a knife or pastry crimper.

11. Gently press the edges together a second time with your fingertips to be surethey stick, and then remove the ravioli to a floured plate. Repeat with the remaining dough and stuffing. If any of the filling is left over, use it as a terrific topping for plain, cooked penne, or spread it on a piece of toast and broil until the ricotta begins to brown.

12. For cooking ideas, see pages 14 and 117.

Ravioli alle Erbe e Noci (Herb and Walnut Ravioli)

These ravioli have a fresh flavor thanks to the herbs, but the nuts make them hearty enough to work as a meal when served with a salad of grilled vegetables. To toast walnuts as needed for the recipe below, spread them on a tray and bake at 350 degrees (a toaster oven works well) for about 8 minutes, shaking the tray often to be sure they don't burn. Feel free to mix and match the herbs in this recipe, although parsley and basil are the major players and should always be included.

Serves 4

1 cup walnuts, toasted	1 cup loosely packed fresh oregano
2 cups loosely packed basil leaves	salt and freshly ground pepper to taste
3 cups loosely packed Italian parsley leaves	1 recipe Pasta Dough (pages 142–143)

1. Chop the toasted walnuts into small crumbs.

2. Rinse the herbs and pat them dry with a paper towel.

3. Grind the herbs into a paste. (The food processor works well for this.)

4. In a small bowl, combine the ground herbs and nuts and season to taste with salt and pepper.

5. Lightly flour your work surface.

6. If you are using a hand-cranked machine, roll out a piece of pasta dough into a strip about 2 inches wide. If you are rolling the dough by hand, roll it out into a sheet and cut sheet into 2-inch strips.

7. Place about 1 teaspoon of the stuffing 1 inch from the top of the strip, and then place additional teaspoon of the stuffing along the strip, all about 1 inch apart.

8. Place a second strip of pasta on top of the first strip.

9. Press the two layers of dough together between the portions of filling. Trim the sides of the strips to make them straight.

10. Cut the ravioli into squares using a knife or pastry crimper.

11. Gently press the edges together a second time with your fingertips to be sure they stick, and then remove the ravioli to a floured plate. Repeat with the remaining dough and stuffing.

12. For cooking ideas, see pages 14 and 117.

Agnolotti di Carne (Meat Agnolotti)

Agnolotti are little half-moons of pasta traditionally stuffed with greens, meat, or both.

Serves 4

1 tablespoon butter
$^1/_4$ lb. ground veal
$^1/_4$ lb. ground pork
$^1/_4$ lb. prosciutto, trimmed of fat and minced
1 egg

$^1/_4$ cup grated Parmesan cheese
$^1/_2$ cup white wine
salt and freshly ground pepper to taste
1 recipe Pasta Dough (pages 142–143)

1. In a large pan, melt the butter and add the ground veal, ground pork, prosciutto, egg, and cheese.

2. Cook over medium heat, breaking up the meats with a spoon like you do with scrambled eggs, until the meats have lost their rawness, about 7 minutes.

3. Add the white wine and continue cooking until the meats are thoroughly cooked, about 10 minutes more.

4. Season to taste with salt and pepper.

5. Lightly flour your work surface.

6. If you are using a hand-cranked machine, roll out a piece of pasta dough into a strip about 3 inches wide. If rolling dough by hand, work with 1 sheet.

7. Cut the dough into circles about 2 $^1/_2$ inches in diameter using a cookie cutter or juice glass.

8. Place $^3/_4$ teaspoon of filling slightly off center in each circle, about $^1/_2$ inch from the edge.

9. Fold the empty half of each circle over the half with the stuffing and seal the edges carefully.

10. Remove the agnolotti to a floured plate. Repeat with the remaining pasta dough and stuffing. You can reuse the remaining trimmings after you cut out the circles for agnolotti. Gather them into a ball and knead for a minute or so to combine. Dough trimmings begin to harden after they have been rolled out repeatedly, however, so save all the trimmings and reuse them at the end. They can probably be rolled out twice before they stiffen.

11. For cooking ideas, see pages 14 and 117.

Agnolotti di Magro
(Agnolotti with Greens)

These agnolotti are considered *magro,* or "lean," because they contain no meat.

Serves 4

2 bunches Swiss chard

1 clove garlic, minced

$1/4$ cup grated Parmesan cheese

$1/2$ cup ricotta cheese

$1/8$ tsp. grated nutmeg

salt and freshly ground pepper to taste

1 recipe Pasta Dough (pages 142–143)

1. Rinse the Swiss chard in several changes of cold water, and then remove and discard the hard stems.

2. Shake excess water off the chard leaves and transfer them to a large frying pan. Cover the pan and steam the chard over medium heat with moisture remaining on leaves until the leaves are cooked, about 7 minutes.

3. When the chard is cool enough to handle, squeeze out as much moisture as possible, and then finely chop them.

4. In a medium bowl, combine the cooked chard, garlic, Parmesan cheese, ricotta cheese, and nutmeg. Season to taste with salt and pepper.

5. Lightly flour your work surface.

6. If you are using a hand-cranked machine, roll out a piece of pasta dough into a strip about 3 inches wide. If you are rolling the dough by hand, work with 1 sheet.

7. Cut the dough into circles about 2 $1/2$ inches in diameter using a cookie cutter or juice glass.

8. Place $3/4$ teaspoon of the filling slightly off center in each circle, about $1/2$ inch from the edge.

9. Fold the empty half of each circle over the half with the stuffing. Seal the edges carefully by pressing gently with your fingertips.

10. Remove the agnolotti to a floured plate. Repeat with the remaining pasta dough and stuffing.

11. For cooking ideas, see pages 14 and 117.

Agnolotti di Scarola (Escarole Agnolotti)

Escarole has a bitter taste when raw but, once cooked, it becomes mild. Prosciutto adds a delicious, salty edge to this dish. Escarole is a type of chicory or bitter lettuce. If you can't find escarole, you can replace it with bitter greens such as broccoli rabe.

Serves 4

4 heads escarole

1 clove garlic, minced

1 tablespoon extra virgin olive oil

$^1/_2$ cup grated Parmesan cheese

$^1/_4$ pound prosciutto, trimmed of fat and minced

salt and freshly ground pepper to taste

1 recipe Pasta Dough (pages 142–143)

1. Rinse the escarole in several changes of cold water.
2. Chop the escarole.
3. In a large pan, sauté the garlic in the olive oil for 1 minute. Add the escarole and cook over medium heat until wilted, about 4 minutes.
4. In a medium bowl, combine the cooked escarole, Parmesan cheese, and prosciutto. Season to taste with salt and pepper.
5. Lightly flour your work surface.
6. If you are using a hand-cranked machine, roll out a piece of pasta dough into a strip about 3 inches wide. If you are rolling the dough by hand, work with 1 sheet.
7. Cut the dough into circles about 2 $^1/_2$ inches in diameter using a cookie cutter or juice glass.
8. Place $^3/_4$ teaspoon of the filling slightly off center in each circle, about $^1/_2$ inch from the edge.
9. Fold the empty half of each circle over the half with the stuffing. Seal the edges carefully by pressing gently with your fingertips.
10. Remove the agnolotti to a floured plate. Repeat with the remaining pasta dough and stuffing.
11. For cooking ideas, see pages 14 and 117.

Tortellini

Tortellini, featured in the recipe below, have a sexy mythology. Supposedly, an innkeeper in Bologna was so besotted with Venus when she spent the night in his establishment that he peeked through the keyhole of her room and saw only her exquisite bellybutton framed there. He rushed to his kitchen and began turning out tortellini as an homage to her navel. Tortellini are probably the best known and most loved stuffed pasta. The best way to enjoy them is to cook and eat them in broth so that all their flavor shines through. You can make the filling for tortellini and most stuffed pastas in advance. The filling benefits from sitting a couple of hours or up to two days in the refrigerator as the flavors blend together.

Serves 4

$1/2$ lb. lean ground beef

2 tablespoon extra virgin olive oil

$1/4$ lb. prosciutto, trimmed of fat and minced

$1/2$ cup grated Parmesan cheese

salt and freshly ground pepper to taste

1 recipe Pasta Dough (page 142–143)

1. Sauté the ground beef in the olive oil over medium heat until cooked through, stirring frequently and breaking up with a fork as you would scrambled eggs. Set aside to cool.
2. Combine the cooked beef, prosciutto, and Parmesan cheese. Season to taste with salt and pepper.
3. Lightly flour your work surface.
4. If you are using a hand-cranked machine, roll out a piece of pasta dough into a strip about 3 inches wide. If you are rolling the dough by hand, work with 1 sheet.
5. Cut the dough into circles about $2^1/2$ inches in diameter using a cookie cutter or juice glass.
6. Place $1/2$ teaspoon of the filling slightly off center in 1 circle, about $1/2$ inch from the edge.
7. Fold the empty half of each circle over the half with the stuffing. Seal the edges carefully by pressing gently with your fingertips.
8. Pick up the circle between your index finger and thumb with the folded edge pointing up.
9. Pull the 2 corners of the semi-circle together around your index finger.
10. Press these 2 corners together to seal and pop up the "skirt."
11. Remove the tortellini to a floured plate. Repeat with the remaining pasta dough and stuffing.
12. For cooking ideas, see pages 14 and 117.

Cappelletti

The word *cappelletti* means "little hats," and once you've made this kind of pasta you'll see why. The finished products look like miniature tri-cornered hats. They are very similar in appearance to tortellini, except they are made with a square piece of dough rather than a round one. Cappelletti are often made with a combination of different kinds of meat or a combination of beef and poultry. A little turkey is especially good in cappelletti.

Serves 4

1 small yellow onion, chopped
2 tablespoons extra virgin olive oil
1 carrot, peeled and minced
1 stalk celery, minced
$1/2$ lb. lean ground beef

$1/4$ lb. prosciutto, trimmed of fat and minced
$1/4$ cup grated Parmesan cheese
$1/4$ teaspoon grated nutmeg
$1/2$ cup white wine
1 recipe Pasta Dough (pages 142–143)

1. In a large pan over medium heat, sauté the onion in the olive oil until softened, about 2 minutes.
2. Add the carrot and celery and sauté until soft, about 2 minutes.
3. Add the ground beef, prosciutto, Parmesan cheese, and nutmeg, and sauté, stirring frequently and breaking up the beef with a fork, until the beef loses its raw color, about 5 minutes.
4. Add the white wine and simmer until it has evaporated and meat is cooked through, about 5 minutes.
5. Set the filling aside to cool.
6. Lightly flour your work surface.
7. If you are using a hand-cranked machine, roll out a piece of pasta dough into a strip about 2 inches wide. If you are rolling the dough by hand, work with 1 sheet.
8. Cut the dough into rectangles 2 inches long and 1 $1/2$ inches wide.
9. Place $1/2$ teaspoon of the filling about $1/2$ inch from the short end of each rectangle.
10. Fold the empty half of one rectangle over the half with the stuffing and seal the edges carefully.
11. Pick up the sealed piece between your index finger and thumb with the folded edge pointing up.
12. Pull the 2 folded corners together around your index finger.
13. Press these 2 corners together to seal and pop up the "skirt."
14. Remove the cappelletti to a floured plate. Repeat with the remaining pasta dough and stuffing.
15. For cooking ideas, see pages 14 and 117.

Cappellacci di Zucca
(Squash Cappellacci)

In Italian, *cappellacci* means "big hats." These are just a larger version of cappelletti. Ferrara is famous for these tasty, slightly sweet treats, which are often served with ragu for a salty-sweet combination.

Serves 4

1 acorn squash	$^1/_4$ teaspoon honey
$^1/_4$ teaspoon nutmeg	1 recipe Pasta Dough (pages 142–143)
$^1/_4$ teaspoon cinnamon	

1. Preheat the oven to 400 degrees.
2. Slice the squash in half the long way. Scrape out and discard the seeds and strings. Place the squash cut-side down in an oiled baking dish and bake until soft, about 45 minutes. Remove the squash from the oven and set aside to cool.
3. When the squash is cool enough to handle, remove the flesh from the shell, and discard the shell. Place the squash flesh, nutmeg, cinnamon, and honey in a small bowl and mash with a fork until well combined.
4. Lightly flour your work surface.
5. If you are using a hand-cranked machine, roll out a piece of pasta dough into a strip about 3 inches wide. If you are rolling the dough by hand, work with 1 sheet.
6. Cut the dough into rectangles 3 inches long and $2^1/_4$ inches wide.
7. Place $^3/_4$ teaspoon of the filling about $^1/_2$ inch from the short end of each rectangle.
8. Fold the empty half of one rectangle over the half with the stuffing. Seal the edges carefully by pressing gently with your fingertips.
9. Pick up the sealed piece between your index finger and thumb with the folded edge pointing up.
10. Pull the 2 folded corners together around your index finger.
11. Press these 2 corners together to seal and pop up the "skirt."
12. Remove the cappellacci to a floured plate. Repeat with the remaining pasta dough and stuffing.
13. For cooking ideas, see pages 14 and 117.

The Least You Need to Know

➤ Making stuffed pasta can be labor-intensive.

➤ All stuffed pastas should be carefully sealed.

Chapter 16

Other Handmade Pasta

In This Chapter

➤ How to make homemade pasta that is not made with regular egg dough

The Runners-Up

Egg pasta (including egg pasta with spinach) is certainly the most common type of homemade pasta, but there are pastas made from other types of dough that can also be made at home. This chapter contains a mismatched bunch of pastas from all over Italy. These pasta types include the following:

➤ Orecchiette

➤ Pizzoccheri

➤ Gnocchi

There's another unusual kind of pasta that I haven't included in this chapter. A recipe for *passatelli*—a pasta made with eggs, Parmesan cheese, and breadcrumbs—is included on page 107 in the Chapter 10, "Pasta + Soup = Comfort[2]." Passatelli are only eaten cooked in broth.

A Nod to Various Italian Noodles

Orecchiette

Orecchiette are probably my favorite pasta to make because they are so very simple. The mix of semolina flour and regular white flour gives them a wonderful, chewy texture. Use orecchiette to make Orecchiette with Broccoli Rabe (page 68) or dress them with a simple tomato sauce. *Orecchiette* means "little ears," and that's just what this pasta—native to the Italian region of Apulia—is shaped like. I've seen recipes for orecchiette that call for a 1:1 ratio of semolina flour to regular flour, and I've seen recipes that call for a 1:2 ratio. Using more semolina and less regular flour won't ruin the recipe, but the orecchiette will take a little longer to cook and will be a little chewier. Experiment with these two flours until you find the balance you like best.

Serves 4

1 cup semolina flour

1 $^1/_2$ cups unbleached all-purpose flour

1 cup warm water

1. Place the flours on a clean work surface and combine.
2. Shape the flours into a well with a deep indentation in the center.
3. Place about 4 tablespoons of the water in the center of the well. The water needn't be extremely hot, but it can't be cold or the pasta dough will remain grainy. Room temperature or slightly warmer is fine.
4. Use your index finger to draw in a little bit of the flour and mix it with the water. A paste should form.
5. When the water has been absorbed, add about 4 tablespoons more water. Draw in some more flour and combine.
6. Continue adding water and drawing in flour a little bit at a time until all the flour has been incorporated into a soft, but not sticky, dough.
7. Clean off your work surface and wash and dry your hands.
8. Return the ball of dough to your clean work surface and begin kneading. Knead until the dough is smooth and consistent, about 7 minutes. If the dough crumbles while you are kneading, wet your hands.
9. Spread a clean dish towel out on the counter (not on your work surface).
10. Cut off a chunk of dough about the size of a golf ball and cover the remaining dough to keep it from drying out.
11. Use your palms to roll the piece of dough into a sausage shape about $^1/_2$ inch in diameter.
12. Slice the dough into disks $^1/_8$ inch thick.
13. Work with one disk at a time. Pick one up and place it in the palm of your left hand. Use your right thumb to press into the center of the disk, swiveling

your thumb once or twice to thin out the center of the disk and enlarge it. The disk should resemble a mushroom cap and should be approximately 1 inch wide. Place the disk on the dish towel. *Note:* These instructions are for right-handed people. If you are left-handed, place the disks in the palm of your right hand and press with your left thumb.

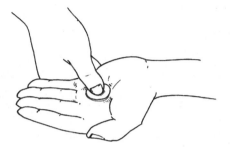

To make orecchiette, place one disk of pasta in your left hand and thin it with your right.

14. Repeat with the remaining disks of pasta. Flour your thumb occasionally if you find it is sticking to the pasta.

15. When you have finished flattening all the disks, sprinkle some flour over them, and then cut another piece of dough and begin again from step 11. You can cook orecchiette right after you finish making them, or you can air dry them. Air-dried orecchiette will keep at room temperature for several months. To air dry orecchiette, spread them on two floured cookie sheets and leave to dry. Orecchiette may take up to 24 hours to dry. Try cutting a few with a knife. If the center is still damp, leave them on the trays. If they are too hard to cut with a knife, they are dry. Once dry, they can be tossed together in a covered container. While just-made orecchiette will cook in about 7 minutes, dried orecchiette may take as long as 20 minutes to cook thoroughly.

Pizzoccheri

Pizzoccheri are buckwheat noodles that come from Italy's Valtellina region. Pizzoccheri are almost always baked in casseroles. Use them to make Pizzoccheri Valtellina Style (page 120) or boil them and toss them with butter and chopped sage leaves.

Serves 4

2 ¹/₂ cups buckwheat flour

1 cup unbleached all-purpose white flour

4 eggs

²/₃ cup milk

2 tablespoons warm water

1. Mix the flours thoroughly and mound them on a large wooden cutting board.
2. Shape the flours into a well with a deep indentation in the center.
3. Crack the eggs into the well.
4. Use a fork or your fingers to break up the yolks and mix the eggs. Add the milk and water.
5. Draw in a little bit of the flour and mix it with the eggs, milk, and water.
6. Continue drawing in a little bit of flour at a time and mixing it in until a paste has formed in the center of the well.
7. When the paste has formed, move all the remaining flour on top of the dough.
8. Squeeze the dough between your fingers to incorporate the remaining flour.
9. At this point you need to evaluate your dough. It should be dry enough that it doesn't stick to the board as you knead. If it still feels somewhat gummy, incorporate more white flour, but only about 1 tablespoon at a time. Remember that it's much easier to add flour to an overly wet dough than it is to moisten a dry dough. If the dough feels too dry, sprinkle on additional water.
10. When the dough has reached the right consistency and forms a ball, clean off your work surface (a dough scraper works best) and wash and dry your hands.
11. Return the ball of dough to your clean work surface and begin kneading.
12. Knead until the dough is soft and firm. It should be uniformly brown with no lumps of flour. The surface of the dough should be soft and smooth. Vigorous kneading by hand will take about 8 minutes. If you prefer to use a food processor to knead this dough, follow the instructions for making egg pasta dough on page 143.
13. Wrap the dough in plastic wrap and refrigerate for about 30 minutes.
14. Roll out the dough using either a rolling pin (page 130) or a hand-cranked pasta machine (page 143).
15. Cut the dough into noodles about ¹/₂ inch wide and 3 or 4 inches long.

Gnocchi di Patate (Potato Gnocchi)

Gnocchi are dumplings, usually made of potatoes and flour. As you will see in the following variations, however, they can also incorporate other ingredients. Gnocchi are suited to both tomato sauces and cream sauces. The word *gnocco* (the singular form) means "lump," like the kind you get when you bang your head, or "blockhead."

Serves 4

3 russet potatoes (about 2 lbs.)

1 $^3/_4$ cups unbleached all-purpose white flour

1. Place the unpeeled potatoes in a large pot.
2. Add water to cover the potatoes.
3. Bring the water to a boil and cook the potatoes until they are easily pierced with a fork, about 15–30 minutes.
4. Remove the potatoes to a colander.
5. As soon as potatoes are cool enough to handle, peel them and discard skins.
6. Place the potatoes in a large bowl and mash with a fork. (Alternately, mash through a ricer.)
7. Add about 1 cup of the flour to the bowl and mix with a wooden spoon.
8. Turn the dough out onto a wooden board. Incorporate the remaining flour a little at a time while kneading. Like pasta, different batches of gnocchi can absorb vastly different amounts of flour. Add the flour slowly and stop as soon as you have achieved a smooth dough that remains just a little tacky. When you roll a bit of dough between your palms, it should form a ball without sticking to your hands or crumbling.
9. When you are satisfied with your dough, form it into sausage shapes about $^1/_2$ inch in diameter.
10. Cut the dough into pieces about 1 inch long. As you cut each piece, squeeze it gently in the middle so that it takes on a slight hourglass shape. Remove the pieces to floured cookie sheets as you finish them. I find that gnocchi cook better if left to dry at air temperature for a couple hours. Sprinkle them with flour and toss them occasionally to be sure they don't stick to the cookie sheets. Gnocchi won't keep at room temperature, and refrigeration makes them gloppy, but they freeze well. Set the cookie sheets in the freezer overnight. When the gnocchi are hard, toss them into a plastic bag. They will keep in the freezer for a month or so.

Gnocchi Verdi
(Green Gnocchi)

Green gnocchi—made with spinach or other leafy greens—are a little lighter than potato gnocchi, and they look beautiful. Top green gnocchi with tomato sauce, or boil them, toss with some butter and Parmesan, and bake them for a few minutes until browned. For an unusual appetizer, brown cooked green gnocchi in a little butter or olive oil and serve on toothpicks. To separate egg yolks, a procedure needed for this recipe, crack an egg over a bowl. Slide the yolk back and forth between the two halves of the egg shell while letting the white slide into the bowl. Egg whites can be refrigerated in a jar for a few days for use in other recipes, such as meringue.

Serves 4

1 lb. spinach

3/4 cup ricotta

2 egg yolks

1/8 teaspoon grated nutmeg

3 tablespoons unbleached all-purpose white flour

1. Soak the spinach in several changes of water.
2. Steam the spinach with some water remaining on leaves. Set aside to cool. To steam spinach, first clean the leaves by soaking them in abundant water in a large bowl or clean sink. Lift the leaves gently out of the water, fill the bowl or sink with clean water, and return the leaves to the clean water until no more sand rests at the bottom of the bowl when you remove the spinach. (Even if you are using pre-cleaned spinach, rinse it once to refresh it.) Shake any excess water off the leaves, place the damp leaves in a pot, and then cook them over medium-low heat, covered, until they have wilted.
3. When the spinach is cool enough to handle, squeeze out as much water as possible and chop finely.
4. In a large bowl, combine the ricotta and the cooked spinach.
5. In a small bowl, beat the egg yolks with a fork, and then add to the spinach mixture. Add the nutmeg and combine thoroughly. (It's best to use your hands.)
6. Incorporate the flour by sprinkling on about a tablespoon at a time and mixing it in before adding more.
7. Pinch a piece of the dough. If it doesn't hold together, add about a tablespoon of flour at a time until the dough forms a ball when pinched.
8. Set the dough aside to rest for about 15 minutes.
9. Roll about 1 teaspoon of dough into a ball between your palms. Set the piece of dough on a floured cookie sheet and repeat with the remaining dough.
10. When all the dough has been used, flour the gnocchi lightly. It's best to allow green gnocchi to set for an hour or so before cooking. They are best, however, if consumed within a day of being made. Green gnocchi do not freeze well.

The Least You Need to Know

➤ Not all homemade pasta is made with egg dough.

Part 5
Asian Noodles

Asian noodles are made in a fast and furious manner; that is, they are usually stir-fried briefly before being served hot. Some types of Asian noodles don't even need to be cooked in boiling water. The dishes in Part 5 are often eaten as snacks or street food rather than at meals, but you can use them as you like.

Take advantage of the different types of Asian noodles available. Although all the noodles in Part 5 are long and ribbon-shaped, they're made with all kinds of funky ingredients.

And if you've put it away, get out the wok. It's handy, it's fast, and it's back. You're going to love the way you can use it to throw together a stir-fried noodle dish in no time. (If you don't own a wok, not to worry—you can also prepare these recipes in a large frying pan.)

Chapter 17

A Pan-Asian Panorama

In This Chapter

➤ Varieties of noodles used in Asia

➤ How to cook Asian noodles

Italians rule when it comes to thinking up fun shapes and creative names for their pasta. Asian noodles are pretty uniform when it comes to shape; they are all long and either thin or thick. The Asian noodle tradition is much more creative when it comes to ingredients.

An Asian Fantasia

Here is a glossary of the various types of Asian noodles available:

➤ *Arrowroot noodles* are slightly sandy-colored noodles made with arrowroot starch. They have a somewhat sweeter taste than regular wheat noodles. Arrowroot noodles hail from China's Szechuan province.

➤ *Bean thread noodles* (also known as *cellophane noodles, mung bean noodles, glass noodles,* and *slippery noodles*) are made from mung bean starch. They are thin like Italian *vermicelli* and are usually lopped together and then dried so that they are entwined in their packages. When uncooked, bean thread noodles are extremely hard and cannot be broken by hand, nor should you attempt to do so; bean thread noodles have a tendency to break into shards and can do serious damage to your skin. Use kitchen shears or a swift chop with a cleaver to break up un-cooked bean thread noodles. Bean thread noodles are clear in color and don't have much taste, but they do absorb flavor from broth quite well. They can also be deep-fried without being cooked first. Bean thread noodles are prized for their texture, which is slippery yet chewy. These noodles are utilized in the cuisines of China, Japan, Thailand, and Indonesia.

Pasta Patter

What a Long, Strange Noodle It's Been: Asian noodles are long for a reason: their length is supposed to imply long life for the eater.

➤ *Broad bean noodles* are bean thread noodles that are flat and wide, similar in shape to Italian *fettuccine.* They are Chinese in origin but are used in most Asian countries.

➤ *Broad rice noodles* are sold both fresh and dried. Sometimes the fresh noodles are sold in sheets and must be cut to the appropriate width. Broad rice noodles have a pleasantly glutinous texture and a sweet taste. They work well in stir fries because they both absorb sauces and retain their shape. Broad rice noodles are featured in most Asian cuisines and are crucial to Vietnamese cooking.

➤ *Cha-soba* are Japanese buckwheat (*soba*) noodles flavored with green tea. They have an unusual color and a delicate taste that can get lost in a heavy sauce. For this reason, cha-soba are usually served cold with a dipping sauce or in a lightly seasoned broth. More unusual soba noodle flavorings include lemon zest and black sesame seeds.

➤ *Rice sticks* are noodles about the same size as Italian *fettuccine*. They are usually flat but can also be round. Like bean thread noodles, rice sticks are wrapped around each other to dry and are hard to break or separate when uncooked. Rice sticks are used in China, Indonesia, Vietnam, and Malaysia, and are the central players in the classic Thai noodle dish *Pad Thai*. They are an opaque white when dry, but as they cook their color lightens and they become transparent.

➤ *Rice vermicelli* are very thin rice noodles. These fine noodles can be used cold in salads or hot in soups and stir-fries. In some dishes, they are fried in one large clump, in which case they expand dramatically and turn quite crunchy.

➤ *Soba noodles* are made of buckwheat flour and are one of Japan's great delicacies. They come in long strands much like Italian spaghetti. Soba are served both hot (in broth) and cold (with dipping sauce on the side). Buckwheat provides an appealing flavor and brown color, and it's a nutritional powerhouse as well.

➤ *Somen* are thin Japanese wheat noodles with a small amount of oil incorporated in the dough. They are very thin and fine, and therefore very fragile. Somen appear most often in cold dishes such as salads. Like soba, they can also be served cold with dipping sauce on the side.

Linguine Lingo

Soba refers both to Japanese noodles made of buckwheat and to the buckwheat itself.

➤ *Thin Chinese egg noodles* are bright yellow in color. Good quality Chinese egg noodles are made with flour and egg, but some lesser quality brands add yellow food coloring, so check the list of ingredients before purchasing anything. Although some cookbooks suggest spaghetti as a substitute, packaged spaghetti are made from a semolina-and-water dough and don't have that same "eggy" flavor. Thin Chinese egg noodles can be served in soups or stir-fries. They are deliciously crisp when fried into a "nest" for vegetables or fish.

➤ *Thin Chinese wheat noodles* are made from the same ingredients as those used for Italian dried pasta, but they are worked in a slightly different manner, with the dough being stretched out in long skeins. In China, thin wheat noodles are eaten primarily in soups and stir-fried dishes.

➤ *Udon* are sturdy Japanese wheat noodles that offer a firm, chewy mouthful. Udon, which are usually as wide as they are high, are available in both dried and frozen forms in Asian groceries. In Japan, udon are served hot in broth in the winter and cold with dipping sauce in the summer.

➤ *Wide Chinese egg noodles* are bright yellow like thin Chinese egg noodles. As with thin Chinese egg noodles, commercial brands sometimes contain food coloring. Additionally, wide Chinese egg noodles are often dipped in oil before being packaged, so they should be rinsed well before being incorporated into any recipe. Wide egg noodles are used in China, Thailand, Malaysia, and Indonesia.

➤ *Wide Chinese wheat noodles* most often appear in soups. They range from $1/4$ inch to $1/2$ inch in width and are widely available in dried form. Some Asian groceries also stock packages of wide Chinese wheat noodles in the refrigerated section.

Noodles Go Soft

Whereas Italian pasta is basically cooked in the same way no matter what the shape, Asian noodles are cooked in different ways depending on their ingredients and how they are to be used. Some noodles are boiled in abundant water like Italian pasta; others are softened in boiling water or simply fried without being cooked first.

Although I provide approximate cooking times, always read the package; noodles can vary in terms of thickness and proportion of ingredients, and both of those factors may affect cooking time. As with Italian pasta, the best way to know whether Asian noodles are done is to taste them.

Boiling Noodles

The rules for boiling noodles are basically the same as those for cooking Italian pasta.

Pasta Patter

Sticky Situation: Traditionally, neither salt nor oil is added to the water when cooking Asian noodles. Stir the noodles often to be sure they don't stick together. A long set of wooden chopsticks is ideal for mixing and separating noodles.

1. Fill a large pot with abundant water.
2. Bring the water to a rapid boil.
3. Add the noodles, stirring often to separate them.
4. Taste the noodles often to check for doneness.
5. Drain and serve the noodles immediately, or toss with a few tablespoons of oil to keep separate if you are cooking the noodles in advance.

Boiling Noodles to Be Stir-Fried

The preceding steps also apply for noodles that are going to be stir-fried later. Because they will finish cooking in a wok, however, noodles for stir-fry should be cooked very al dente. Drain the noodles when the center of each noodle still offers resistance and appears slightly uncooked.

Boiling Japanese Noodles

Japanese noodles (udon and soba) are cooked in a slightly different way, as follows:

1. Fill a large pot with abundant water until about three-fourths full.
2. Bring the water to a rapid boil.
3. Add the noodles, stirring often to separate.

4. When the water returns to a boil, add a glass of cold water and stir the noodles.

5. When the water returns to a boil, add another glass of cold water and stir the noodles.

6. When the water returns to a boil, taste the noodles. If they are not ready, add another glass of cold water and stir the noodles.

7. When the noodles are cooked, drain them, rinse them with hot or cold water (depending on whether they are meant to be served hot or cold), and serve them immediately. If you are preparing the noodles in advance, toss them with a few tablespoons of oil to keep separate.

Pasta Patter

Drink It Down: The water used to cook soba is usually served at the end of the meal. It is quite refreshing, has a sweet taste, and contains many of the nutrients of buckwheat.

Soaking Noodles

Some types of thin noodles cook so quickly that rather than dropping them into boiling water, you pour boiling water over them. This method is usually used for rice noodles and bean thread noodles.

Some Asian noodles are cooked by soaking them in boiling water.

1. Place the noodles in a large, heat-proof bowl.

2. Pour on enough boiling water to cover the noodles.

3. Set the bowl aside until the noodles have softened. This should take anywhere from 8 to 15 minutes.

4. When noodles are cooked, drain them.

Pasta Practice

Don't Overdo It: If you will be using the noodles in a stir-fry or adding them to a soup, drain them while they are still firm; they will cook further in those preparations.

Frying Noodles

Sometimes you will want to fry noodles to serve as a bed for a dish. Only thin noodles such as bean thread noodles and thin rice stick noodles can be fried. They are not cooked first.

1. Heat a wok or skillet (any skillet you use should be deep and heavy, preferably cast iron) over high heat until a drop of water dances on the surface.

2. Fill the wok or skillet with enough oil to submerge the noodles halfway (about 2 cups should be enough for a 2-oz. bundle).

3. Heat the oil until almost smoking, about 425 degrees.

4. Add the noodles to pan. Be very careful to avoid splatters.

5. When the noodles have browned and puffed, which should take about 5 seconds, use a large spatula to turn them over.

6. When the noodles are cooked on both sides, remove them with a skimmer or slotted spoon.

7. Transfer the noodles to a brown paper bag or paper towels to drain.

Pasta Practice

Frying Wise: As a rule, Asian chefs don't use olive oil for anything. Safflower oil is best for frying. It doesn't impart any real flavor to the noodles, which is best since you want them to serve as a backdrop.

Browning Noodles

You can also pan-fry noodles rather than deep-frying them. The noodles should be cooked or softened in water and then drained. They should be patted dry with paper towels as well, mostly for safety reasons. If you dip wet noodles into hot oil, they will splatter all over.

1. Cook or soften the noodles.

2. Drain the noodles and pat them dry.

3. Toss the noodles with a small amount of oil.

4. Shape the noodles as you wish. You can use them in a single disk (use a pie plate for shaping them this way), in individual baskets (called "bird's nests"), or in one large basket. Asian groceries and cooking equipment stores sell special basket-shaped wire spoons for this purpose, or you can use an appropriate size wire strainer.

5. Pan-fry noodle disks in a wok. Immerse bird's nests in oil.

6. Brown the noodles on one side (about 7 minutes) and then flip and brown on the other side. If you are making bird's nests, remove them from the wire baskets after they are browned on one side, and then brown the remaining sides. They should hold their shape.

7. Keep the browned noodles warm in an oven until needed.

Noodle cakes can also be prepared this way and then browned in the broiler rather than pan-fried.

Pasta Practice

Temperature Techniques: There are several ways to check the temperature of oil. The most obvious is to use a thermometer. If you don't have a kitchen thermometer, you can drop in a small cube of bread. At 425 degrees, it should brown immediately and bob about in the oil. You can also stick in the tip of a chopstick, which should cause large bubbles to rise up, or the tip of a scallion, which should both cause bubbles and turn brown.

Reheating Asian Noodles

It is acceptable to cook Asian noodles in advance and then reheat them before using. You do need to reheat them, though, or they will form a single clump and be impossible to stir-fry or use in soup. To reheat noodles, place them in a large wire strainer or colander and set the strainer in boiling water so that the noodles are immersed. Stir the noodles with a long-handled wooden fork. They should take about 20 seconds to heat up and separate. Remove the strainer immediately and rinse the noodles.

To reheat Asian noodles, set them in a strainer over boiling water.

Keep It Flexible

While Italians are stuck on matching shapes and sauces and would never top certain homemade noodles in anything but the traditional way, Asian cooks (and as a result, Asian dishes) are a lot more flexible. If you don't have bean thread noodles on hand, thin rice noodles will probably take their place quite well. If you have a hard time finding Asian noodles, check the resources provided in Appendix B or substitute dried Italian pasta. As a rule, use vermicelli for very thin noodles and linguine for thin, flat noodles. Wide rice noodles are hard to replace. You can achieve the same shape with wide ribbon noodles such as pappardelle, but the taste won't be quite the same.

How to Stir-Fry

Many Asian noodle recipes require stir-frying. Stir-frying is a cooking technique that is exactly what it sounds like: you will be "frying" food (albeit in a very small amount of oil) while stirring it constantly. The stir-fry motion is as follows: Use a stir-fry spatula to push food out of the center of the wok (or very large skillet) and up against the walls, and then remove the spatula and allow the food to fall back down to the bottom. It's very simple but yields spectacular results. When you are stir-frying noodles, use two forks or chopsticks to stir the noodles and make sure they are coated evenly with any sauce; otherwise, they tend to form a clump.

A wok (or large skillet) and spatula are used for stir-frying.

The Least You Need to Know

➤ All Asian noodles are long and of varying widths.

➤ Asian noodles often consist of unusual ingredients such as rice flour or green tea.

➤ Asian noodles are cooked in various ways, depending on their ingredients and use.

Much more!

Chapter 18

More Than Lo Mein: Chinese Noodles

> **In This Chapter**
>
> ➤ A look at Chinese noodles
>
> ➤ Recipes for Chinese noodle dishes

Noodles in Chinese Cooking

Chinese cuisine, like Italian cuisine, really consists of a lot of different regional cuisines. It is only natural that such a large country should have various ways of eating in its different parts. The northern and southern halves of China are usually defined as wheat- and grain-eating, and rice-eating, respectively. In the north, wheat noodles (as well as buns and dumplings) are served with every meal. Noodles are less popular in the south, but rice noodles do appear there.

Most of the noodles eaten throughout Asia today originated in China. The following are the types of noodles used in Chinese cuisine:

➤ Arrowroot noodles
➤ Bean thread noodles
➤ Broad bean noodles
➤ Broad rice noodles

➤ Chinese egg noodles
➤ Chinese wheat noodles
➤ Rice sticks
➤ Rice vermicelli

Wheat noodles reign supreme in northern China; southern China favors rice and rice noodles.

Pasta Patter

Past the Expiration Date: Flour mills already existed in China during the Han Dynasty, which lasted from 206 B.C. to 220 A.D.

Going for a Wok

The following items are crucial to cooking Chinese noodle dishes:

➤ A wok

➤ A wok cover

➤ A wok ring

➤ A stir-fry spatula

➤ A skimmer

All these items are usually packaged together.

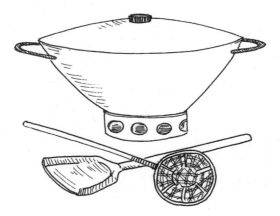

Generally, a wok, wok cover, wok ring, stir-fry spatula, and skimmer are sold in a single unit.

Like most dishes in China, noodles are prepared in a wok (or in the case of soups, a pot). If you've never used a wok, you're in for a treat. These pots, shaped like inverted domes, heat up quickly and are extremely fuel efficient. Generally, a wok is heated dry and then oiled before it is used. Very little oil is necessary in a wok. The oil pools at the bottom, and as you stir-fry, the items being cooked are tossed in and out of it. A wok sits on a ring, which is set around a burner (preferably a gas stove). Vegetables cooked in a wok are ready quite quickly and retain a nice crunch. Each ingredient (aside from the noodles) needs to be sliced into small pieces before being cooked in the wok. When you stir-fry, be sure all your ingredients are prepared before you place the wok over the heat; most stir-fry dishes are ready in 10 minutes or less. You won't have the spare time to prepare ingredients once the cooking process is in motion.

Pasta Practice

It's a Little Wok-y: If you don't have a wok, don't despair. In a pinch, you can substitute a large frying pan. You'll probably need to use a little more oil when cooking stir-fry dishes in a frying pan (enough to coat the entire surface), and the pan needs to be very large, or you'll be pushing stuff over the sides. I recommend a pan that's at least 12 inches in diameter. If you do use a frying pan, you can place it directly over the burner and skip the wok ring.

Pasta Patter

Working Hard for the Money: Early noodle shops in China were known as "workers' shops" because noodles were served as snacks during the work day (much like today's coffee breaks).

189

Chinese Chewables

Chicken Lo Mein

In the 1950s, when Chinese restaurants were just beginning to make inroads in North America (almost all of those restaurants were Cantonese), lo mein was *the* Chinese dish. Even now that our palates have been exposed to so many different regional cuisines and dishes, it still tastes great. *Lo mein* refers to all stir-fried noodle dishes coated with a sauce. Chinese wheat noodles are also called *lo mein*. The best way to grate ginger is to use—no big surprise here—a ginger grater. A ginger grater is a ceramic utensil with bumps but no holes. Minced ginger can be somewhat stringy, but when you grate ginger on a ginger grater, you get all the pulp and juice and leave the stringy flesh behind.

Serves 4

2 teaspoons fresh grated ginger

3 cloves garlic, minced

3 tablespoons soy sauce

3 tablespoons Chinese rice wine

1 teaspoon toasted sesame oil

3/4 lb. chicken breast, cut into 1-inch-by-2-inch strips

2 tablespoons cornstarch

1 lb. wide Chinese wheat noodles

3 tablespoons safflower oil or other vegetable oil

1 bunch scallions (greens included), sliced

10 oyster mushrooms, sliced, or 10 dried black mushrooms, soaked until soft, drained, and then thinly sliced

1. In a medium bowl, combine the ginger, garlic, soy sauce, rice wine, and sesame oil.

2. Use about half of this mixture as a marinade for the chicken. Place the chicken in a non-reactive dish and pour the marinade over it. Cover the dish and refrigerate for at least 30 minutes and up to 2 hours, turning the chicken occasionally.

3. Add the cornstarch to the remaining sauce, stir until dissolved, and then set the sauce aside.

4. When you are ready to cook, prepare the egg noodles following the instructions on page 12.

5. Heat 2 tablespoons of oil in the wok over high heat until sizzling.

6. Remove the chicken from the marinade. Stir-fry the chicken until cooked through, about 7 minutes. Remove the chicken with a slotted spoon and set aside.

7. Heat the remaining 1 tablespoon of oil in the wok. Add the scallions and mushrooms and stir-fry until the scallions are wilted and the mushrooms are soft, about 1 minute.

8. Add the cooked noodles to the wok, pour on the reserved sauce, and toss briskly over high heat until the sauce is absorbed.

9. Add the chicken to the wok and cook 1 additional minute. *Note:* To test whether a wok is hot enough, sprinkle a few drops of water onto the surface. They should sizzle. If the food begins to brown very quickly or burn while you are stir-frying, lower the heat to medium-high.

Shrimp Chow Mein

Chow mein is one of those dishes that never comes out the same way twice. There is no set recipe for it—in China the idea of writing down a chow mein recipe is laughable—so be as flexible as you like with both the amounts and the ingredients in this recipe. Water chestnuts are available in cans in Asian grocery stores and regular grocery stores. Simply remove them from their liquid and rinse briefly. Bok choy comes in bunches. Chop off and discard the hard core where all the leaves meet. You can eat both the leaves and the white stems.

Serves 4

1 lb. thin Chinese egg noodles

1 tablespoon soy sauce

1 tablespoon Chinese rice wine

1 teaspoon chili paste

1 tablespoon sherry

1 tablespoon cornstarch

2 tablespoons safflower oil or other vegetable oil

1 teaspoon grated ginger

1 clove garlic, minced

2 carrots, peeled and sliced diagonally

$^1/_2$ lb. shrimp, peeled and deveined

4 dried black Chinese mushrooms, soaked until soft and thinly sliced

1 bunch scallions (greens included), sliced

10 snow peas, stemmed and cut in half

4 water chestnuts, sliced

1 oz. bamboo shoots, drained and sliced

4 heads bok choy, sliced

1. Cook the noodles following the instructions on page 182.
2. Combine the soy sauce, rice wine, chili paste, sherry, and cornstarch. Stir to combine and set aside.
3. Heat the safflower oil in a wok until sizzling.
4. Add the ginger and garlic and stir-fry for 30 seconds.
5. Add the carrots and stir-fry until softened, about 4 minutes.
6. Add the shrimp, mushrooms, scallions, snow peas, water chestnuts, and bamboo shoots. Stir-fry until the shrimp are pink and cooked through, about 4 minutes.
7. Add the bok choy and stir-fry until wilted, about 1 minute.
8. Add the noodles, pour on the prepared sauce, and toss until all the ingredients are combined.

One-Dish Beef Noodles

This filling meal is served in a bowl and is typical of hearty Chinese soups in that it contains enough meat and vegetables to be considered a meal in itself. I make it in a wok, but you can also use a large, heavy soup pot. Your best bet here is flank steak, trimmed of fat and then cut into thin strips. Any type of lean beef will do, however. You can also substitute chicken breast, lean pork, or even cubes of tofu. The most commonly available type of Chinese cabbage is the pale green Napa cabbage. You may also run across celery cabbage (sometimes called Chinese leaves), which is the same color but has much narrower leaves. Either of these is a good addition to this recipe, as is bok choy. Try to avoid regular white cabbage, however, which has a strong taste.

Serves 4

1 tablespoon soy sauce

1 tablespoon Chinese rice wine

1 tablespoon cornstarch

$^1/_2$ lb. beef, cut into 1-inch-by-2-inch strips

2 tablespoons safflower oil or other vegetable oil

2 cloves garlic, minced

1 bunch scallions (greens included), sliced

1 head Chinese cabbage, sliced

10 dried black Chinese mushrooms, soaked until soft and thinly sliced

6 cups chicken or beef broth

8 oz. rice stick noodles, softened

salt and freshly ground pepper to taste

1. Combine the soy sauce, rice wine, and cornstarch in a small bowl.
2. Marinate the beef in the soy sauce mixture for about 30 minutes, turning occasionally.
3. Heat 1 tablespoon of safflower oil in the wok until sizzling.
4. Remove the beef from the marinade with a slotted spoon and stir-fry until cooked through, about 4 minutes.
5. Remove the beef from the wok with a slotted spoon and set aside.
6. Add the remaining tablespoon of oil to the wok, if necessary.
7. Add the garlic and scallions and stir-fry for 30 seconds.
8. Add the Chinese cabbage and black mushrooms and stir-fry until the cabbage is wilted, about 4 minutes.
9. Pour in the broth and bring to a boil. Add the noodles and simmer until the flavors are combined and noodles are soft, about 2 minutes. Season to taste with salt and pepper.

Seafood on Crispy Noodles

The crispy fried noodles in this recipe are not combined with ingredients as they are in a stir-fry, but instead serve as a bed for a dish that is prepared separately.

Serves 4

1 teaspoon cornstarch

1 tablespoon water

1 teaspoon sesame oil

$1/4$ teaspoon sugar

salt and freshly ground pepper to taste

2 tablespoons safflower oil or other vegetable oil

1 clove garlic, minced

1 teaspoon grated ginger

2 carrots, cut into $1/2$-inch dice

12 snow peas, stemmed and halved

4 scallions (greens included), sliced

1 cup canned baby corn, drained and rinsed

5 water chestnuts, drained, rinsed, and sliced

12 medium shrimp, shelled and deveined

6 large scallops, quartered

1 fillet firm white fish, such as cod, cut into 1-inch pieces

1 lb. thin Chinese egg noodles, boiled and formed into a browned disk following the instructions on page 184

1. Combine the cornstarch, water, sesame oil, and sugar, and season to taste with salt and pepper. Set aside.

2. Heat the safflower oil in the wok until sizzling.

3. Add the garlic and ginger and stir-fry for 30 seconds.

4. Add the carrots and stir-fry until softened, about 4 minutes.

5. Add the snow peas, scallions, baby corn, water chestnuts, shrimp, scallops, and white fish, and stir-fry until the fish are cooked, about 8 minutes. (Flake a piece of the white fish to be sure it's cooked all the way through.)

6. Pour on the prepared cornstarch mixture and stir-fry until all the ingredients are coated, about 2 minutes.

7. Place the browned noodles on a serving plate. Ladle the fish mixture in the center of the noodle disk.

Szechuan Noodles
with Vegetables

China's Szechuan province is known for its hot, hot, hot foods. Spicy kung pao chicken comes from this province, as does this very piquant vegetarian dish.

Serves 4

1 lb. thin Chinese egg noodles

1 tablespoon soy sauce

1 teaspoon black Chinese vinegar

$1/2$ teaspoon five-spice powder

1 teaspoon chili paste

1 tablespoon Chinese rice wine

2 tablespoons safflower oil or other vegetable oil

2 cloves garlic, minced

1 teaspoon grated ginger

1 bunch scallions (greens included), sliced

2 carrots, peeled and grated

2 oz. green beans, trimmed

1 oz. bamboo shoots, drained and sliced

$1/2$ teaspoon chili oil

$1/2$ teaspoon toasted sesame oil

1. Cook the noodles as instructed on page 182.
2. Combine the vinegar, five-spice powder, chili paste, and rice wine, and set aside.
3. Heat the wok over high heat. Add the safflower oil and heat until sizzling.
4. Add the garlic and ginger and stir-fry for 30 seconds.
5. Add the scallions, carrots, green beans, and bamboo shoots, and stir-fry until softened, about 4 minutes.
6. Add the cooked noodles and prepared chili sauce. Toss until all the sauce has been absorbed and the ingredients are evenly distributed, about 2 minutes.
7. Sprinkle on the chili oil and sesame oil.

The Least You Need to Know

➤ Noodles are especially popular in the northern part of China.

➤ Most Asian noodles were born in China.

➤ Chinese noodle dishes are stir-fried in a wok.

Chapter 19

Serenity in a Bowl: Japanese Noodles

> **In This Chapter**
>
> ➤ A look at Japanese noodles
>
> ➤ Recipes for Japanese noodle dishes

Chinese noodles are flashy; they're cooked quickly in a wok and eaten quickly, too. *Menrui,* or Japanese noodle dishes, are the opposite of Chinese noodles. When I visit my favorite Japanese soba house I'm filled with a sense of calm and well-being. The noodles—whether served cold with a dipping sauce or hot in broth—are "earthy" tasting. I breathe easier for the hour or two that I'm there.

Soba, So Good

The buckwheat noodles called *soba* are practically an object of cult-like adoration in Japan, and for good reason: They are delicious. Buckwheat lends them a slightly sweet taste and makes them very satisfying.

Soba noodles have been made in Japan for more than 400 years. Japan has more than 6,000 soba factories and more than 40,000 soba shops. Some of these are fine restaurants that serve freshly made soba, but more of them are simple stands that serve dried noodles.

Part of the reverence for soba in Japan stems from buckwheat's nutritional profile. It is high in protein and vitamins B1 and B2. Since it is used in whole form, it provides a large amount of fiber as well. In Japan, soba are believed to ease tension and aid digestion. Eating buckwheat also has been proven to lower cholesterol.

Dried Japanese soba come wrapped in little individual bundles within their package. You can figure on one bundle per person; cook them according to the instructions on page 182.

In Japan, noodles are more than a cuisine; they are a culture.

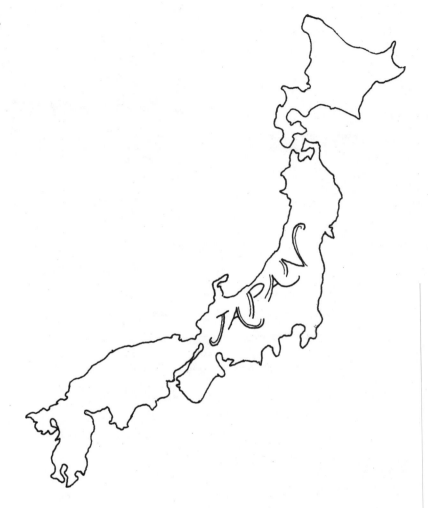

Pasta Patter

The Good Neighbor Policy: It is traditional for Japanese people who have moved to present soba noodles to their new neighbors as a gift. The word *soba* is a homonym for the Japanese word for "close." Also, the narrow, elongated shape of soba noodles is meant to mimic ideal neighborly relations: long-lasting, yet restrained.

Pasta Patter

Heed the Master: Serious soba restaurants are run by a soba master, who trains his under-lings in the making of fine soba. The rule is that apprentices spend the first year mixing the dough, the second year rolling the dough, and the third year cutting the noodles. That's some education!

You Do Udon

Udon noodles and soba noodles are the most popular types of noodles in Japan. Whereas soba noodles are made of buckwheat, udon noodles are thick wheat noodles that can be either round, square, or flat. Soba noodles are popular in the north of Japan, where the majority of buckwheat grows; udon noodles are popular in the south.

Udon noodles are most commonly available in dried form, but the fresh variety may also be found in Asian groceries. (I've also found very good packages of frozen udon noodles at my local Asian grocery.) In any case, udon noodles should be cooked according to the instructions on page 182. Like soba noodles, udon noodles are served hot in broth or cold with a dipping sauce. Udon noodles have a particularly satisfying mouth feel.

That's Not All, Folks

While soba and udon noodles are the most popular types of noodles in Japan, somen noodles, bean thread noodles, and thin noodles with yam incorporated into the dough are eaten as well.

Somen noodles are very thin wheat noodles similar to vermicelli. They are most often served in salads.

Japanese also make frequent use of *ramen*, which are instant noodles available in all kinds of flavors and shapes. You simply add hot water to them to make noodle soup. You can purchase your own ramen (just follow the package's instructions about adding boiling water), but read their labels carefully. Some brands of ramen have excessive amounts of salt, oil, or MSG.

Linguine Lingo

In Japan, bean thread noodles are known as *harusame*, which means "spring rain." Presumably this refers to their light texture and subtle flavor.

197

Bow Down to Noodles

Cold Soba
with Dipping Sauce

This is the classic cold soba preparation. I usually spring for imported Japanese soba noodles because the quality tends to be a little better, but you can also find good quality domestic soba noodles in health food stores. *Mirin* is sweet Japanese cooking wine. It differs from sake because it is distilled after fermentation. *Wasabi* is often confused with horseradish because it has the same strong, sinus-clearing taste. Fresh wasabi root is unavailable outside of Japan, but you can buy either wasabi paste in a tube or pale green wasabi powder, which needs to be mixed with water. (I prefer the latter.) Wasabi powder loses strength as it is exposed to air, so opt for small, individual foil packets rather than a larger tin. *Nori* is the seaweed that's wrapped around sushi. Sheets of toasted nori are usually available in health food stores and Asian groceries. To shred nori, tear it into strips, and then crumble the strips into smaller pieces.

Serves 4

4 bundles (14 oz.) dried soba noodles	1 tablespoon wasabi paste
1 teaspoon chicken broth	1 bunch scallions (greens included), sliced
1 teaspoon mirin or sherry	1 sheet toasted nori, shredded
3 tablespoons soy sauce	2 tablespoons grated daikon radish
$^{1}/_{2}$ cup water	

1. Cook the soba noodles following the instructions on page 182.

2. Drain the noodles and rinse with cold water. Place them in a bowl of ice water until very cold, about 2 minutes.

3. Meanwhile, make the dipping sauce by combining the broth, mirin, soy sauce, and water, and then placing in individual dipping bowls. In Japan, dipping sauces are placed in small, flat, cleverly decorated dishes that are often shaped like animals or vegetables. If you don't have a set, pour your dipping sauce into saucers.

4. Divide the wasabi, scallions, shredded nori, and grated daikon radish onto 4 separate small dishes.

5. Drain the noodles and serve immediately with the dipping sauce and garnishes on the side (the garnishes are added to the dipping sauce). Don't forget to drink the noodle cooking water afterwards, if desired. For an unusual dish, replace the soba in this recipe with *cha soba* (soba noodles with green tea). In Japan, cold soba noodles are served on special lacquered trays that spread the noodles out. A bowl will do just as well, however.

Soba in Broth

This is the classic *hot* soba preparation. (You can use any vegetables you like, however.) After I've eaten rich foods for a few days and want something light yet substantial, this always does the trick. *Kombu* is seaweed that is added to stocks for its slightly salty flavor. It is also thrown into the pot with grains or beans because it both boosts their nutritional content and adds flavor. To use *kombu*, break off a strip about 6 inches long and rinse it briefly under cold water. *Kombu* is available in Asian groceries and health food stores. *Bonito flakes* are shavings of dried fish. (*Bonito* is from the tuna family.) You can purchase them in Asian grocery stores and some health food stores. *Bonito flakes* will go bad if they absorb too much moisture, so be sure to keep them in a dry place.

Serves 4

4 bundles (14 oz.) dried soba noodles

6 cups water

1 piece kombu

1 cup bonito flakes

3 tablespoons soy sauce

2 tablespoons mirin or sherry

4 dried shiitake mushrooms, softened and sliced

1 carrot, grated

1 cup green beans, trimmed and cut into ¹/₂-inch pieces

2 tablespoons toasted sesame seeds

1 sheet toasted nori, shredded

4 scallions (greens included), sliced

1 tablespoon cayenne pepper

1 tablespoon wasabi paste

1 tablespoon grated ginger

2 tablespoons grated daikon radish

1. Cook the soba noodles following the instructions on page 182.

2. Meanwhile, to make the stock, combine the water and kombu in a pot and bring to a boil.

3. When the water reaches a boil, fish out the kombu and discard.

4. Add the bonito flakes to the boiling water, stir, and remove from heat.

5. When the bonito flakes have sunk to the bottom of the pot, about 1–2 minutes, strain the stock and discard the bonito flakes. Return the stock to the pot.

6. Add the soy sauce and mirin to the stock.

7. Add the carrot and green beans and simmer until they are cooked through but firm, about 5 minutes.

8. To serve, divide the noodles among 4 bowls. Ladle the soup over the noodles and sprinkle sesame seeds and nori on top. Serve the scallions, cayenne, wasabi, ginger, and daikon radish on the side so that people can add garnishes to the soup. In Japan, soba noodles are eaten traditionally on the last day of the year to usher out the old year and welcome in the new.

Hot Soba with Shrimp

You can embellish the preceding two recipes with a lot of different ingredients, including shrimp tempura placed on top. I like the way shrimp marries perfectly with the salty broth and sweet soba. Tempura makes this easy dish too complicated, however, so I just cook it right in the stock.

Serves 4

4 bundles (14 oz.) dried soba noodles

6 cups water

1 piece kombu

1 cup bonito flakes

3 tablespoons soy sauce

2 tablespoons mirin or sherry

24 medium shrimp, peeled and deveined, tails left intact

2 tablespoons toasted sesame seeds

1 sheet toasted nori, shredded

4 scallions (greens included), sliced

1 tablespoon cayenne pepper

1 tablespoon wasabi paste

1 tablespoon grated ginger

2 tablespoon grated daikon radish

1. Cook the soba noodles following the instructions on page 182.
2. Meanwhile, to make the stock, combine the water and kombu in a pot and bring to a boil.
3. When the water reaches a boil, fish out the kombu and discard.
4. Add the bonito flakes to the boiling water, stir, and remove from the heat.
5. When the bonito flakes have sunk to the bottom of the pot, about 1–2 minutes, strain the stock and discard the bonito flakes. Return the stock to the pot.
6. Add the soy sauce and mirin to the stock.
7. Add the shrimp and simmer until they are cooked through, about 4 minutes.
8. To serve, divide the noodles among 4 bowls. Ladle the soup and shrimp over the noodles and sprinkle sesame seeds and nori on top. Serve the scallions, cayenne, wasabi, ginger, and daikon radish on the side so that people can add garnishes. It is traditional to slurp Japanese noodles noisily while eating them in broth. Far from being considered impolite, slurping is considered a compliment to the chef, whereas eating quietly is considered an insult. Slurping also helps to cool the noodles, since you suck in cold air as you do it.

Cold Udon with Dipping Sauce

Udon, like soba, can be eaten hot in broth or cold with a dipping sauce.

Serves 4

1 lb. udon noodles
1 teaspoon chicken broth
1 teaspoon mirin or sherry
3 tablespoons soy sauce
1/2 cup water

1 tablespoon wasabi paste
1 bunch scallions (greens included), sliced
1 sheet toasted nori, shredded
2 tablespoons grated daikon radish

1. Cook the udon noodles following the instructions on page 182.
2. Drain the noodles, rinse with cold water, and then place them in a bowl of ice water until very cold, about 2 minutes.
3. Meanwhile, make dipping sauce by combining the broth, mirin, soy sauce, and water. Place the mixture in individual dipping bowls.
4. Divide the wasabi, scallions, shredded nori, and grated daikon radish onto 4 separate small dishes.
5. Drain the noodles and serve immediately with the dipping sauce and garnishes on the side.

Udon in Broth

Although the recipes for soba in broth and udon in broth are the same, the taste is noticeably different. Udon noodles are blander than soba noodles and they absorb more flavor from the broth.

Serves 4

1 lb. udon noodles
6 cups water
1 piece kombu
1 cup bonito flakes
3 tablespoons soy sauce
2 tablespoons mirin or sherry
4 dried shiitake mushrooms, soaked in hot water to soften, drained, and sliced
1 carrot, grated

1 cup green beans, trimmed and cut into 1/2-inch pieces
2 tablespoons toasted sesame seeds
1 sheet toasted nori, shredded
4 scallions (greens included), sliced
1 tablespoon cayenne pepper
1 tablespoon wasabi paste
1 tablespoon grated ginger
2 tablespoons grated daikon radish

continues

continued

1. Cook the udon noodles following the instructions on page 182.

2. Meanwhile, to make the stock, combine the water and kombu in a pot and bring to a boil.

3. When the water reaches a boil, fish out the kombu and discard.

4. Add the bonito flakes to the boiling water, stir, and remove from the heat.

5. When the bonito flakes have sunk to the bottom of the pot, about 1–2 minutes, strain the stock, discard the bonito flakes, and then return the stock to the pot.

6. Add the soy sauce and mirin to the stock.

7. Add the carrot and green beans and simmer until they are cooked, about 5 minutes.

8. To serve, divide the noodles among 4 bowls. Ladle the soup over the noodles and sprinkle sesame seeds and nori on top. Serve the scallions, cayenne, wasabi, ginger, and daikon radish on the side so that people can add garnishes to soup.

Udon with Sesame Sauce

In addition to being served cold with dipping sauce on the side, udon can be combined with a dressing to make a cold noodle salad.

Serves 4

1 lb. udon noodles

2 cloves garlic

1/2 cup sesame seeds, toasted

1 teaspoon grated ginger

1/2 cup chicken stock or water

4 tablespoons soy sauce

1 tablespoon toasted sesame oil

2 tablespoons mirin or sherry

1/4 teaspoon cayenne pepper (optional)

1 bunch scallions (greens included), sliced

1 cucumber, peeled and grated

1. Cook the udon noodles following the instructions on page 182.

2. Drain the noodles, rinse with cold water, and then place them in a bowl of ice water until very cold, about 2 minutes.

3. Meanwhile, to make the sauce, equip a food processor with a metal blade. Drop the garlic through the feed tube with machine running to mince.

4. Add the sesame seeds and run the machine until they are finely ground.

5. With the machine running, add the stock, soy sauce, sesame oil, mirin, and cayenne pepper (if using) through the feed tube. Process until the sauce is the consistency of thin sour cream. If necessary, add a small amount of water.

6. Toss the cold noodles with the sauce. Garnish with the scallions and grated cucumber.

Cold Somen with Broccoli

Somen are very thin and white wheat noodles that are usually served cold. They have little flavor of their own but absorb the flavors of sauces and stocks. In summer when asparagus is in season, it makes an interesting substitute for the broccoli. Asparagus doesn't need to cook as long as broccoli, either.

Serves 4

1 lb. broccoli

1 lb. somen

3 tablespoons soy sauce

3 tablespoons toasted sesame oil

2 tablespoons mirin or sherry

2 teaspoons grated ginger

1 clove garlic, minced

1 bunch scallions (greens included), sliced

3 tablespoons sesame seeds

1. Cut the broccoli into stems and florets. Cut up any florets larger than about 2 inches. Peel the stems and cut them into $1/2$-inch slices.
2. Bring a large pot of water to a boil.
3. Add the broccoli stems to the water and boil about 1 minute.
4. Add the broccoli florets and boil until the stems and florets are soft but still firm, about 2 additional minutes.
5. Remove the broccoli with a slotted spoon and blanche under cold water.
6. Cook the somen in boiling water following the instructions on page 182.
7. While the somen are cooking, whisk together the sesame oil, mirin, ginger, and garlic in a small bowl.
8. When the noodles are done, drain, rinse with cold water, and then place them in a bowl of ice water until very cold, about 2 minutes.
9. Drain the noodles and toss with the dressing, broccoli, and scallions. Allow the mixture to sit at room temperature from 30 minutes to 2 hours.
10. Sprinkle on the sesame seeds before serving.

Somen on Ice

On the hottest summer days, cold somen are served on ice. This dish is not only refreshing to eat, but also refreshing to make since it takes very little effort. If you have small glass bowls, use them to serve this dish. The side view of the noodles floating in water is quite striking. Here's a simple way to make those ice cubes visually appealing: drop a parsley leaf into the center of each cube when you are filling the ice tray.

Serves 4

1 lb. somen
2 teaspoons chicken broth
2 teaspoons mirin or sherry
6 tablespoons soy sauce
$1/2$ cup water

12 ice cubes
4 sprigs watercress
1 tablespoon wasabi paste
1 bunch scallions (greens included), sliced

1. Cook the noodles following the instructions on page 182.
2. To make the dipping sauce, combine the broth, mirin, soy sauce, and water. Set aside.
3. Drain the cooked noodles and then rinse them in cold water.
4. Divide the somen among 4 serving bowls and add fresh, cold water to cover them. Drop 3 ice cubes into each bowl. Garnish each bowl with a sprig of watercress.
5. Divide the wasabi and scallions onto 4 separate small dishes.
6. Drain the noodles and serve immediately with individual plates of dipping sauce and garnishes on the side. This is a very strong dipping sauce that becomes weaker as the water from the somen mixes with it; you may want to replenish the dipping sauce on the individual plates once or twice during the meal.

Harusame Salad

Harusame is the Japanese name for bean thread noodles. Like Chinese bean thread noodles, harusame are made from mung bean starch. The Japanese version are slightly wider and flatter than the Chinese, but they are basically interchangeable.

Serves 4

8 oz. bean thread noodles	salt to taste
3 tablespoons orange juice	2 carrots, peeled and cut into matchsticks
1 tablespoon mirin or sherry	1 cucumber, peeled and grated
2 tablespoons sesame oil	10 snow peas, stemmed, blanched, and halved
1 tablespoon soy sauce	1 red bell pepper, seeded and diced
1 teaspoon grated ginger	4 scallions (greens included), sliced

1. Cook the noodles following the instructions on page 182.

2. To make the dressing, combine the orange juice, mirin, sesame oil, soy sauce, and ginger, and salt to taste.

3. When the noodles are done, drain them and rinse with cold water. Place them in a bowl of ice water until very cold, about 2 minutes.

4. Drain the noodles and then toss with the dressing, carrots, cucumber, snow peas, bell pepper, and scallions. Allow the dish to sit at room temperature for about 10 minutes before serving.

The Least You Need to Know

➤ Japanese noodles are eaten hot in broth, cold with dipping sauce, or cold in salads.

➤ The major types of Japanese noodles are soba (buckwheat) and udon (thick, wheat noodles).

Chapter 20

Slurping It Up: Noodles from Other Asian Countries

> ### In This Chapter
>
> ➤ Noodle traditions in Asian countries other than China and Japan
>
> ➤ Recipes for noodle dishes from Asian countries other than China and Japan

Everybody's Got a Noodle

So far, we've looked at noodle habits in China and Japan. Almost every Asian country has at least one noodle dish to its name, however, most of which are modeled on the Chinese classics but with little twists. Many are quite spicy.

Thai Me Up

Thai food, in general, is revved up. It's flavors are strong: the hottest chili peppers, the sourest limes, the sweetest coconut, the most aromatic Jasmine rice. Thai noodle dishes are no exception; they often have enough chili in them to make you cry.

While Thai cuisine is distinct and unique—one reason for this is that Thailand has never been colonized—it is influenced heavily by both China (stir-fries) and India (curry). One thing to remember: If you're trying for that truly authentic Thai touch, don't serve chopsticks. In Thailand, people eat with spoons and forks.

Many Asian countries have their own traditional noodle dishes.

Pad Thai, which literally means "soft noodles," is one of Thailand's signature dishes (a stir-fry of rice noodles, vegetables, shrimp, and sometimes chicken), and is the first recipe we'll present from this geographical region.

Pad Thai

It's sort of silly to write down a recipe for Pad Thai, since you can really make it any way you like. I've left out chicken, but you can add that in addition to shrimp or any vegetables that you happen to like. Thai fish sauce, known as *nam pla,* is similar to soy sauce but is made with dried fish. Although it smells fishy in the bottle, it doesn't have a strong fish taste. Tofu (soy bean curd) soaks up sauces better and fries faster if it's been pressed first to expel as much water as possible. To do this, place the block of tofu between two plates and weight the top plate with something heavy, such as a full can or a bag of beans. Let the tofu sit like this for about 30 minutes, tilting the plates every 10 minutes or so to drain the water. Dicing tofu couldn't be easier: Use a serrated knife to cut the pressed tofu into slabs, then turn the slabs on their side and slice through them to make strips. Finally, cut the strips into cubes. Don't be put off by the large amount of garlic in this dish. Once stir-fried and browned, it turns sweet. If you're concerned about garlic breath, distribute fresh stalks of cilantro or parsley to chew on after the meal.

Serves 4

1 lb. rice sticks

6 scallions

2 tablespoons fish sauce

1 tablespoon sugar

$1/4$ cup water

1 tablespoon Thai chili paste

$1/2$ cup safflower oil or other vegetable oil

1 cup firm or extra-firm tofu, pressed and diced

6 cloves garlic, peeled and minced

12 medium shrimp, peeled and deveined

$1/2$ cup loosely packed broccoli rabe or spinach

1 cup bean sprouts

1 beefsteak tomato, peeled and seeded

2 eggs, beaten

$1/4$ cup chopped cilantro

coarsely ground unsalted peanuts (garnish)

lime wedges (garnish)

additional fish sauce (garnish)

hot pepper flakes (garnish)

sugar (garnish)

1. Soften the rice noodles following the instructions for soaking noodles on page 184.
2. Chop the scallions, keeping white and green portions separate, and set aside.
3. In a small bowl, combine the fish sauce, sugar, water, and chili paste and set aside.
4. Place about half of the oil in a wok and fry the tofu cubes until browned, about 5 minutes. Remove the tofu with a slotted spoon and set aside on paper towels or brown paper bags to drain.
5. Pour out the oil and wipe the wok clean.
6. Add the remaining oil to the wok and heat until almost smoking.
7. Add the garlic and stir-fry until brown, about 30 seconds.
8. Add the shrimp and white portion of scallions and stir-fry until the shrimp are pink and cooked through, about 2 minutes.
9. Add the broccoli rabe, sprouts, and tomato and stir-fry until the tomato is soft and the sprouts and greens have wilted, about 2 minutes.
10. Add the eggs and stir until cooked into bits of scrambled egg (the end of a chopstick can be useful for keeping the egg pieces separate), about 30 seconds.
11. Immediately add the softened noodles. Pour the prepared sauce over the noodles and stir-fry until the ingredients are combined and the sauce is absorbed, about 2 minutes.
12. Sprinkle with chopped cilantro and serve the garnishes, including the scallion greens, in small bowls on the side.

Lard Nar

This dish also can be varied by changing the vegetables or including chicken rather than beef.

Serves 4

1 lb. broad rice noodles

1 tablespoon fish sauce (see page 208)

1 tablespoon fermented black bean sauce

2 tablespoons water

$^1/_2$ teaspoon cornstarch

2 tablespoons safflower oil or other vegetable oil

$^1/_2$ teaspoon sugar

2 cloves garlic, minced

$^1/_2$ lb. beef, cut into strips

12 snow peas

3 cups loosely packed bok choy

salt and freshly ground pepper to taste

1. If you are using fresh rice noodles, rinse them under hot water. If you are using dried rice noodles, soak them according to instructions on page 184.

2. Combine the fish sauce, black bean sauce, water, cornstarch, and sugar. Stir to dissolve the cornstarch, and then set aside.

3. Heat the oil in a wok. Stir-fry the garlic 1 minute. Add the beef strips and stir-fry until cooked through, about 5 minutes. Remove the beef with slotted spoon and set aside.

4. Stir-fry the snow peas and bok choy until soft, about 2 minutes.

5. Add the noodles to the wok. Drizzle on the prepared sauce and stir-fry until the noodles, sauce, and vegetables are well combined.

6. Add the cooked beef and cook, stirring constantly, 2 additional minutes. Season to taste with salt and pepper.

Mee Krob

Mee Krob is usually served as an appetizer or snack. This recipe doesn't make quite enough to serve as an entrée, although you could accompany it with a salad and a vegetable stir-fry and call it a night. If you want more noodles, fry them in two batches to keep from crowding the wok. The primary feature of Mee Krob is the contrast between the different tastes: crunchy, sweet, sour, and salty. To crush noodles, place them in a plastic freezer bag, close the bag securely, and break them with a rolling pin.

Serves 4

3 $^1/_4$ cups safflower oil or other vegetable oil

8 oz. rice vermicelli, crushed

1 cup pressed and diced firm or extra-firm tofu

2 tablespoons white vinegar

2 tablespoons fish sauce (see page 208)

2 tablespoons sugar

2 tablespoons water

2 eggs, beaten

2 cloves garlic, minced

1 bulb shallot, minced

3 scallions, sliced

2 small red chili peppers, minced

1. Heat 3 cups of the oil in a wok until almost smoking. To test whether the oil is hot enough to fry the noodles, drop a few pieces in. If they bubble up to the surface immediately and are nicely browned, the oil's ready; if they sink to the bottom, it's not.

2. Carefully drop the noodles into the oil and fry until they are puffed up and brown, about 10 seconds. With a slotted spoon, remove the noodles to paper towels or brown paper bags to drain. Fry the noodles in batches, if necessary.

3. Pour out the hot oil and wipe out the wok. You cannot pour hot oil into the garbage (it will melt the garbage bag), and you can't pour it down the drain (it will sputter and clog up the drain). The best thing to do is to pour it into a small bowl or an empty can that you plan to throw away, set it aside to cool, and then dispose of it with your regular trash.

4. Place the remaining oil in the wok and brown the tofu on all sides. Remove the tofu with a slotted spoon and set aside on paper towels or brown paper bags to drain.

5. Wipe out the wok again. Remove the wok from the heat and, in the wok, combine the vinegar, fish sauce, sugar, and water. Stir to dissolve the sugar.

6. Bring the fish sauce mixture to a boil and simmer until reduced slightly, about 2 minutes.

7. Pour in the eggs and stir with a spatula or chopstick to scramble. For a more substantial Mee Krob, add some minced chicken breast or pork along with the eggs. in step 7.

8. Add the garlic, shallot, scallions, chili peppers, noodles, and tofu, and toss in the wok until thoroughly combined, about 2 minutes. Mee Krob is one of those dishes that cannot be kept warm for a half hour after cooking. The noodles begin to get soggy very quickly, so serve this dish immediately.

Vietnamese Victuals

Vietnamese cuisine makes extensive use of noodles (mostly rice noodles). This is no surprise considering the vast rice fields that cover much of the country.

The Vietnamese are quite fond of soups and even eat them for breakfast. Beef is prevalent in Vietnamese food, as are pork and shrimp. While much of Vietnamese cooking can trace its roots back to China, there is still a French influence in Vietnam as well—a remnant of the French colonization that lasted for 70 years, ending in 1954.

It's up to the diner to personalize Vietnamese meals, which are almost always served with a salad of fresh greens and pickled vegetables and accompanied by a choice of sauces. These are appropriate with noodles soups as well. Vietnamese sauces include the following:

➤ *Nuoc mam,* or Vietnamese fish sauce, differs slightly from Thai fish sauce but may be used interchangeably.

➤ *Nuoc leo,* or peanut sauce, is normally used for dipping items such as vegetables wrapped in rice papers.

➤ *Tuong ot* is a hot chile sauce that is similar to Thai chili paste.

➤ *Mom tom* is a very salty, fishy shrimp sauce.

Pho

Pho is often referred to as Vietnam's national dish. This spicy noodle soup is eaten at almost any meal and can also serve as a snack. Traditionally, Pho contains pig's feet and tripe, but I've altered it a little to make it more palatable to North American tastes. Pho is sometimes known as "Hanoi soup" because it is so closely associated with that city. In Vietnam, this soup is always made with fresh rice noodles. If you can find fresh rice noodles, by all means use them. Simply rinse them under hot water to heat and then place them in the bowls. Obviously, using homemade broth will up the quality of this dish, but since the broth is simmered briefly with other seasonings to refresh it, canned broth is okay, too. Traditionally, the beef is sliced very thin and then placed in bowls; when the broth is ladled over it, it is supposed to cook from that heat. I'm wary of eating any meat that's not cooked well, and I also like the slightly charred flavor that grilling or broiling the meat adds. If you prefer the traditional version, you can skip this step. To broil steak, heat your broiler at the highest temperature. Place the steak strips in the broiler pan. Insert the pan close to the broiler flame and cook the steak strips until well done, about 5 minutes per side. To grill steak, heat your grill and grill the steak strips until well done, about 5 minutes per side. Whether you are using a broiler or a grill, turn the steak strips with tongs.

Serves 4

8 oz. dried rice sticks

1/2 lb. steak, cut into 2-inch strips

3 qt. beef broth

1 onion

2 whole cloves

2 pieces star anise

1 cinnamon stick

1 1/2-inch × 1/2-inch piece ginger, peeled

2 tablespoons fish sauce

1/4 cup chopped cilantro

3 scallions, sliced

2 small red chile peppers, minced

1. Soften the rice noodles following the instructions for soaking noodles on page 184.

2. Broil or grill the steak and set aside.

3. Place the broth in a large soup pot. Stick the cloves into the sides of the onion and place in the pot. Add the anise, cinnamon stick, ginger, and fish sauce to the broth.

4. Bring the broth to a boil and simmer about 10 minutes.

5. Meanwhile, bring a pot of water to a boil. Boil the rice noodles until al dente, about 1 minute. Drain the noodles, rinse with cool water, and set aside.

6. When the broth is ready, remove and discard the onion, anise, cinnamon stick, and ginger.

7. To serve, divide the noodles among serving bowls, top with beef, and then ladle on the broth. Sprinkle on cilantro, scallions, and chile peppers.

Bun Bo

Bun Bo is a spicy soup that originates in Hue, the one-time imperial capital of Vietnam. It is similar to Pho but uses rice vermicelli rather than rice sticks. Fresh lemongrass has much more flavor than dried lemongrass, which tends to taste more like potpourri than the real thing. It is available at all Asian groceries and sometimes even in mainstream grocery stores. To release the flavor of lemongrass, smash it with the side of a cleaver as you would a clove of garlic.

Serves 4

8 oz. dried rice vermicelli	1 teaspoon hot pepper flakes
$1/2$ lb. pork, cut into 2-inch strips	2 tablespoons fish sauce
3 qt. beef broth	1 cup bean sprouts
1 stalk lemongrass, smashed	2 cups loosely packed spinach
1 small onion, coarsely chopped	$1/4$ cup cilantro
1 tablespoon chili paste	3 scallions, sliced

1. Soften the rice noodles following the instructions for soaking noodles on page 184.
2. Broil or grill the pork and set aside.
3. Place the broth in a large soup pot. Add the lemongrass and onion.
4. Bring the broth to a boil and simmer about 10 minutes.
5. When the broth is ready, remove and discard the lemongrass. Add the chili paste, pepper flakes, and fish sauce.
6. Add the bean sprouts and spinach to the soup and simmer until wilted, about 2 minutes. Add the pork and keep at a low simmer while you cook the noodles.
7. Bring a pot of water to a boil. Boil the rice vermicelli until al dente, about 1 minute. Drain the noodles, rinse with cool water, and set aside. To keep rice vermicelli from overcooking, it is best to place them in a large wire strainer, lower the strainer into the pot, and then simply remove the strainer when the noodles are cooked. They should be ready quite quickly.
8. To serve, divide the noodles among serving bowls and ladle on the broth. Sprinkle on cilantro and scallions. Serve additional hot sauce on the side.

Philippines

Pansit

Pansit can serve as a snack or a meal in the Philippines. It lends itself to endless variations. This dish is differentiated from other stir-fry dishes by its flour-thickened sauce. The Philippines consist of 7,000 islands and boast a cuisine influenced by sources as diverse as Spain, China, Malaysia, Japan, and the United States. A dish of pansit is usually garnished with either chopped scallions, lemon wedges, hard-boiled eggs, or pork cracklings. You can serve any or all of these with your pansit (crumbled bacon makes a good substitute for cracklings), along with hot sauce. It's also delicious without any embellishment.

Serves 4

1 lb. thin, round rice noodles or rice sticks

3 cups chicken broth

2 tablespoons unbleached white flour

2 tablespoons soy sauce

2 tablespoons safflower oil or other vegetable oil

2 cloves garlic, minced

1 onion, peeled and chopped

12 medium shrimp, peeled, deveined, and roughly chopped

1/2 lb. lean pork, cut into cubes

1 cup shredded cabbage

2 carrots, cut into matchsticks

salt and freshly ground pepper to taste

1. Soften the rice noodles following the instructions for soaking noodles on page 184.
2. Combine about 1/2 cup of the chicken broth, the white flour, and the soy sauce, stir until the flour is dissolved, and set aside.
3. Place the oil in the wok and heat over high heat until almost smoking.
4. Stir-fry the garlic and onions until softened, about 30 seconds.
5. Add the cabbage and carrots and stir-fry until the carrots are softened and the cabbage is wilted, about 5 minutes.
6. Add the shrimp and pork and stir-fry until cooked through, about 4 minutes.
7. Add the remaining 2 1/2 cups of broth to the wok and bring to a boil.
8. Rinse the softened noodles and add to the wok. Continue stirring the noodles and vegetables until the noodles are cooked through and the broth has been absorbed, about 5 minutes.
9. Pour the reserved broth mixture over the noodles, season to taste with salt and freshly ground pepper, and stir-fry until the noodles are coated with the sauce, about 2 minutes. Pansit is usually a yellow-orange color due to the addition of annato seeds. Since these seeds can be hard to find and are basically flavorless, I haven't included them in this recipe. If you want to use annato seeds, soak them in some warm water until the water is brightly colored, 30 minutes or so, strain the water, and then discard the seeds. Add the water to the flour-thickened broth in step 2.

Indonesia

Bahmi Goreng

Indonesia's bahmi goreng is a spicy, stir-fried noodle dish that can include a mix of meats and vegetables. A soupier version of this same dish is known as *bahmi godog*. Indonesia is best known for its role in the spice trade. (This archipelago includes the aptly named Spice Islands). Cinnamon, nutmeg, cloves, and ginger all originated in Indonesia. *Ketjap manis* is Indonesian soy sauce. It is sweeter and more viscous than regular Chinese or Japanese soy sauce. You can purchase *ketjap manis* in an Asian grocery store. If you cannot find it, combine 2 tablespoons of soy sauce with 1 tablespoon of brown sugar and stir until the sugar is dissolved.

Serves 4

1 lb. round, thin egg noodles	1 stalk celery, minced
1 teaspoon ground ginger	12 shrimp, peeled and deveined
1/4 teaspoon cinnamon	1 whole, boneless chicken breast, skinned and cut into cubes
2 tablespoons ketjap manis	
2 tablespoons safflower oil or other vegetable oil	1 cup bean sprouts
	2 tomatoes, peeled, seeded, and cut into quarters
1 small onion, thinly sliced	
2 cloves garlic, minced	
1 or 2 small green chili peppers, minced	

1. Cook the noodles following the instructions for boiling noodles on page 182.
2. Stir the ginger and cinnamon into the ketjap manis and set aside.
3. Heat the oil in a wok over high heat until almost smoking.
4. Add the onion, garlic, chili peppers, and celery and stir-fry until soft, about 30 seconds.
5. Add the shrimp and chicken and stir-fry until cooked through, about 5 minutes.
6. Add the bean sprouts and tomatoes and stir-fry until soft, about 2 minutes.
7. Add the cooked noodles, drizzle on the prepared ketjap manis mixture, and toss over high heat until the sauce is absorbed and evenly distributed, about 2 minutes.

Like almost all Indonesian dishes, bahmi goreng is served with a spicy condiment called *sambal ulek*. You can either serve chili paste on the side or make your own *sambal ulek* by combining chile peppers, salt, and lime juice in a blender. You can include some tomatoes in the mixture if you like.

Malaysia

Malaysian cuisine is divided into Chinese, Indian, and Malay. The three categories don't intermingle but coexist happily. Typical Indian-influenced fare includes thin, crepe-like pancakes with various fillings and dishes with curry sauces. Chinese-style dishes include noodle soups and stir-fried noodle dishes. Malay cuisine offers grilled skewers of meat, rice with chicken, and *mee rebus*. Malaysia is also famous for its many food stalls selling dishes such as *laksa* (fish soup over noodles), *hokkien mee* (noodles with shrimp), and *wan tan mee* (pork dumplings in soup).

Mee Rebus

The inclusion of sweet potatoes in the Malaysian dish mee rebus might strike you as strange, but they provide a wonderful balance to the saltiness of the other ingredients. Leave out the shrimp for an equally delicious vegetarian version. Mee Rebus is usually very, very hot. You can adjust the cayenne to your own taste.

Serves 4

6 shrimp, peeled and deveined

1 teaspoon grated ginger

4 cloves garlic

2 shallots

2 teaspoon cayenne

$1/2$ cup safflower oil or other vegetable oil

1 cup pressed and diced firm or extra-firm tofu

1 sweet potato, boiled, peeled, and mashed

2 tablespoons flour

2 tablespoons corn flour

1 tablespoon sugar

salt to taste

1 cup water

1 lb. thin, round egg noodles

1 cup bean sprouts, blanched

$1/4$ cup ground peanuts

1. Combine the shrimp, ginger, garlic, shallots, and cayenne in a food processor, grind to a paste, and set aside.
2. Heat all but 2 tablespoons of the oil in a wok until almost smoking. Fry the diced tofu until browned, about 5 minutes, and then remove to paper towels or brown paper bags to drain.
3. Wipe out the wok, and then add the remaining 2 tablespoons of oil.
4. Add the reserved paste and stir-fry until the shrimp are completely cooked, about 1 minute.
5. Add the mashed sweet potato to the wok and combine with the paste with a fork. Sprinkle on the flours and sugar, combine thoroughly, and season to taste with salt. Add the water, mix until water is thoroughly incorporated, bring mixture to a boil, and then simmer until thickened slightly, about 10 minutes.
6. Boil the noodles following the instructions on page 182. When cooked, drain the noodles and place them on a large platter. Top the noodles with the bean sprouts and fried tofu, pour on the sweet potato mixture, and top with the ground peanuts.

The Least You Need to Know

➤ Every Asian country has at least one noodle dish.

➤ Noodles in Asian countries are often served as "street food," not entire meals.

Part 6
Strange Food in a Strange Land

Pasta originated in Italy and China, most likely, so why are people eating noodles in Malaysia and Malibu? The answer is simple: people move around and take their foods with them. The poverty that drove Italians from their country for many years propelled pasta around the world. Italian immigrants have brought pasta with them everywhere they've gone. And wherever it lands, pasta always seems to catch on.

In Part 6, you'll sample pasta dishes from Greece and France. You'll feast on the couscous of North Africa, learn the ultimate matzoh ball soup recipe, and check out some American favorites.

Chapter 21

No Longer Greek to You

In This Chapter

➤ Greek pasta dishes

Laid Back Greek Pasta

Venetians occupied parts of Greece in the fourteenth century and even built a castle in the city of Astipalaia. They can't take credit for introducing pasta to Greece, however. It was there long before they were.

Greeks eat almost as much pasta per capita as Italians. They're not famous for their pasta, however, and the reason is simple. Whereas Italians have developed all sorts of rules and regulations and more than 500 different pasta shapes, Greeks are laid back about their pasta. They eat basically a few different shapes (orzo, macaroni such as penne, and spaghetti) and don't have a lot of different sauces. They don't have rules about mixing and matching pasta and sauces; they just sit back, relax, and enjoy their pasta. Here are a few Greek pasta recipes so that you can do the same.

Greeks eat mainly orzo, macaroni, and spaghetti.

Greek Eats

Pastitsio

Pastitsio is a big baked pasta dish that is great for a casual party. It resembles the Italian dish Pasticcio, but with the Greek flavor imprints of cinnamon and goat cheese. *Kefalotyri* is considered the Greek version of Italy's Parmesan cheese. It is a semi-hard yellow cheese that is usually grated. *Kasseri* is a fresh Greek cheese. It is soft and crumbly and has a mild taste.

Serves 10

2 tablespoons extra virgin olive oil

1 onion, minced

1 clove garlic, minced

1 lb. ground beef

3 cups chopped, peeled tomatoes and their juice

1 teaspoon cinnamon

salt and freshly ground pepper to taste

1 lb. dried penne or other short, dried pasta

3 teaspoons butter

$^1/_2$ cup unbleached white flour

5 cups milk

$^1/_2$ cup grated kefalotyri or other hard goat cheese

$^1/_2$ cup crumbled kasseri or other soft goat cheese

1. Preheat the oven to 350 degrees. Oil a 9×13-inch baking pan with 1 tablespoon of the oil, and set aside.

2. In a large pan, sauté the onion and garlic in the remaining 1 tablespoon olive oil until softened, about 2 minutes.

3. Crumble the meat into the pan and sauté until cooked through, about 7 minutes.

4. Add the tomatoes to pan. Stir in the cinnamon and season to taste with salt and pepper. Simmer the sauce until almost all the liquid has evaporated, about 15 minutes.

5. Meanwhile, cook the pasta in abundant boiling water, following the instructions on page 12.

6. To make a white sauce, melt the butter in a medium pan over low heat. Whisk in the flour a little at a time. Once all the flour has been added, cook for 2 minutes, stirring constantly. Add the milk, a little at a time, allowing the sauce to return to a simmer after each addition. When all the milk has been added, simmer the sauce, stirring constantly, until it has thickened to the consistency of sour cream, about 8 minutes.

7. When the pasta is ready, toss it with about $^1/_2$ of the white sauce.

8. Pour $^1/_2$ of the pasta into the prepared pan and distribute evenly. Top this first layer of pasta with all the tomato sauce, using the back of a spoon to distribute it evenly. Top with half of the kefalotyri and half of the kasseri. Pour the remaining pasta over the cheese. Use a spatula to spread the remaining white sauce on top of the pasta. Top with the remaining kefalotyri and kasseri.

9. Bake until the top is browned, about 35–40 minutes. Allow to settle about 15 minutes before cutting.

Orzo with Feta and Tomatoes

Orzo, a small pasta shaped like rice, is usually used in soups. It is particularly popular in Greece. This dish is delicious when hot, but it also makes a nice room-temperature dish on a lazy summer afternoon. *Orzo* means "barley" in Italian. These small pieces of pasta do look like grains; they are small and almond-shaped. *Feta* is a salty, white, sheep's milk cheese from Greece. Fortunately, it is widely available; there is no substitute for its distinctive taste. *Feta* means "slice" in Greek, because this cheese is cut into large slices before being stored in brine for a month.

Serves 4

1 lb. orzo	1 clove garlic, minced
4–6 beefsteak tomatoes, chopped	$^1/_2$ cup crumbled feta cheese
$^1/_4$ cup extra virgin olive oil	salt and freshly ground pepper to taste

1. Cook the orzo following the instructions on page 12.

2. Meanwhile, combine the tomatoes, olive oil, garlic, and feta cheese in a large serving bowl. Season to taste with salt and pepper. Be sure to taste this mixture before adding salt. Feta can be very salty, so you may not want to add any salt at all.

3. When the pasta is cooked, drain and toss it with the sauce. If this were an Italian recipe you'd expect to see basil leaves added to the dish at the end. Greeks don't eat basil, however. If you must add a fresh herb, use the leaves from a sprig or two of fresh oregano.

Macaroni with Yogurt Sauce

This is the ultimate no-brainer recipe. As long as you remember to drain the yogurt in advance (about a day, so plan ahead), you can't go wrong. Try to get the best, freshest yogurt you can. In Greece, yogurt is usually made with sheep's milk. Drained yogurt (sometimes referred to as "yogurt cheese") is a wonderful ingredient that can be used as a substitute for cream cheese and other spreadable dairy products. To drain yogurt, fit a double thickness of cheesecloth or a coffee filter inside a strainer, and set the strainer in a bowl large enough that the bottom of the strainer doesn't touch the bottom. Pour the yogurt into the lined strainer and let sit overnight in the refrigerator. Be sure the yogurt has no gelatin or other thickeners, or it won't drain correctly.

Serves 4

1 lb. dried macaroni or other dried pasta

2 sprigs fresh oregano

2 sprigs fresh dill

3 tablespoons extra virgin olive oil

1 ¹/₂ cups plain yogurt, drained

salt and freshly ground pepper to taste

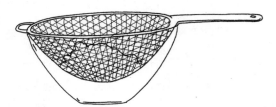

To make yogurt cheese, drain yogurt in a strainer.

1. Cook the macaroni following the instructions on page 12.
2. Meanwhile, strip the oregano and dill leaves and chop.
3. When the pasta is cooked al dente, drain and transfer it to a serving bowl.
4. Drizzle on the olive oil and toss.
5. Pinch off pieces of drained yogurt and add to the pasta. Stir until the yogurt has melted and is evenly distributed.
6. Sprinkle on the chopped herbs.

Macaroni with Olives

Greeks are justifiably proud of their olives and olive oil. A mix of various green and black olives makes this simple dish very visually appealing.

Serves 4

1 lb. dried macaroni or other dried pasta

1/2 cup extra virgin olive oil

1 tablespoon lemon juice

1 cup pitted olives, roughly chopped

1 tablespoon capers, rinsed

salt and freshly ground pepper to taste

1. Cook the macaroni following the instructions on page 12.
2. Meanwhile, whisk together the olive oil and lemon juice.
3. When the pasta is cooked al dente, drain and transfer it to large serving bowl.
4. Pour on the olive oil mixture and toss. Add the olives and capers, toss again, and season to taste with salt and pepper.

The Least You Need to Know

➤ Greeks eat almost as much pasta as Italians, but their repertoire of pasta dishes is more limited.

Chapter 22

The French Do It, The Germans Do It, Even The Spanish Do It

In This Chapter

➤ A few more pasta recipes scattered across Europe

Cleverly Continental

Other European countries (in addition to Italy and Greece) also serve pasta. Although the pasta traditions of countries such as France, Germany, and Spain don't have the breadth of Italy's, they do offer some excellent recipes that you shouldn't pass up.

Provençal, But Not Provincial

If you check out a map, you'll see it's no coincidence that pasta has made its way to Provence; this southern region of France lies along the Italian border. The French, however, have their own way with pasta. They favor vegetable mixtures over straight tomato sauces. Both of the following recipes contain typical Provençal flavors and ingredients.

Pasta Provence Style

Provence's *ratatouille*—a mash of zucchini, eggplant, bell pepper, and tomato—is justifiably famous. It tastes as great tossed with pasta as it does with crusty bread.

Serves 4

1 eggplant, diced (no need to peel)

3 tablespoons extra virgin olive oil

1 red bell pepper, cored, seeded, and diced

1 green bell pepper, cored, seeded, and diced

1 small yellow onion, chopped

1 clove garlic, minced

salt and freshly ground pepper to taste

1 zucchini, diced

1 ¹/₂ cups peeled tomatoes and their juice

¹/₄ cup red wine vinegar

fresh tagliatelle for 4 people (see page 148) or 1 lb. dried pasta

¹/₂ cup chopped basil leaves

1. Place the eggplant pieces in a colander. Sprinkle both sides liberally with salt and allow the bitter juices to drain off for at least 1 hour.
2. Rinse the eggplant and pat it dry.
3. Heat the olive oil in a large skillet.
4. Add the peppers, onion, and garlic, and season to taste with salt and pepper. Cook, covered, over low heat until very soft, about 30 minutes.
5. Add the zucchini, tomatoes, and drained eggplant, and continue cooking until the eggplant and zucchini are soft, about 20 minutes.
6. Stir in the vinegar and cook an additional 2 minutes.
7. Meanwhile, cook the pasta in abundant salted water following the instructions on page 12.
8. When the pasta is cooked al dente, drain and transfer it to serving bowl. Pour on the vegetable mixture and toss to combine. Top with basil leaves.

Pasta with Truffles

This is so simple it can hardly be deemed a recipe. It's the best way to showcase the unusual taste of truffles. *Truffles* are a kind of fungus with a distinctive taste and smell. They are similar to mushrooms but with a much headier perfume. Fresh truffles are extremely expensive. Canned truffles are more reasonable, but still not cheap, and can be found in gourmet stores. Truffle oil is available in gourmet stores. When choosing truffle oil, opt for a vegetable oil base rather than an olive oil base. The taste of the truffle will be lost in the strong taste of the olive oil.

Serves 4

fresh fettuccine for 4 people (see page 148)

2 tablespoons butter

4 tablespoons truffle oil

salt and freshly ground pepper to taste

1 1-oz. can of truffles, drained and diced (or 12 morel mushrooms)

1. Cook the fettuccine in abundant salted water as instructed on page 12.
2. Meanwhile, melt the butter in a large skillet. Add the truffle oil and stir to combine. Season to taste with salt and pepper.
3. Add the diced truffles to the butter mixture and sauté 2 minutes. (If using morel mushrooms, sauté until tender, about 5 minutes.)
4. When the pasta is cooked al dente, drain and toss it with the butter mixture in the skillet. If you have access to fresh truffles—which cost an arm and a leg—by all means use them. Simply shave fresh truffles over the pasta, or diners can add truffle shavings to taste at the table.

Spaetzle

In Germany, spaetzle are usually served as a side dish. Like all small buttered noodles, they are terrific with stews. In German, *spaetzle* means "little sparrow."

Serves 4

3 cups unbleached white flour	4 eggs, lightly beaten
1 pinch nutmeg	$^1/_4$ cup milk or water
$^1/_2$ teaspoon salt	4 tablespoons butter, melted

1. Place the flour, nutmeg, and salt in a large bowl and whisk to combine.
2. Make a well in the flour mixture and pour the eggs into it.
3. Add about half of the milk and mix with a wooden spoon until smooth.
4. The spaetzle dough should be stiff enough to form clumps when dropped from a spoon but not as stiff as regular pasta dough. Add more milk if necessary to achieve the correct consistency.
5. Bring a large pot of water to a boil.
6. Use a spaetzle machine or potato ricer to squeeze noodles directly into the boiling water. There are a number of ways to make spaetzle. I recommend putting them through a potato ricer. You can also slice them off of a wooden board and simultaneously push them into the boiling water (wet the board first and use a slightly stiffer dough) or grate them using a special spaetzle machine, which is kind of a cross between a mandolin and a grater.
7. Boil the spaetzle until they rise to the surface and are soft, about 5 minutes.
8. Remove the spaetzle with a slotted spoon and transfer to serving bowl. Top with melted butter and toss. There are lots of ways to dress spaetzle up a little bit more. Try tossing buttered spaetzle with any or several of the following: thinly sliced cooked mushrooms, fresh herbs, grated Emmenthaler cheese, browned chopped onion, beef gravy.

Fidellos with Tomatoes

Fidellos, sometimes spelled *fideos* or *fideus,* are very fine Spanish noodles that are sautéed briefly before being cooked. If you can't find real fidellos, buy the thinnest angel hair or cappellini that you can find. Fidellos are very versatile. Although this dish is usually served as a side dish, it can easily become a main course if topped with a piece of white fish, such as cod, or with some cooked shrimp. In that case, you might want to substitute fish broth for the chicken stock.

Serves 4

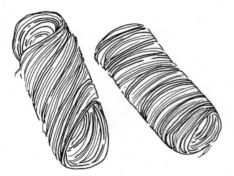

Fidellos are usually available in "nests."

1 lb. fidellos or angel hair

$^{1}/_{2}$ cup extra virgin olive oil

1 onion, chopped

1 clove garlic, minced

1 cup peeled and seeded tomatoes, chopped

5 cups chicken broth

salt and freshly ground pepper to taste

$^{1}/_{4}$ cup chopped parsley

1. Break the fidellos into approximately 2-inch pieces and set aside. Preheat the broiler.

2. In a large skillet, heat $^{1}/_{4}$ cup of the olive oil over medium heat. Add the noodles and sauté until just browned. (The noodles will continue to cook after you remove them, so be sure to keep a close eye on them.) Remove the noodles with a slotted spoon and set aside on paper towels or brown paper bags to drain.

3. Wipe the skillet clean. Add the remaining olive oil and sauté the onion and garlic until soft.

4. Add the tomatoes and broth and bring to a boil. Add the toasted fidellos.

5. Season to taste with salt and pepper and turn down to a simmer. Simmer until most of the liquid is absorbed and the noodles are cooked through.

6. Place the skillet in the preheated broiler as close to the heat source as possible. Broil until the noodles are browned on top, about 3 minutes. Allow the noodles to set for 10 minutes, sprinkle on the parsley, and cut into wedges. Fidellos can be served either at room temperature or hot. If you prefer individual servings, put the fidellos into individual ramekins before proceeding with step 6.

The Least You Need to Know

➤ Pasta is eaten all across Europe.

Chapter 23

A Kreplach By Any Other Name.... Ashkenazic Jewish Noodles

In This Chapter

➤ Recipes for Ashkenazic Jewish noodle dishes

A History of Movement

Jews have been nomads for so long that they've served as magnets for the world's cuisines. Dishes have stuck to them and been transferred around the world along with the Diaspora. Pasta is no exception.

In this chapter I look specifically at Ashkenazic Jewish dishes. The Jewish community can be divided (very roughly) into two groups: Ashkenazic Jews and Sephardic Jews. The former had roots in France and Germany, the latter in Spain. Ashkenazic Jewish recipes tend to resemble Polish and German cooking, with the obvious exception that they follow the rules of kashrut and therefore contain no pork or seafood products. If you are interested in a Sephardic recipe, take a look at the recipe for Fidellos with Tomatoes on page 228. It is a typical Sephardic Jewish dish that traveled from Spain to Latin America (not the version with shrimp, of course).

Pasta Patter

While Judaism is certainly not the first religion that most people associate with Italy, Italian Jews have lived in Rome since the time of the Roman Empire. There are about 50,000 Jews living in Italy today, approximately half of them in Rome. Italian Jews eat pasta regularly, but since Jews are forbidden to cook on the Sabbath, they often resort to room temperature pasta on Saturdays. The Pasta Salad with Tomatoes on page 249 was inspired by these make-ahead Italian-Jewish dishes.

Is It Kosher?

While the following recipes are not kosher, they can be prepared in a kosher manner. The following are the basics of the laws of kashrut. For greater detail, see a rabbi.

➤ No eating meat from animals with cloven hooves. (That's why pig products are not allowed.)

➤ Any fish eaten must have scales (that is, no shellfish).

➤ No mixing of dairy products and meat (that is, no cheesecake after your steak).

Ashkenazic Pasta

Chicken Soup with Kreplach

Kreplach are easier to make than most stuffed pastas because the filling is quite simple (despite the long recipe) and the pasta squares are just folded in half. In the interest of authenticity, I feel I should point out that the most common cooking fat in Ashkenazic Jewish cooking is *schmaltz*, or chicken fat. Since schmaltz is hard to find and none too healthy, I'd substitute canola oil or some other vegetable oil in this recipe. If you love the flavor and don't mind the fat, go with an equal amount of schmaltz.

Serves 6

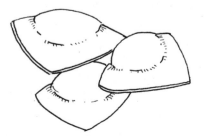

Kreplach are triangles of dough that enclose a filling.

2 tablespoons vegetable oil

1 onion, chopped

1 lb. ground beef

salt and freshly ground pepper to taste

3 ¹/₂ cups unbleached white flour

4 eggs

3 qts. chicken broth

1. Heat the vegetable oil in a large skillet over medium heat.
2. Add the onion and sauté until soft.
3. Add the ground beef, breaking it up with a fork, and sauté until cooked through, about 5 minutes.
4. Remove the cooked beef with a slotted spoon and set aside.
5. To make the pasta, mound the flour on a large wooden cutting board.
6. Shape the flour into a well with a deep indentation in the center.
7. Crack the eggs into the well.
8. Use a fork or your fingers to break up the yolks and mix the eggs.
9. Draw in a little bit of the flour and mix it with the eggs.
10. Continue drawing in a little bit of flour at a time and mixing it in until a paste has formed in the center of the well.
11. When the paste has formed, move all the remaining flour on top of the dough.
12. Squeeze the dough between your fingers to incorporate the remaining flour.
13. At this point you need to evaluate your dough. It should be dry enough that it doesn't stick to the board as you knead. If it still feels somewhat gummy, incorporate more flour, but only about 1 tablespoon at a time. Remember that it's much easier to add flour to an overly wet dough than it is to moisten a dry dough.
14. When the dough has reached the right consistency and forms a ball, clean off your work surface (a dough scraper works best) and wash and dry your hands.
15. Return the ball of dough to your clean work surface and begin kneading.
16. Knead until the dough is soft and firm. It should be a bright, consistent yellow color with no lumps of flour. The surface of the dough should be soft and smooth. Vigorous kneading by hand will take about 8 minutes.
17. Dust your work surface (wooden cutting board) very lightly with flour.
18. Place the ball of dough on the center of the work surface.
19. Use your hands to flatten the ball of dough slightly.
20. Place the rolling pin on the center of the dough and roll it away from you.
21. Turn the dough a quarter-turn and repeat.
22. Continue rolling the dough away from you and turning a quarter-turn each time until you have a large circle about ¹/₈-inch thick.
23. Cut the dough into 2 ¹/₂-inch squares.

continues

continued

24. Re-roll any extra pieces of dough and cut into 2 $\frac{1}{2}$-inch squares.

25. Place a scant tsp. of filling in the middle of each piece.

26. Fold the dough pieces in half to form triangles, pressing the edges firmly to close.

27. Allow kreplach to rest for 30 minutes or so, then bring the broth to a boil, add the kreplach, and simmer until the kreplach are tender, about 12 minutes. If you prefer not to use kreplach in soup, you can simply cook them in water (they take slightly longer than Italian stuffed pasta, since they are thicker) and then toss them with melted butter. Meat kreplach are the most common, but you can also fill kreplach with cheese or jam. Cheese kreplach are delicious with melted butter. Sweet jam kreplach can be topped with cinnamon, sugar, and melted butter, and served as a dessert or snack. If you are in a hurry, you can buy wonton wrappers and use them in place of the homemade pasta in this recipe. They don't have quite the same taste, but they save time.

Noodle Kugel

The variations on noodle kugel are endless, but this one—the one my mother always made—is my all-time favorite because it is so plain and so good. A *kugel* is an Eastern European Jewish baked pudding that can be made with potatoes, bread, rice, noodles, or other ingredients. A kugel can be sweet or savory.

Serves 6

1 lb. wide egg noodles

8 tablespoons (1 stick) butter

1 lb. cottage cheese

1 cup milk

1 pint sour cream

salt to taste

1. Preheat the oven to 375 degrees.

2. Cook the egg noodles in abundant boiling water until soft.

3. Melt 6 tablespoons of the butter and set aside.

4. Grease a 9×13-inch baking dish with 1 tablespoon butter and set aside.

5. In a large bowl, combine the melted butter, cottage cheese, milk, and sour cream. Season to taste with salt.

6. When the noodles are cooked, drain and add them to the cottage cheese mixture, and stir to combine well.

7. Pour the noodles into the prepared baking dish and dot them with the remaining 1 tablespoon butter.

8. Bake until the top is crusty and brown, about 60–75 minutes. This is no diet dish, but I indulge in it every once in a while. I've also had great success using skim and low-fat dairy products.

Vegetable Noodle Kugel

Here's another kugel that has vegetables added. Kugel is usually served as a side dish, but you can use this as a vegetarian entrée as well.

Serves 6

1 lb. wide egg noodles	1 cup sour cream
2 tablespoons butter	1 cup milk
1 medium onion, chopped	1 cup cottage cheese
8 oz. mushrooms, sliced	1 teaspoon paprika
6 cups loosely packed spinach leaves	salt and freshly ground pepper to taste

1. Preheat the oven to 375 degrees.
2. Cook the egg noodles in abundant boiling water until soft.
3. Grease a 9×13-inch pan with 1 TB. butter and set aside.
4. Meanwhile, in a medium skillet over medium heat, sauté the onion in the remaining 1 TB. butter until soft, about 2 minutes.
5. Add the mushrooms and sauté until they are soft and their liquid has evaporated. With a slotted spoon, remove the mushrooms to a large bowl.
6. Soak the spinach leaves in several changes of water until the water runs clean. Add them to the pan and cook until wilted.
7. When the spinach is cool, squeeze out as much liquid as possible and chop. Add them to the bowl with the mushrooms.
8. Add the sour cream, milk, cottage cheese, and paprika to the vegetables and season to taste with salt and pepper.
9. When the noodles are cooked, add them to bowl and stir to combine all the ingredients thoroughly.
10. Pour the noodles into the prepared dish.
11. Bake the noodles until the top is brown and crusty, about 60–75 minutes.

Matzoh Ball Soup

It's funny to call matzoh balls pasta; the idea of boiling matzoh balls and topping them with some kind of sauce is unheard of. But matzoh balls, integral ingredients in "Jewish penicillin" (matzoh ball soup) are a kind of dumpling. *Matzoh meal* is made by grinding *matzoh,* the unleavened bread that Jews eat during Passover. Although matzoh is served only during Passover, matzoh ball soup is eaten year long.

Serves 6

2 eggs	3 tablespoons vegetable oil
1 egg white	3 tablespoons cold water
salt to taste	3 qts. chicken broth
$^3/_4$ cup matzoh meal	

continues

continued

1. To make the matzoh balls, in a medium bowl, beat together the eggs and egg white. Season to taste with salt.

2. Add the matzoh meal, oil, and water, and mix with your hands until combined. Cover the bowl and refrigerate at least 3 hours and up to 24 hours.

3. Bring a large pot of water to a boil.

4. Wet your hands. Roll a small amount of matzoh ball dough between your palms to make a ball about the size of a golf ball.

5. Drop the ball into the boiling water. Repeat until you have used up all the dough. (You may have to wet your hands a few times.)

6. Lower the heat to a simmer, cover the pot, and cook the matzoh balls until firm, about 30 minutes. Do not lift the lid.

7. Bring the broth to a boil in a separate pot. Remove the matzoh balls with a slotted spoon, add them to the broth, and simmer until they are heated through. You can prepare the matzoh balls through step 6 and refrigerate them right in the cooking liquid for a few days. You can also freeze them in their cooking liquid for a month or so.

Chicken Soup with Farfel

Farfel is the Jewish version of Italy's *pastina*. For a really fast lunch, replace the fresh farfel in this recipe with any small dried pasta. *Farfel* are small pieces of egg pasta most often served in soup. *Farfel* is sometimes labeled "egg barley," not because it contains barley, but because its small pieces resemble that grain. Don't be misled by matzoh farfel, which is crumbled pieces of matzoh.

Serves 6

2 ¹/₂ cups unbleached white flour

3 eggs

3 qts. chicken broth

1. To make the dough, mound the flour on a large wooden cutting board.

2. Shape the flour into a well with a deep indentation in the center.

3. Crack the eggs into the well.

4. Use a fork or your fingers to break up the yolks and mix the eggs.

5. Draw in a little bit of flour and mix it with the eggs.

6. Continue drawing in a little bit of flour at a time and mixing it until a paste has formed in the center of the well.

7. When the paste has formed, move all the remaining flour on top of the dough.

8. Squeeze the dough between your fingers to incorporate the remaining flour.

9. At this point you need to evaluate your dough. Farfel dough is slightly drier than other pasta doughs. If it still feels somewhat gummy, incorporate more flour, but only about 1 tablespoon at a time.

10. When the dough has reached the right consistency and forms a ball, clean off your work surface (a dough scraper works best) and wash and dry your hands.

11. Return the ball of dough to your clean work surface and begin kneading.

12. Knead until the dough is soft and firm. It should be a bright, consistent yellow color with no lumps of flour. The surface of the dough should be soft and smooth. Vigorous kneading by hand will take about 8 minutes.

13. Set the dough aside and allow it to dry until no longer pliable, about 45 minutes.

14. Grate the dough on the largest holes of a 4-sided grater. Spread the farfel out on lightly floured cookie sheets and allow to dry, about 2 hours.

15. Bring the chicken broth to a boil. Add the farfel and simmer until cooked through, about 8 minutes. You can prepare the farfel in advance, allow it to dry, and then store it in an airtight container for a couple of weeks. If you're in a hurry, you can grate the farfel directly into the boiling chicken broth and skip the drying (although if the dough isn't dry enough, fresh farfel may stick together). If you prefer, you can cook the farfel in boiling water and serve with a little melted butter. For toasted farfel, spread the dried farfel on clean cookie sheets (not floured) and toast at 350 degrees until browned, about 15 minutes. Toasted farfel has a nutty flavor.

The Least You Need to Know

➤ Ashkenazic Jewish cuisine has been influenced by many other cultures.

➤ The laws for keeping kosher have also influenced Ashkenazic Jewish cooking.

Chapter 24

The Couscous Coup: North Africa's Pasta

In This Chapter

➤ What is couscous?

➤ Recipes using couscous

Couscous: Pasta or Grain?

Although couscous is often mistaken for a whole grain, it is really a type of pasta made from small pellets of durum semolina flour. The word derives from the Arabic word meaning "to pound," because couscous is made by pounding a semolina dough through a sieve. Couscous originates in the North African countries of Morocco, Algeria, and Tunisia, where it is still prized today as a special food for celebrations.

Making couscous is such a pain and so time-consuming that few people aside from truly dedicated North Africans continue to do so. You can buy excellent couscous in grocery stores, Middle Eastern groceries, and health food stores. In North Africa, couscous is available in various grain sizes; in the United States, it is generally a medium-grain size. You can also purchase whole-wheat couscous for a nutritional boost.

Couscous is a very fine type of pasta.

One of the reasons why making couscous is such a long-term project is that it needs to be steamed as many as seven times. The couscous is placed in a special piece of equipment called a *couscoussier*, which is a large pot with a colander that fits inside. The colander and lid are sealed to the pot very tightly—either with a piece of cloth or some clay—so that no steam escapes. The couscous rests in the colander with the boiling broth below both cooking it with steam and infusing it with flavor.

You can make couscous this way if you like, but there's really no need to steam it more than once. Since the couscous you buy has been pre-steamed, I don't think it adds any more flavor than my preferred method: mixing the couscous with boiling liquid. The following recipes contain recommended cooking times, but if you buy couscous in a box you may prefer to follow the manufacturer's instructions.

Couscous is extremely versatile: it stands up well to fish, vegetables, meat, and is even used to make sweet, dessert-like dishes. (In North Africa, these often serve as a special course between entrée and dessert.)

Use Your Noodle

Don't Get Burned: Hot steam can burn your skin just as badly as boiling water. When you open a pot that contains steam-cooked food, wear an oven mitt to lift the lid, keep your face out of the way, and tilt the lid away from yourself as you lift it to direct the steam in the other direction.

Pasta Patter

A Two-Way Street: The southern part of Italy and the northern part of Africa are not very far from each other, which explains why spaghetti is eaten in Tunisia, and why couscous is an integral part of the food of Sicily, where it is known as *cuscusu*.

Couscous Concoctions

Couscous with Fish

You can use any type of firm, white fish for this recipe. I also like it with bluefish or mackerel fillets.

Serves 4

1 onion, chopped

2 tablespoons butter

3 cups peeled, seeded tomatoes and their juice

1 tablespoon tomato paste

$1/4$ cup raisins

$1/2$ teaspoon cinnamon

salt and freshly ground pepper to taste

1 lb. fillets of firm fish, such as cod, cut into 1-inch pieces

$1 1/2$ cups water

1 cup couscous

$1/4$ cup chopped cilantro

1. In a skillet large enough to hold the fish in a single layer, sauté the onion in butter over medium heat until softened, about 2 minutes.

2. Add the tomatoes, tomato paste, raisins, and cinnamon to the skillet and stir to combine. Season to taste with salt and pepper and place the fillets on top of the sauce.

3. Cover the skillet and simmer gently until the fish is cooked through. The thickness of the fish will dictate the amount of time required. When cooked, the fish will be opaque in the center.

4. When the fish is cooked, remove it from the heat and put the lid on to keep it warm. Bring the water to a boil in a medium pot. Add the couscous and stir to combine. Lower the heat to a simmer, cover the couscous, and simmer until all the water has been absorbed, about 2 minutes.

5. Let the couscous stand for 5 minutes.

6. To serve, spread the couscous on a serving platter, fluffing it with a fork as you remove it from the pot. Place the fish fillets and sauce on top of the couscous. Sprinkle with cilantro.

Couscous with Chick Peas

North African cuisine is a rich source of delicious vegetarian foods, including this dish. Compared with other beans, chick peas take a really long time to cook. That's why I almost always use canned chick peas. I find the organic brands now available are nice and firm and perfect for adding to recipes in which the chick peas will be cooked a little further. *Harissa* is a spicy Tunisian sauce that enlivens many North African dishes (and others as well). Cans of harissa are available in specialty stores, Middle Eastern groceries, and some supermarkets. It is also available in a tube. Serve harissa on the side, allowing guests to add as much as they like.

Serves 4

2 tablespoons butter

2 onions, chopped

1 clove garlic, chopped

2 carrots, peeled and chopped

2 cups cooked chick peas

1 teaspoon saffron threads, dissolved in ¹/₄ cup water

salt and freshly ground pepper to taste

1 ¹/₂ cups water

1 cup couscous

¹/₄ cup chopped parsley

harissa

1. In a large skillet, melt the butter over medium heat and sauté the onion and garlic until softened, about 2 minutes.

2. Add the carrots and sauté until softened, about 5 minutes.

3. Add the chick peas and sauté 1 minute. Pour on the saffron water and season to taste with salt and pepper. Allow the chick peas to simmer gently, stirring occasionally, until the water has evaporated.

4. Once the chick peas are simmering, bring the water to a boil in a medium pot. Add the couscous and stir to combine. Lower the heat to a simmer, cover the couscous, and simmer until all the water has been absorbed, about 2 minutes.

5. Let the couscous stand for 5 minutes.

6. To serve, spread the couscous on a serving platter, fluffing with a fork as you remove it from the pot. Place the chick pea stew in the center of the couscous, sprinkle with parsley, and serve harissa on the side.

Vegetable Couscous

The "rule" on this couscous dish—which hails from Morocco—is that there must be at least seven different vegetables incorporated. (It doesn't much matter, however, which vegetables.) For more eye appeal, and to be sure they are cooked at the same time, chop the vegetables into equal-sized pieces.

Serves 4

6 cups chicken broth

5 carrots, peeled and chopped

1 onion, chopped

2 turnips, peeled and chopped

1 stalk celery, chopped

1 bulb fennel, chopped

1 cup peas

1 cinnamon stick

$1/2$ teaspoon ground cumin

$1/2$ teaspoon dried oregano

salt and freshly ground pepper to taste

2 zucchini, chopped

1 red bell pepper, seeded and chopped

$1 1/2$ cups water

1 cup couscous

$1/4$ cup chopped parsley

1. Place the broth in a large pot and bring to a boil. Add the carrots, onion, turnips, celery, fennel, peas, cinnamon stick, cumin, and oregano. Season to taste with salt and pepper.

2. Return the broth to a boil, lower the heat to a simmer, and cook the vegetables until tender, about 20 minutes.

3. Add the zucchini and pepper and simmer until tender, about 10 minutes.

4. Once the vegetables are cooked, bring the water to a boil in a medium pot. Add the couscous and stir to combine. Lower the heat to a simmer, cover the pot, and simmer until all the water has been absorbed, about 2 minutes.

5. Let the couscous stand for 5 minutes.

6. To serve, spread the couscous on a serving platter, fluffing with a fork as you remove it from the pot. Remove the vegetables from the broth with a slotted spoon and place in the center of the couscous. Moisten the couscous with some of the broth. Sprinkle with parsley. While you can feel free to eat couscous with a spoon, traditionally it is scooped up with a piece of bread or vegetable and eaten by hand.

Sweet Couscous

Couscous makes a terrific dessert. I like to reheat leftover Sweet Couscous for breakfast, too. Normally, the couscous is cooked and the dried fruit is plumped and mixed into it. That method doesn't make much sense to me, however, so I cook the couscous with the fruit already mixed in. That way, the fruit plumps while the couscous is cooking. If you've got cooked couscous on hand, you can make it the usual way.

Serves 4

1 ¹/₂ cups water	1 teaspoon cinnamon
1 cup couscous	1 tablespoon sugar
¹/₂ cup raisins	3 tablespoons butter
¹/₂ cup chopped dates	¹/₂ cup milk
¹/₂ cup chopped dried apricots	¹/₄ cup slivered almonds

1. Bring the water to a boil in a medium pot. Add the couscous, raisins, dates, and apricots, and stir to combine. Lower the heat to a simmer, cover the couscous, and simmer until all the water has been absorbed, about 2 minutes.

2. Stir in the cinnamon, sugar, butter, and milk, and let couscous stand for 5 minutes.

3. Top with slivered almonds.

The Least You Need to Know

➤ Couscous is a pasta consisting of small pellets of semolina flour.

➤ The recipes in this chapter use pre-steamed couscous.

Chapter 25

Ingenuity Strikes: Pasta in the United States

> ## In This Chapter
>
> ➤ A few newfangled types of pasta available in the United States
> ➤ American-style pasta recipes

Pasta, American Style

Culinarily speaking, Americans could not be more opposite from Italians. Whereas Italians share great reverence for certain foods—chiefly pasta—Americans revel in experimentation. Italians proudly identify with the foods grown in their own regions; Americans ship produce across our much larger nation with abandon.

So it's only natural that when pasta arrived in the United States, we took a different tack than Italians. Not only do we serve pasta in ways that are different from what you'd see on an Italian table (such as spaghetti with meatballs and pasta salad with broccoli), but we've invented some new kinds of pasta as well.

Amber Waves of Grain

Although you can use regular semolina pasta for any of the recipes in this chapter, one of the clever things Americans have done in the pasta arena is to create pasta made from grains other than durum wheat, as well as whole-wheat pasta made with all of the durum wheat. You can find a variety of whole-grain pastas in health food stores, including the following:

Brown rice-flour pasta	Pasta made with brown rice flour has an excellent flavor but a slightly sandy texture.
Emmer pasta	Emmer, often indicated by its Italian name, *farro,* is a grain that has been around since Roman times and has recently experienced a resurgence in Italy as well as in the United States. You can sometimes find Italian *farro* pasta in gourmet specialty stores.
Kamut pasta	Kamut pasta is one of the best whole-grain pastas available because it doesn't tend to disintegrate when cooked. Kamut is a grain similar to wheat but with much larger grains.
Mixed whole-grain pasta	A few companies in Italy and the United States combine various whole-grain flours to make pasta. These whole-grain pastas have a pleasant, nutty flavor.
Quinoa pasta	Quinoa (pronounced *keen-wa*) is a tiny grain with an excellent nutritional profile. (It can be a godsend for those allergic to wheat.) Quinoa pasta is made by grinding the grain into flour and then making pasta in the usual way. Quinoa pasta tends to be slightly gritty, which is sometimes an advantage.
Spelt pasta	Spelt is actually a type of wheat, but because of slight differences from regular wheat, it is usually tolerated much better by people who are allergic or sensitive to wheat. Widely available in health food stores and some supermarkets, spelt pasta tastes quite similar to whole-wheat pasta.
Whole durum wheat pasta	The best whole-wheat pasta is made from whole semolina flour. Since Italy is currently experiencing a health food revival, you can sometimes find imported whole-wheat pasta as well as American-made brands. Whole wheat Japanese-style noodles are also tasty but are slightly different; they are made with softer flour and, therefore, result in a more limp texture.

Whole-grain pasta usually cooks more quickly than regular pasta. It also tends to fall apart if it gets even slightly overcooked, so be sure to remove it from the heat as soon as it's *al dente.*

Yankee Doodle Style

Pasta Patter

Stuck a Feather in His Hat: While you may have thought the lyrics to the song *Yankee Doodle Dandy* ("Yankee Doodle went to town/ Riding on a pony/ Stuck a feather in his hat/ And called it macaroni") were a simple nonsense rhyme, they actually had meaning during the American Revolution when the song became popular. In those days, a "macaroni" was a man who dressed in a dapper fashion and often took on a somewhat silly air. The song is teasing Yankee Doodle for believing that simply placing a feather in his hat would make him elegant.

Spaghetti with Meatballs

Many Americans are shocked to learn that this dish, which was once served in every "Italian" restaurant, is unknown in Italy. It's actually a combination of an Italian first course (spaghetti with tomato sauce) and a second course (meatballs) that was most likely cooked up by someone eating in a hurry. For very light-tasting meatballs, replace some or all of the beef with ground veal. To add extra flavor, replace no more than $^1/_4$ lb. of the beef with ground pork.

Spaghetti with meatballs is a wholly American invention.

Serves 4

1 lb. lean ground beef
1 egg, lightly beaten
1 pinch nutmeg
$^1/_2$ cup breadcrumbs
$^1/_2$ cup grated Parmesan cheese
salt and freshly ground pepper to taste

$^1/_4$ cup extra virgin olive oil
3 tablespoons chopped onion
1 clove garlic, minced
3 cups peeled, seeded tomatoes and their juices
1 lb. dried spaghetti

continues

continued

1. To make the meatballs, in a medium bowl combine the beef, egg, nutmeg, breadcrumbs, and Parmesan cheese. Season to taste with salt and pepper. Combine thoroughly using your hands.
2. Shape the meat mixture into meatballs the size of golf balls. Roll them between your hands to make them round.
3. Pour the extra virgin olive oil into a large skillet, and sauté the onion and garlic over medium heat until softened, about 2 minutes.
4. Add the meatballs and cook over medium heat until browned on all sides.
5. Pour off any excess fat. Pour the tomatoes and juices over the meatballs and simmer until the meatballs are cooked through, about 20 minutes.
6. When the meatballs are cooked, cook the spaghetti in abundant boiling water following the instructions on page 12.
7. When the spaghetti is cooked, drain and remove it to a serving bowl. Top with the meatballs and tomato sauce.

Macaroni and Cheese

I don't know why you would eat the orange macaroni and powdered cheese that comes in a box when you can make this recipe. My mother always made this recipe in a deep casserole, but I find that spreading out the macaroni and cheese in a lower, wider pan has two advantages: the dish cooks more quickly, and there's more of that good brown crust.

Serves 6

1 lb. elbow macaroni

6 tablespoons butter

4 tablespoons unbleached flour

4 cups milk

2 cups grated cheddar cheese

2 cups grated mozzarella cheese

salt and freshly ground pepper to taste

1. Preheat the oven to 350 degrees.
2. Cook the macaroni in abundant boiling water following the instructions on page 12.
3. While the macaroni is cooking, use 1 TB. of the butter to grease a 9×13-inch baking pan.
4. Melt 4 tablespoons of butter in a small saucepan. Slowly whisk in the flour. Add the milk a little at a time, stirring between additions. Simmer this mixture until thickened slightly, about 3 minutes.
5. In a large bowl, combine the cooked macaroni, milk mixture, and grated cheese. Mix to combine and season to taste with salt and pepper.
6. Pour the macaroni mixture into the prepared pan. Dot with the remaining 1 tablespoon of butter and bake until the top is browned and crusty, about 35 minutes.

Pasta Salad with Tomatoes

Pasta salad is another one of those pasta dishes that Americans can take credit for. This version, however, may have been influenced by an Italian Jewish dish prepared on Friday afternoon to be eaten on Saturday. You can use almost any short, dried pasta in a pasta salad. Just don't try this with spaghetti or any homemade egg pasta; they get too sticky.

Serves 4

1 lb. dried rotelle or other pasta

$^1/_4$ cup extra virgin olive oil

2 teaspoons balsamic vinegar

4 beefsteak tomatoes, seeded and chopped

1 clove garlic, minced

salt and freshly ground pepper to taste

1 cup loosely packed basil

1. Cook the pasta in abundant boiling water following the instructions on page 12.
2. While the pasta is cooking, whisk together the olive oil and vinegar.
3. Combine the tomatoes and garlic in a serving bowl, season to taste with salt and pepper, and dress with half of the olive oil and vinegar combination.
4. When the pasta is cooked, drain and add it to the bowl. Dress with the remaining olive oil and vinegar and toss to combine.
5. Set the pasta salad aside and allow it to reach room temperature.
6. Just before serving, check that the pasta is not sticking together. If it is, add a small amount of extra virgin olive oil and toss gently. Tear the basil leaves and sprinkle on the pasta. I know a lot of pasta salad recipes call for cooking the pasta and then running it under cold water to cool it off. I've never done that without ending up with pasta that sticks together and tastes slightly slimy. This salad is meant to be served at room temperature; it shouldn't be ice cold! For that same reason (and because it does a disservice to tomatoes) don't refrigerate this salad. Simply make it an hour or two before you wish to serve it.

Rice Pasta Salad with Broccoli

Here's a pasta salad that uses Asian flavors.

Serves 4

1 head broccoli

1 lb. dried brown rice penne or other dried pasta

4 scallions, sliced

juice of 1 lemon

$^1/_3$ cup sesame oil

1 tablespoon toasted sesame oil

salt and freshly ground pepper to taste

2 tablespoons toasted sesame seeds

1. Separate the broccoli florets and stalks. Break the florets into small pieces. Cut the stalks into slices about $^1/_2$-inch thick and 1-inch long.

continues

249

continued

2. Bring a large pot of water to a boil and add the stalks. Allow the water to return to a boil and cook for 1 minute. Add the florets and cook for an additional 4 minutes, or until the stalks and florets are tender.

3. Use a slotted spoon to remove the broccoli to a colander. Shock the broccoli with cold water and drain.

4. When the water returns to a boil, cook the pasta following the instructions on page 12.

5. In a large serving bowl, toss the broccoli, cooked pasta, and scallions with the lemon juice, sesame oil, and toasted sesame oil. Season to taste with salt and pepper. Set the pasta salad aside to cool.

6. Just before serving, check that the pasta is not sticking together. If it is, add a small amount of oil and toss gently. Sprinkle the sesame seeds on the pasta. This is a very simple, "lemony" pasta salad. You can make the Asian flavors more pronounced by adding some grated ginger, soy sauce, or rice vinegar.

Whole Wheat Pasta with Roasted Vegetables

There is nothing quite like the aroma of roasting vegetables. Although this recipe requires a lot of cutting and chopping, once the vegetables are in the oven, your work is practically finished.

Serves 4

2 carrots, peeled and chopped

1 small butternut squash, peeled, seeds and strings discarded, chopped

1 bulb fennel, trimmed and chopped

2 parsnips, peeled and chopped

1 onion, chopped

5 cloves garlic, peeled

4 tablespoons extra virgin olive oil

1 tablespoon balsamic vinegar

salt and freshly ground pepper to taste

1 lb. whole wheat penne or other short pasta

1/4 cup chopped parsley

1. Preheat the oven to 450 degrees.

2. In a large baking pan, toss the carrots, squash, fennel, parsnips, onion, and garlic cloves with 3 tablespoons of the olive oil and the vinegar. Season to taste with salt and pepper.

3. Roast the vegetables until they are caramelized and soft, about 1 hour.

4. When the vegetables are almost ready, cook the pasta in abundant boiling water following the instructions on page 12.

5. In a serving bowl, toss the pasta with the roasted vegetables. Drizzle on the remaining 1 tablespoon of olive oil and sprinkle with parsley. Don't be alarmed by the whole garlic cloves in this recipe. Once roasted they turn sweet and are not at all sharp-tasting. Feel free to substitute any other root vegetables (beets, rutabagas, sweet potatoes) or to double the batch and eat the roasted vegetables on their own the next day. They are fabulous.

Southwestern Quinoa Pasta

The spicy flavors of the American southwest lend themselves particularly well to whole-grain pastas. Canned beans work well in this recipe. One 15-oz. can equals just about 2 cups. Rinse canned beans well before using.

Serves 4

1 lb. quinoa pasta or other whole-grain pasta	1 cup fresh or frozen corn kernels
2 cloves garlic, minced	2 cups cooked black beans
2 scallions, sliced	1 tablespoon lime juice
1 small red chile pepper, minced	salt and freshly ground pepper to taste
1/4 cup extra virgin olive oil	

1. Cook the pasta in abundant boiling water following the instructions on page 12.
2. Meanwhile, in a large skillet over medium heat, sauté the garlic, scallions, and chile pepper in the olive oil until softened, about 2 minutes.
3. Add the corn kernels and sauté until cooked through, about 4 minutes.
4. Add the black beans to the skillet and heat through.
5. When the pasta is cooked, drain and transfer it to the skillet. Toss briefly over medium heat to coat the pasta. Drizzle on the lime juice and toss again. Season to taste with salt and pepper.

The Least You Need to Know

➤ Pasta made from a wide range of flours other than wheat is available.

Stuck a Feather in His Hat and Called It *What?*

Al Dente in Italian literally means "to the tooth," indicating that pasta cooked in this manner should still boast some resistance so that it sticks to your teeth a little as you eat it rather than simply dissolving into mush on your tongue.

Arrabbiata is the Italian word for "angry." When talking about pasta, it refers to a type of tomato sauce with a large quantity of hot pepper.

Arrowroot Noodles are slightly sandy-colored noodles made with arrowroot starch. They have a somewhat sweeter taste than regular wheat noodles. Arrowroot noodles hail from China's Szechuan province.

Balsamic Vinegar is made from Italian Trebbiano grapes aged through a highly specialized process. It has a distinctive, slightly sweet flavor. You can purchase balsamic vinegar in gourmet specialty stores.

Bean Thread Noodles (also known as *cellophane noodles, mung bean noodles, glass noodles,* and *slippery noodles*) are made from mung bean starch. They are thin like Italian *vermicelli* and are usually looped together and then dried so that they are entwined in their packages. Bean thread noodles are used throughout Asia.

Bonito Flakes are shavings of dried fish (bonito is from the tuna family). They can be purchased in Asian grocery stores and some health food stores.

Borlotti Beans are brown beans with red markings related to kidney beans. They are sometimes labeled as cranberry or romano beans. Borlotti beans are available dried year-round and may be purchased fresh in their pods in some areas in the spring.

Broad Bean Noodles are bean thread noodles that are flat and wide, similar in shape to Italian *fettuccine.* They are Chinese in origin but used in most Asian countries.

Broad Rice Noodles are sold both fresh and dried. Sometimes the fresh noodles are sold in sheets and must be cut to the appropriate width. Broad rice noodles have a pleasantly glutinous texture and a sweet taste. They work well in stir fries because they both absorb sauces and retain their shape. Broad rice noodles are featured in most Asian cuisines and are crucial to Vietnamese cooking.

Brown Rice Flour Pasta has a slightly sandy texture, but an excellent flavor.

Cannellini Beans are about $1/2$ inch long, white, and creamy and nutty when cooked. Cannellini beans are available dried year-round and may be sold fresh in their pods in the spring in some areas.

Cannelloni means "tubes" or "pipes," which perfectly describes the shape of these large, cylindrical pieces of Italian pasta.

Cappellacci means "big hats" in Italian. They are a larger version of *cappelletti*.

Cappelletti means "little hats," and once you've made this kind of pasta you'll see why. The finished product looks like miniature tri-cornered hats.

Cha-Soba are Japanese buckwheat (soba) noodles flavored with green tea. They have an unusual color and a delicate taste that can get lost in a heavy sauce. Therefore, cha-soba are usually served cold with a dipping sauce or in a lightly seasoned broth. Other, more unusual soba noodle flavorings include lemon zest and black sesame seeds.

Couscous is a North African pasta consisting of small pellets of semolina flour. The word derives from the Arabic word meaning "to pound," because couscous is made by pounding a semolina dough through a sieve.

D.O.C. stands for *denominazione di origine controllata*, or "regulated title." D.O.C. (pronounced "doak") has also come to mean "excellent" in Italian slang. To say, for example, that friends have a D.O.C. house is to pay them a great compliment. Look for this abbreviation on wine labels and some other Italian products.

Durum Wheat (its Latin name is *triticum durum*) is a spring wheat that yields a hard flour used mostly to make pasta. The word *durum* is Latin for "hard."

Emmer, often indicated by its Italian name, *farro,* is a grain that has been around since Roman times and has recently experienced a resurgence in Italy as well as in the United States. You will sometimes find Italian farro pasta in gourmet specialty stores.

Erbe Aromatiche are the Italian herbs oregano, basil, and parsley in their fresh (not dried) form. As the name implies, they possess a heavenly smell.

Farfalle are butterfly-shaped pasta (sometimes called "bow ties" in the United States).

Farfel are small pieces of egg pasta most often served in soup. A farfel box is sometimes labeled "egg barley," not because it contains barley, but because its small pieces resemble that grain.

Fennel is a versatile vegetable that comes in the form of a bulb with fern-like fronds. It tastes like licorice when eaten raw but is much milder when cooked.

Feta is a salty, white, sheep's milk cheese from Greece. *Feta* means "slice" in Greek. Feta cheese is cut into large slices before being stored in brine for a month.

Fettuccine are medium-width egg noodles. Their name in Italian literally means "little ribbons."

Fidellos, sometimes spelled *fideos* or *fideus,* are very fine Spanish noodles that are sautéed briefly before being cooked.

Fontina is a very mild cheese from northern Italy's Val d'Aosta region. It is similar to Swiss cheese in taste but less tangy and without the holes. Slices of fontina melt very well, making it ideal for omelets and grilled sandwiches.

Formaggio Parmigiano Reggiano literally translates as "cheese from Parma and Reggio." True Parmesan cheese (in English we've dropped the reference to Reggio) comes from the provinces of those two cities in the Emilia region. Buy your Parmesan cheese in large blocks from a cheese store rather than in a tin from the supermarket.

Gemelli is the Italian word for "twins." This thick pasta gets its name from the two strands that twist together to form each individual piece.

Gnocchi are Italian dumplings, usually made of potatoes. The word *gnocco* (the singular form) means "lump," like the kind you get when you bang your head, or "blockhead."

Gorgonzola is an Italian blue cheese best identified by its pungent smell. Gorgonzola can be used very sparingly in salads. It is crumbly, with greenish veins running through it. Gorgonzola is usually made in the region of Lombardy (where the town of Gorgonzola is located).

Grana Padano is a hard Italian cheese similar to Parmesan cheese. It can sometimes serve as a substitute when Parmesan is not available.

Harissa is a spicy Tunisian sauce that enlivens many North African dishes (and others as well).

Harusame is the Japanese name for bean thread noodles. Presumably, the name, which means "spring rain," refers to the light texture and subtle flavor of these noodles.

Kamut Pasta is one of the best whole-grain pastas available, as it doesn't tend to disintegrate when cooked. Kamut is a grain similar to wheat but with much larger grains.

Kasseri is a fresh Greek cheese. It is soft and crumbly and has a mild taste.

Kefalotyri is considered the Greek version of Italy's Parmesan cheese. It is a semi-hard yellow cheese that is usually grated.

Ketjap Manis is Indonesian soy sauce. It is more viscous and sweet, however, than regular Chinese or Japanese soy sauce.

Kombu is seaweed that is added to stocks for its slightly salty flavor. It is also thrown into the pot when grains or beans are cooking because it both boosts their nutritional content and adds flavor.

Kugel is an Eastern European Jewish baked pudding that can be made with potatoes, bread, rice, noodles, or other ingredients. A kugel may be sweet or savory.

Lo mein refers to all stir-fried noodle dishes coated with a sauce. Chinese wheat noodles are also called *lo mein.*

Macaroni (the Italian spelling is *maccheroni,* but the pronunciation is basically the same) refers to noodles of all types made from flour and water.

Maltagliati are irregular pieces of pasta that are usually cooked in soup. The Italian word means "poorly cut."

Matzoh meal is made by grinding matzoh, the unleavened bread that Jews eat during Passover.

Mirin is sweet Japanese cooking wine. It differs from sake because it is distilled after fermentation.

Mixed Whole Grain Pasta is made by a few companies in Italy and the United States. These whole grain pastas have a pleasantly nutty flavor.

Mom Tom is a very salty and fishy shrimp sauce from Vietnam.

Mozzarella is probably best known in the United States for its use on pizza. In Italy, however, the best mozzarella—*mozzarella di bufala,* or buffalo's milk mozzarella—is sliced and served as a table cheese either on its own or with sliced tomatoes.

Nam Pla, or Thai fish sauce, is similar to soy sauce but made with dried fish. While it smells fishy in the bottle, it doesn't have a strong fish taste.

Noodles usually refers to all kinds of long, ribbon-like pastas. The word derives from the German *nudel,* which in turn probably came from the Latin *nodus,* meaning "node."

Nori is the seaweed that is wrapped around sushi.

Nuoc Leo, or Vietnamese peanut sauce, is normally used for dipping items such as vegetables wrapped in rice papers.

Nuoc Mam, or Vietnamese fish sauce, differs slightly from Thai fish sauce (*nam pla*), but they may be used interchangeably.

Orecchiette means "little ears," and that's just what this pasta—native to the Italian region of Apulia—is shaped like.

Orzo means "barley" in Italian. These small pieces of pasta do look like grains; they are small and almond-shaped.

Pad Thai literally means "soft noodles." This stir-fry of rice noodles, vegetables, shrimp, and sometimes chicken is one of Thailand's signature dishes.

Pancetta, rolled and cured Italian bacon, makes a savory addition to many dishes. It is available in specialty stores.

Panna is the Italian word for cream.

Parmesan cheese, see **Formaggio Parmigiano Reggiano**

Pasta Artigianale is dried pasta that is made with brass-coated machinery and then air dried. It is usually made of higher quality semolina flour than regular dried pasta.

Pasticciato, in Italian, indicates something that has been made a mess of. A pasta dish with this name usually has a little of everything that might be thrown over pasta: olive oil, tomato, garlic, and cream.

Pastina is the generic term for small types of pasta made for soup. There are endless varieties, with most of their names ending *-ini* or *-ine* (the Italian diminutive). Some of the more common types are *acini di pepe, anellini, ditalini, stelline, farfalline,* and *quadratini.*

Pecorino is sheep's milk cheese (*pecora* is the Italian word for sheep). It comes in many forms. Fresh pecorino is mild and soft, almost white in color. Pecorino can also be aged; it not only grows harder but develops a sharper flavor as well. Usually, what we see labeled as "pecorino" is really *pecorino romano,* a very tangy grating cheese.

Perciatelli are long pasta, similar to spaghetti, with a hole running down the middle. They are sometimes called *bucatini.*

Pomodoro is the Italian word for "tomato." It literally means "golden apple."

Prosciutto cotto is ham that has been baked rather than salted and air-cured like *prosciutto crudo.*

Quinoa pasta is made from quinoa (pronounced *keen wa*), a tiny grain with an excellent nutritional profile. Quinoa pasta is made by grinding the grain into flour and then making pasta in the usual way. Quinoa pasta tends to be slightly gritty—sometimes an advantage—and can be a godsend for those who are sensitive or allergic to wheat.

Ragú (tomato-flavored meat sauce) is an ancient food, with recipes dating all the way back to the sixteenth century. Early versions were usually sweet.

Ravioli are square pillows of pasta usually filled with some type of greens. The name derives from the Genoese dialect word *rabiole,* meaning "rubbish." Presumably, these tasty squares were a handy way for using leftovers.

Rice Sticks are noodles about the same size as Italian *fettuccine.* They are usually flat but can also be round. Like bean thread noodles, rice sticks are wrapped around each other to dry and are hard to break or separate when uncooked. Rice sticks are used in China, Indonesia, Vietnam, and Malaysia; they are the central players in the classic Thai noodle dish Pad Thai. They are an opaque white when dry, but as they cook their color lightens and they become transparent.

Rice Vermicelli are very thin rice noodles. These fine noodles can be used cold in salads or hot in soups and stir-fries. In some dishes, they are fried in one large clump, in which case they expand dramatically and turn quite crunchy.

Ricotta is actually not a cheese in itself, but is made from whey, a byproduct of cheese making. Both cow's milk and sheep's milk ricotta are available.

Rotelle are small, circular pasta that are sometimes called "wagon wheels."

Sale Grosso, literally "big salt," is the rock salt used for cooking pasta.

Sale Tino is table salt.

Savoy Cabbage, also known as *curly cabbage,* is a ruffled, green cabbage. It remains bright green when cooked and has a less gassy aroma than other cabbages.

Semolina Flour is milled from durum wheat. It has a coarser consistency than all-purpose white flour, as well as a rich yellow color. Occasionally, packages of semolina flour are labeled simply "pasta flour," although it is also used in certain breads and desserts, usually in combination with white flour.

Soba noodles are made of buckwheat flour and are one of Japan's great delicacies. They come in long strands much like Italian spaghetti. Soba are served both hot (in broth) and cold (with dipping sauce on the side). The buckwheat provides an appealing flavor and brown color, and it's a nutritional powerhouse as well. *Soba* refers both to Japanese noodles made of buckwheat and to the buckwheat itself.

Somen are thin Japanese wheat noodles with a small amount of oil incorporated in the dough. They are very thin and fine and, therefore, very fragile. Somen appear most often in cold dishes such as salads. Like soba, somen can also be served cold with dipping sauce on the side.

Spaetzle are small noodles that are usually served as a side dish. The word *spaetzle* means "little sparrow" in German.

A **spaghettata** is a late-night snack in Italy consisting of simply prepared spaghetti, usually shared after a night on the town.

Spelt pasta is made from spelt, a type of wheat that, because of slight differences from regular wheat, is usually tolerated much better by people who are allergic or sensitive to wheat.

Stracchino, which is also known as *crescenza,* is a smooth, slightly tangy Italian cheese that has a consistency somewhere between cream cheese and sour cream. It is most often eaten on its own, spread on bread or crackers, but it can also be used in baked pasta dishes.

Stracci are irregular pieces of pasta, usually cooked in soup. The Italian word means "rags."

Thin Chinese Egg Noodles are bright yellow in color. Good quality Chinese egg noodles are made with flour and egg, but some lesser quality brands add yellow food coloring, so check the list of ingredients before purchasing anything. Although some cookbooks suggest spaghetti as a substitute, packaged spaghetti are made from a semolina-and-water dough and won't have that same eggy flavor. Thin Chinese egg noodles can be served in soups or stir-fries. They are deliciously crisp when fried into a "nest" for vegetables or fish.

Thin Chinese Wheat Noodles are made from the same ingredients as those used for Italian dried pasta but are worked in a slightly different manner, with the dough being stretched out in long skeins. In China, thin wheat noodles are eaten primarily in soups and stir-fried dishes.

Trenette are noodles that are slightly more narrow than tagliatelle.

Truffles are a kind of fungus with a distinctive taste and smell. They are similar to mushrooms but with a much headier perfume. Fresh truffles are extremely expensive, but canned truffles—more reasonable but still not cheap—can be found in gourmet stores.

Tuong Ot is a hot chile sauce from Vietnam that is similar to Thai chili paste.

Udon are sturdy Japanese wheat noodles that offer a firm, chewy mouthful. Udon, which are usually as wide as they are high, are available dried in Asian groceries or are often sold in frozen form as well. In Japan, udon are served hot in broth in the winter months and cold with dipping sauce in the summer.

Wasabi is often confused with horseradish because it has the same strong, sinus-clearing taste. Fresh wasabi root is unavailable outside of Japan, so you have the choice of either buying wasabi paste in a tube or pale green wasabi powder, which needs to be mixed with water. (I prefer the latter.) Wasabi powder loses strength as it is exposed to air, so opt for small individual foil packets of powder rather than a larger tin.

Whole Durum Wheat Pasta is made from whole semolina flour. Since Italy is currently experiencing a health food revival, you can sometimes find imported whole wheat pasta as well as American-made brands. Whole wheat Japanese noodles are also tasty but slightly different; they are made with softer flour and, therefore, result in a limper texture.

Wide Chinese Egg Noodles are bright yellow like thin Chinese egg noodles. As with thin Chinese egg noodles, commercial brands sometimes contain food coloring. Wide Chinese egg noodles are often dipped in oil before being packaged, so they should be rinsed well before incorporated into any recipe. Wide egg noodles are used in China, Thailand, Malaysia, and Indonesia.

Wide Chinese Wheat Noodles most often appear in soups. They range from $1/4$ inch to $1/2$ inch in width and are widely available in dried form. Some Asian groceries may also stock packages of wide Chinese wheat noodles in the refrigerated section.

Pasta By Special Delivery: Mail-Order Sources

Balducci's
424 Sixth Avenue
New York, NY 10011
800-225-3822

Dean & DeLuca
560 Broadway
New York, NY 10012
212-226-6800

Sunrise Mart
43 East 9th Street
New York, NY
212-598-3040

Vivande
2125 Fillmore Street
San Francisco, CA 94115
415-346-4430

Zingerman's
422 Detroit Street
Ann Arbor, MI 48104
888-636-8162

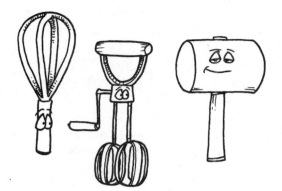

Kitchen Tools and Techniques

Here is some general cooking information that may help you with the recipes in this book.

Baking is cooking food in an oven.

A **baking dish** may be made of glass, ceramic, or even cast iron.

Blanching means immersing food in boiling water for a few minutes, then immersing it in cold water to stop cooking.

To **boil Asian noodles**, bring a large pot of water to a rapid boil. Add the noodles then stir often to separate them. Taste often to check for doneness. Drain and serve immediately, or toss with a few tablespoons of oil to keep separate.

To **boil Japanese noodles**, fill a large pot about 3/4 full with water. Bring the water to a rapid boil before adding noodles. Add the noodles then stir often to separate them. When water returns to a boil, add a glass of cold water and stir noodles. When water returns to a boil, add another glass of cold water and stir noodles. When water returns to a boil, taste noodles. If they are not ready, add another glass of cold water and stir noodles. When noodles are cooked, rinse with hot or cold water (depending on whether they are meant to be served hot or cold), drain, and serve immediately, or toss with a few tablespoons of oil to keep separate.

Boiling is cooking food in boiling water for an extended period.

Foods that are **browned** are cooked—in a skillet, oven, or broiler—until the surface turns brown.

To **brown Asian noodles,** cook or soften noodles. Drain noodles and pat dry. Toss noodles with a small amount of oil. Shape noodles as you wish. You can either use them in a single disk (use a pie plate for shaping them this way) or in individual baskets (called bird's nests) or one large basket. Pan-fry noodle disks in wok. Immerse bird's nests in oil. Brown on one side (this should take about 7 minutes), then flip and brown on the other side. If making bird's nests, remove from wire baskets after they are browned on one side and brown on remaining sides. They should hold their shape. Browned noodles can be kept warm in an oven until needed.

Chopping is cutting food into pieces. Sometimes a recipe will specify whether to chop roughly (into large pieces) or finely (into small pieces). If no size is specified, chop the food into medium pieces.

To **clean anchovies preserved in salt**, rinse off the salty coating, then use a small paring knife to slice off the head and tail. Finally, slice the anchovy in half and remove the spine and bones. Don't worry too much about any small bones left behind; they tend to dissolve when cooked.

To **clean and bone fresh sardines**, chop off the heads and pull off the fins. With the tip of a small paring knife, cut a slit down the belly-side of each sardine. Open the fish up and lift out the spine and attached bones. They should come out cleanly.

To **clean baby artichokes**, work with one at a time. First, remove all of the hard outer leaves (you will feel as though you are throwing away a lot, but don't worry), then slice off the pointy top. There should not be any fuzzy choke inside baby artichokes, but occasionally a downy layer does grow there. Use the tip of a small paring knife to remove any hairy growth. Peel the stem and bowl-like bottom of the artichoke. Drop prepared artichokes into a bowl of cold water with a liberal dose of lemon juice to keep them from discoloring.

To **clean clams**, soak them in several changes of cold water until no sand appears at the bottom of the bowl. Scrub each clam briefly under cold running water.

To **clean mussels**, scrub each one under cold running water with a stiff brush. Remove the thick beard from each mussel with a knife, or simply by yanking it firmly with one hand while holding the mussel with the other.

A **colander** is a large bowl made of either metal or plastic and poked with holes. It's used for draining cooked pasta. You place the colander in the sink and pour the cooked pasta and water out of the pot. The water runs through the holes and down the drain. The pasta is ready to go.

To **cook lentils**, rinse them, check through them for any small pebbles, then simmer them in water (or stock if you prefer) until they are tender, about 30 to 45 minutes. Test a spoonful of lentils when checking for doneness.

Coring is cutting a fruit or vegetable and cutting out the inedible core.

You will **crumble** certain cheeses before using them. You can use your hands to do this, or break the cheese up with a knife and it will crumble into smaller pieces.

To **crush a clove of garlic**, remove the papery skin on the outside of the garlic. Place the clove flat on a cutting board. Rest the side of a cleaver on the clove and press down firmly with the heel of your hand.

Some leafy greens are **cut into ribbons** before being added to a dish. Stack the leaves in a pile and use a sharp knife to slice them into strips about 1/2-inch wide.

Dicing is cutting a food into cubes. The sides of the cubes should be about 1/2 inch unless otherwise specified.

A **double boiler** has two parts: the bottom of the double boiler is filled with water so that food can be reheated gently in the top.

Draining is allowing liquid to run out of something. Usually pasta is drained in a colander.

A **dry measuring cup** should be a scoop made of metal or plastic with "1 cup" marked on it somewhere. To use it, either sweep the measuring cup into a container of flour and bring it up full, or gently spoon flour into the measuring cup until it is full. The flour should rest in a mound that is higher than the top of the measuring cup. Hold the measuring cup over the flour container (or over a sheet of wax paper). Grasp a knife in your other hand and hold the blade vertically with the blunt side against the edge of the measuring cup closest to you. Briskly sweep the knife across the top of the measuring cup so that the excess flour either spills back into the flour container or onto the wax paper. If using the wax paper method, pinch one side of the piece of paper to create a "spout" and pour the flour back into your flour container.

When you are told to **drizzle** a liquid onto a dish (usually olive oil), you should add it slowly in a thin stream, moving your hand around as you pour so that it doesn't pool in one place.

An **electric pasta machine** is a gadget that kneads pasta dough and extrudes it to form noodles.

A **food mill** simultaneously purées food and removes any seeds or skins. A food mill is often preferable to a food processor because it creates a coarser purée. In addition to tomato purée, food mills are handy when making applesauce and soup.

A **food processor** is an electric machine that grates, kneads, chops, minces, and does even more if you outfit it with various blades.

To **fry Asian noodles**, heat a wok or skillet (any skillet you use should be deep and heavy, preferably cast-iron) over high heat until a drop of water dances on the surface. Fill the wok or skillet with enough oil to submerge the noodles halfway (about 2 cups should be enough for a 2-ounce bundle). Heat the oil until almost smoking, about 425 degrees. Add noodles to pan. Be very careful to avoid splatters. When noodles have browned and puffed, which should take about 5 seconds, use a large spatula to turn them over. When noodles are cooked on both sides, remove with a skimmer or slotted spoon. Transfer noodles to a brown paper bag or paper towels to drain.

A **grater** is a piece of metal with holes that are rough on one side. You rub the item—usually cheese—to be grated against the rough side of the holes, and bits of it fall through onto a plate. Each side of a four-sided grater has differently sized holes; the smallest are ideal for grating hard cheeses such as Parmesan, while the largest are better for shredding soft cheeses such as mozzarella.

Grilling is cooking food close to an open flame.

A **hand-cranked pasta machine** both flattens out pasta dough and cuts the dough into noodles. The slot for flattening out pasta dough is opened and closed in increments using a notched wheel. The machine should be outfitted with various size cutters; you choose the size by setting the crank in the correct indentation.

To **knead pasta dough**, press into the ball of dough with the heel of your hand and push away from yourself. Next, fold the far end of the dough back over the top of the dough and turn it a quarter-turn. Repeat this action of pushing into the dough, folding it, and turning it. This will go fastest if you use one hand to press and the other to fold. The dough may feel resistant at first, but it will grow more tender as you work it. Kneading takes a fair amount of strength—don't worry about being too rough with your dough.

A **ladle** is a spoon with a very deep bowl usually used to serve soup.

A **liquid measuring cup** is made of glass or plastic and has a spout and has various measurements marked on its side.

Mincing is chopping food very finely. Garlic is often minced.

A **mortar and pestle** are ancient tools—basically a fancy bowl and a stubby stick—used to pound and rub ingredients into a paste.

A **paring knife** is a knife with a small, thin blade that can be used not only for paring, but for mincing, slicing, and dicing. It is indispensable.

A **pastry crimper** is a small wheel with a handle. The crimper cuts and seals at the same time.

Peeling is removing the outer layer of a fruit or vegetable. In most cases, you can do this with a vegetable peeler or a paring knife.

A **pinch** is just what it sounds like: the amount of an ingredient that you can pick up between your index finger and thumb.

To **pit olives**, make a slit in each olive using a paring knife and squeeze out the pits. Alternately, you can use a specially designed olive pitter to squeeze out the pits.

To **press tofu**, place the block of tofu between two plates and weight the top plate with something heavy (a full can or a bag of beans). Let the tofu sit like this for about 30 minutes, but tilt the plates to drain the water every 10 minutes or so.

Reducing a sauce means simmering it so that some of the liquid evaporates. The sauce then thickens.

To **reheat Asian noodles**, place them in a large wire strainer or colander and set the strainer in boiling water so that the noodles are immersed. Stir noodles with a long-handled wooden fork. It should take about 20 seconds for them to heat up and separate. Remove the strainer immediately and rinse noodles.

A **ricer** is a press that includes a disk with holes. Food (usually potatoes) is placed inside the press and forced through the holes.

You will need to **rinse** some canned and salted foods (such as capers) before adding them to a dish. To do this, place the item in question in a strainer and run water over it. Allow the water to drain out, shaking the strainer a few times to facilitate this. If you want the food to be absolutely dry, blot it with paper towels.

Roasting is cooking food in the oven.

Sautéing food is cooking it on a stove with some form of fat over medium or medium-high heat.

Seeding means removing the seeds from a fruit or vegetable.

A **serrated knife** has a ridged blade with teeth.

To **shell and devein shrimp,** insert a small paring knife under the back of the shell and pull upwards. The shell should split, and you can now remove it easily. Next, cut a slit down the back of the shrimp with the knife and remove the thin black thread (the shrimp's intestinal tract). Pull off tail unless recipe indicates otherwise.

Shredding means cutting food into long, thin strips.

When food is **simmering**, it is hot but not boiling. A few bubbles should rise to the surface at a time.

A **skillet** (sometimes called a frying pan) is a wide pan with low sides. A well-stocked kitchen will probably have both a 10-inch and a 12-inch skillet. The larger size is preferable for recipes in which pasta is cooked and then tossed in a skillet with its sauce. The smaller size is fine for sautéing vegetables and reducing cream sauces.

A **slotted spoon** has holes in it so that liquid drains out.

To **soak Asian noodles,** place noodles in a large, heat-proof bowl. Pour on enough boiling water to cover the noodles. Set bowl aside until noodles have softened. This should take anywhere from 8 to 15 minutes. When noodles are cooked, drain.

To **soak dried beans** before cooking, first look through the beans and eliminate any small pebbles. Then, rinse the beans once or twice to remove dust. Place beans in a large bowl and add a large amount of cold water. The beans should be well covered. (If you live in a warm climate or will be soaking the beans for more than eight hours, refrigerate them to avoid the growth of bacteria. If bacteria do grow in your bean bowl, the water will smell sour.) Before cooking the beans, drain the soaking water and rinse the beans one more time.

Steaming is usually cooking food in a basket set above boiling water. Sometimes tender greens such as spinach are steamed in the water that remains on their leaves after rinsing. In that case, you don't need a basket. To steam tender greens, first clean the leaves by soaking them in abundant water in a large bowl or tub. Continue to lift the leaves gently out of the water, fill the bowl or tub with clean water, and return the leaves to the clean water until no more sand rests at the bottom of the bowl when you remove the spinach. (Even if you are using pre-cleaned greens, rinse them once.) Shake excess water off the leaves, then place the damp leaves in a pot and cook over medium-low heat, covered, until leaves have wilted.

Stir-frying is a cooking technique that is exactly what it sounds like: you will be "frying" food (albeit in a very small amount of oil) while stirring it constantly. The stir-fry motion is as follows: use a stir-fry spatula to push food out of the center of the wok or very large skillet and up against the walls of the wok, then remove the spatula and allow the food to fall back down to the bottom.

A **stock pot** is a large pot with high sides and a capacity of about 8 quarts.

A **strainer** is usually a cup-shaped piece of equipment made of wire woven together so that you can scoop items out of water. It works like a colander—liquid runs through the holes and the items you are scooping remains in the strainer.

When you cut something into **strips**, the pieces should be about 2 inches long and 1 inch wide, unless the recipe indicates otherwise.

When a recipe calls for **tomatoes and their juice**, you don't want to use all the juice from a can of tomatoes. If you are using 2 or 3 cups, about 1/4 cup should be juice.

To taste means that you can add as much or as little of an ingredient (usually salt and pepper) as you like. In most cases, 1/4 to 1/2 teaspoon of salt and 1/8 to 1/4 teaspoon of pepper is about right, but "to taste" really means just that—taste the food and add a small amount of salt and pepper at a time until you like the balance.

To **toast nuts and seeds**, spread them on a tray and bake at 350 degrees (the toaster oven works well) for about 4 to 8 minutes, shaking the tray often to be sure they don't burn. Alternately, toast nuts and seeds in a small skillet over low heat. Shake the skillet often and remove nuts and seeds before they are fully toasted as they will continue to cook until cool.

Pork products such as prosciutto are often **trimmed.** This just means that you should cut off any visible fat, especially around the edge, before using them.

A **well of flour** is a mound of flour with a deep indentation in the center.

Whisking is stirring with a wire whisk.

A **wok** is a pot shaped like an inverted dome. It heats up quickly and is extremely fuel efficient.

Wooden spoons are essential for cooking pasta and noodles. They can also be used for sautéing and they will not damage metal pots and pans.

Some Suggested Menus

Virtually any recipe in this book would pair up with a salad and some fruit to make a nice light meal. If you are feeling more ambitious, try one of the following menus:

Traditional Sunday Dinner

Lasagne (Chapter 11, page 113)
roasted rabbit or chicken
roasted potatoes
spinach sautéed with garlic
pastries

Italian Vegetarian Lunch

vegetable antipasto
Pasta with Lentils (Chapter 8, page 92)
baked apples

Lunch at the Beach House

seafood salad
Linguine with Clams (Chapter 6, page 63)
grilled shrimp on skewers
ice cream

Sick-in-Bed Dinner

Pasta in Bianco (Chapter 5, page 52)
fruit-flavored gelatin

Diet-Is-Over Dinner

chicken liver crostini
Maccheroncini with Four Cheeses (Chapter 4, page 39)
breaded veal cutlets
chocolate mousse

Warm-Me-Up Winter Dinner

Pizzoccheri Valtellina Style (Chapter 11, page 120)
eggplant Parmesan
mashed potatoes
pears in syrup

Sophisticated Dinner

onion tartlets
Tagliatelle with Caviar (Chapter 14, page 156)
cheese course
biscotti and vin santo

Sophisticated-But-Easy Dinner

Maccheroncini with Radicchio (Chapter 9, page 96)
salad of fennel, beets, and Parmesan cheese
fruit compote

Country-Style Lunch

varied sliced meats (prosciutto, salami, and so forth)
Pasta and Bean Soup (Chapter 14, page 152)
roasted chicken
green salad
fresh fruit

City-Style Lunch

Fusilli with Spicy Carrots (Chapter 6, page 65)
grilled chicken breasts
arugula salad
pears and Parmesan cheese

Japanese Relaxation Dinner

sweet omelet
Soba in Broth (Chapter 19, page 199)
green tea ice cream with red bean sauce

Chinese Celebration Lunch

Chicken Lo Mein (Chapter 18, page 190)
beef with orange sauce
stir-fried string beans
plain rice
pineapple

Thai Buffet

Pad Thai (Chapter 20, page 208)
Lard Nar (Chapter 20, page 210)
stir-fried vegetables
stir-fried shrimp
ice cream

Greek Family Get-Together

Pastitsio (Chapter 21, page 220)
roasted lamb
green salad with grated carrots
honey-flavored cookies

American Lunch on the Patio

Rice Pasta Salad with Broccoli (Chapter 25, page 249)
grilled zucchini and eggplant
strawberry shortcake

Additional Sources

These are some of my favorite books about pasta and noodles.

Asian Noodles, by Nina Simonds (New York: Hearst Books, 1997). This is a fun introduction to the various Asian noodles. It's a beautifully designed book as well.

The Authentic Pasta Book, by Fred Plotkin (New York: Simon & Schuster, 1985). Unfortunately, this book is out-of-print and difficult to find. If you see a used copy, snatch it up.

The Book of Soba, by James Udesky (New York: Kodansha International, 1988). This book is the top resource on the history and preparation of Japan's famous noodles.

Essentials of Classic Italian Cooking, by Marcella Hazan (New York: Knopf, 1992). This is, in my opinion, the best book ever written in English about Italian cooking. Naturally, the sections on pasta are extremely complete.

The Splendid Table, by Lynne Rossetto Kasper (New York: William Morrow and Company, 1992). This impressively wide-ranging book covers the food of Italy's Emilia-Romagna region and that region's homemade pasta.

Zuppa!: Soups from the Italian Countryside, by Anne Bianchi (New York: Ecco, 1996). Anne Bianchi writes fabulous books about honest, hearty Italian cooking; this one is no exception.

Index

284

Spaghetti con il Tonno
(Spaghetti with Tuna), 89
Spaghetti with Meatballs,
247–248
Spinach Pasta Dough,
144–145
Sweet Couscous, 244
Szechuan Noodles with
Vegetables, 194
Tagliatelle al Caviale
(Tagliatelle with
Caviar), 156
Tagliatelle con i Fagioli
(Tagliatelle with
Beans), 155
Tortellini (Tortellini), 168
Trenette al Pesto (Trenette
with Pesto), 156–157
Udon in Broth, 201–202
Udon with Sesame
Sauce, 202
Vegetable Couscous, 243
Vegetable Noodle Kugel, 235
Whole Wheat Pasta with
Roasted Vegetables, 250
Zuppa di Cannellini e
Bietole (Cannellini Bean
and Chard Soup), 109
Zuppa di Ceci (Chick Pea
Soup), 153–154
reducing, 266
regional pasta, 124–126
reheating, Asian noodles,
185, 266
Rice Pasta Salad with Broccoli,
American cuisine (recipe),
249–250
rice sticks, 180
Asian cuisine, 257
rice vermicelli, 180
Asian cuisine, 257
ricers, 267
ricotta, 37, 258
rinsing, 267
roasting
cooking techniques, 60
cooking terms, 267

rock salt, 10
rolling out homemade pasta,
146–148
rolling pins, 130
Roma tomatoes, 72
Romans, olive oil, 45
Ronzoni, 21–22
rotelle, 258
Rotelle con Lenticchie e Bietole
(Rotelle with Lentils and
Swiss Chard), recipe, 69
Rustichella d'Abruzzo, Artisanal
pasta, 22

S

safety
canning food, 76
food processors, 134
homemade pasta,
cutting, 149
salmonella, 138
steam, 240
sale grosso, 258
sale tino, 258
salmonella, 138
salt, 9–10
saltare in padella, 61
San Marzano tomatoes, 73
sardines, 264
sauces
cooking time, tomatoes,
84–85
harissa, Tunsinia, 242
matching with pasta
shapes, 27–28
tomatoes, 84–85
Vietnamese sauces, 211–212
sauteing
cooking techniques, 60
cooking terms, 267
savoy cabbage, 258
sea salt, 10
Seafood on Crispy Noodles,
Chinese cuisine (recipe), 193
seeding, 267

semolina flour, 258
Artisanal pasta, 20
dried pasta, 139
durum wheat, 18–19
Sephardic Jewish pasta
Fidellos with Tomatoes,
recipe, 228
history of, 231–232
serving raw, cooking
techniques, 61
shapes, dried pasta, 24–26
sheets, rolling out homemade
pasta, 146–147
shredding, 267
shrimp, 267
Shrimp Chow Mein, Chinese
cuisine (recipe), 191
simmering, 267
skillets, 267
slippery noodles, *see* bean
thread noodles
slotted spoons, 267
soaking
Asian noodles,
183–184, 267
beans, dried, 104–105, 267
soba, 180–181, 195–196
Japanese cuisine, 258
nutritional information, 195
Soba in Broth, Japanese cuisine
(recipe), 199
somen, 181
Japanese cuisine, 258
Japanese noodles, 197
Somen on Ice, Japanese cuisine
(recipe), 204
soups
bean soup, 104–105
broth, 103
cooking, 105
homemade pasta, 127
recipes
Basic Broth, 106
Minestrone (Vegetable
Soup), 108
Passatelli in Brodo (Broth
with Passatelli), 107